PLAYING FOR KNIGHT

MY SIX SEASONS WITH COACH KNIGHT

Steve Alford

WITH

John Garrity

A FIRESIDE BOOK
Published by Simon & Schuster Inc.
New York   London   Toronto   Sydney   Tokyo   Singapore

Fireside
Simon & Schuster Building
Rockefeller Center
1230 Avenue of the Americas
New York, New York 10020

Copyright © 1989 by Steve Alford, John Garrity, and Super Talents Ltd.

First Fireside Edition, 1990

FIRESIDE and colophon are registered trademarks
of Simon & Schuster Inc.

Designed by Irving Perkins Associates
Manufactured in the United States of America

10   9   8   7   6   5   4   3
10   9   8   7   6   5   4   3   2   1   Pbk.

Library of Congress Cataloging in Publication Data

Alford, Steve.
Playing for Knight : my six seasons with Coach Knight / Steve Alford with
John Garrity.
p.   cm.
1. Alford, Steve. 2. Basketball players—United States—Biography.
3. Knight, Bobby. 4. Basketball—United States—Coaches—Biography.
5. Indiana University, Bloomington—Basketball—History. I. Garrity,
John II. Title.
GV884.A43A3   1989
796.323.'092—dc20
[B]   89-37911
            CIP
ISBN 0-671-67771-3
ISBN 0-671-72441-x Pbk.

To all those who have helped my career along:
my family, my coaches, my teammates,
and the thousands of fans who have supported me.

Acknowledgments

In addition to the many friends and teammates who helped refresh, and sometimes correct, my memory of the incidents in this book, I would like to thank Kit Klingelhoffer and Eric Ruden of the Indiana University Sports Information Department; the staff at the Indiana University Library; Bernard and Todd Morgan of *Super Talents*; and my mom and dad, who patiently checked the manuscript for errors and saved all the scrapbooks and photographs that helped make this book possible.

Contents

PLAYING FOR
KNIGHT

Foreword

Michael Jordan had a mischievous gleam in his eyes.

"I'll bet you a hundred dollars," he told Steve Alford, "you don't stay the whole four years with Coach Knight."

It was the summer of 1984. Jordan and Alford were playing cards in the players' quarters of the Los Angeles Olympic Village, resting up from another grueling practice with Bob Knight, head coach of the U.S. Olympic basketball team.

Jordan, a sensational junior forward from the University of North Carolina, was still reeling from three months of boot-camp-style training under the loud, domineering Knight. He felt sorry for Alford, who had just finished his freshman year at the Indiana University, where Knight was head coach. Alford faced three more years of Knight moves: three years of screaming, glowering, arm waving, and foot stomping; three years of admonitions and threats; three years of benchings and banishings. It wasn't lost on Jordan that Knight hectored Alford, his own player, more than anyone else on the U.S. team.

"One hundred dollars," Jordan goaded. "You'll never last four years at Indiana."

Alford, the only college freshman on the Olympic team, was certain that he would finish at Indiana. Sure, he said, it was tough to play for Knight. But the man was a basketball genius, a perfectionist. Put yourself in his hands and you simply had to improve. And that's what Alford said he wanted most of all—to improve.

Jordan shook his head. He had heard the stories about Indiana's program, tales about brilliant basketball recruits who buckled under Knight and never fulfilled their promise. Or who dropped out. Or who transferred to other schools. Who could forget Isiah Thomas, the scintillating point guard who led Indiana to the national championship in 1981? Hadn't Thomas passed up his junior and senior years because he felt stifled by Knight?

Isiah was a special case, Alford replied. And even Isiah admitted he was a better player because of Coach Knight.

"Take the bet!" Jordan yelped. "I'm tellin' you, man, you'll never go the whole three years."

"Okay," Alford finally said, laughing. "I'll bet you."

If you follow basketball, you know that Alford won the bet. Three years later, when he walked off a court in New Orleans after his last game in an Indiana uniform, Alford was not just an all-America, not just one of the great shooting guards in college basketball history, and not just the floor leader of the new NCAA champions. Alford, in the end, was the most beloved player in the Indiana basketball pantheon, the quintessential Hoosier hoopster.

It was storybook stuff: handsome, straight-arrow Indiana kid grows up practicing his shot on a basket in the driveway; breaks the all-time state tournament scoring record and is voted "Mr. Basketball"; goes to State U and drives his team to the Final Four; stands tall and proud with his teammates as "The Star-Spangled Banner" plays, an Olympic gold medal hanging from his neck.

Funny thing, though. Today, the question Alford always gets is "Was it worth it?"

The question, like Jordan's wager, is grounded in the public's fascination with basketball's most paradoxical personality—Robert Montgomery Knight. Since he took over the Indiana University program in 1971, Knight's adventures have captured headlines:

1979: INDIANA COACH ARRESTED AT PAN AM GAMES; SOCKS PUERTO RICAN COP

1985: BATTLING BOBBY HURLS CHAIR ON COURT; CONFERENCE, SCHOOL PONDER PUNISHMENT

1987: ENRAGED KNIGHT YANKS TEAM OFF FLOOR WITH 11:07 LEFT, FORFEITS GAME WITH RUSSIANS

1988: KNIGHT QUOTE ANGERS WOMEN'S GROUPS; APOLOGY DEMANDED

The man behind the headlines, insiders know, is as volatile as the headlines suggest. Former Indiana players and coaches share battle stories, often with a knowing grin or a telling groan. Just to have survived playing for Knight is a badge of courage. Former Indiana center Uwe Blab had a two-word answer when asked why he stayed at Indiana: "I'm stubborn."

Then came John Feinstein's 1986 best-seller, *A Season on the Brink*. Suddenly, the Bob Knight the insiders knew was on public display, pinned like a bug under glass. Feinstein captured Knight as a man with little dynamic range—tyrannical and obsessive on page 1, and still tyrannical and obsessive on page 311, with intermittent episodes of petulance, hysteria, and outright meanness. And there was this shocker: a favorite target of Knight's scathing tongue was none other than Steve Alford, the all-American boy.

Was Feinstein's account of Indiana basketball accurate? In these pages, Alford answers bluntly: "Yes. *A Season on the Brink* was one hundred percent fact. I know. I lived it."

But Alford says Feinstein didn't—couldn't—get all of the

story. The dimension beyond Feinstein's reach was the players' view. By taking the reader into player meetings and bull sessions closed to Feinstein, Alford reveals the genius side of Bob Knight. Through his relationships with teammates, Alford explains why some players thrive at Indiana, while others wilt under Knight's stare. And by recounting not one season under Knight but six—if you count the Olympic summer of 1984 and the Hoosiers' around-the-world tour in 1985—Alford shows the cyclical, often contrived nature of Knight's outbursts.

Alford is a believer in Coach Knight and his methods, even as he admits there were times he hated Knight, feared Knight, and blamed Knight for taking the fun out of basketball. Alford says, "People are always coming up to me and saying, 'I'm glad I read A Season on the Brink, because now I can appreciate all you had to go through.' And I look back at them and say, 'Hey, you read one year's worth. There's three others back there you haven't even *seen*.' "

In these pages, Alford pulls back the curtain on those years and shows how one angry coach took fourteen tough youngsters from a season on the brink to the highest peak of college basketball—the 1987 NCAA championship.

A word of warning. Don't take Alford's self-appraisal in these pages at face value. He is his own severest critic, and he tends to take blame more often than he takes credit. When he grudgingly admits here that he "played better" in some game or another, you can translate that to mean he was Big Ten Player of the Week or MVP of the tournament. He won't tell you, so I will: Steve Alford was the national high school player of the year for 1983, as voted by the National High School Athletic Coaches Association. He was Big Ten freshman of the year in 1984, a first-team all–Big Ten selection three times, and a consensus first-team all-America his junior and senior seasons. He was voted Most Valuable Player at Indiana four times, the first player to accomplish that feat at any Big Ten school. "He's just tremendous, that's all," coach-turned-color-commentator Al McGuire said of Alford in his senior year. "He represents four years of perfection."

Alford's is a story filled with short tempers and loud voices, but also with humor, affection, and ultimate triumph.

Was it worth it? Alford says yes. "If you stick with Coach Knight, you eventually see the method in his madness. I truly believe I am a better player and a better person because of him."

Sorry, Michael Jordan. You lose.

JOHN GARRITY
Kansas City, Missouri, April 1989

Prologue

My dad, who was also my high school coach, drove me the 110 miles from New Castle to Bloomington one afternoon in October 1982. I had a season of high school basketball yet to play, but I was ready to make a verbal commitment. That's what we were on our way to do. Coach Bob Knight was waiting in Bloomington.

Dad was all for it. He shared my longtime dream that I would one day play for Indiana University. We talked with excitement about my future as we drove through the beautiful fall foliage of south-central Indiana.

It was late afternoon when we reached Bloomington. Dad parked the car in the vast, empty parking lot surrounding the IU basketball arena, Assembly Hall. We walked up the steps and entered by the doors at the south end.

To reach Coach Knight's office we had to walk up a switchback ramp. From the bottom of the ramp we could hear the muffled sounds of a very angry man shouting upstairs. As we got closer, we recognized the angry voice as that of Coach Knight.

17

Dad knocked on the door of the basketball office, which served as Knight's outer office. Coach Jim Crews, one of Knight's assistants, opened the door and recognized us. "Come on in, have a seat," he said. He looked embarrassed. He gestured toward the closed door, which practically vibrated from the noise within. "Something happened."

The thing that had happened was that two Indiana players, Winston Morgan and John Flowers, had played that summer in a church league and had accepted trophies. That was against the rules, and Coach had just learned that the NCAA had suspended both players for the first game of the season.

Crews shook his head. "Coach is very upset with them."

Upset? An understatement! Coach Knight continued to scream behind the door. Nobody yelled back. The only voice we heard was his.

Pretending to ignore the ruckus, I thumbed through some sports magazines. Dad looked at photographs of former Indiana all-Americas on the wall.

Suddenly, the shouting stopped and the door opened. Morgan and Flowers came out and practically ran onto the concourse. They were both in tears.

Dad must have sensed how tense I was. He raised an eyebrow and said, "Are you sure you want to go through with this?"

I cleared my throat noisily and said, "Yeah, I'm sure."

The door to Coach Knight's office remained open. Coach Crews had his arm out to usher us in. "Coach is ready for you now."

And that's how it began. Dad and I got up and walked into the red-carpeted office...and I closed the door behind me.

CHAPTER ONE

WAR STORIES

"Alford!"

Coach Knight spun around and glared at me. "Alford," he shouted, "I can't believe how *stupid* that play was!"

With a forceful kick, he sent a trash can across the locker room. It spun to a halt, dented badly.

He resumed pacing. "We were not gonna leave Duncan, no matter what, remember? I showed you how good a shooter he is. How did I tell you to play him?"

Coach expected an answer. I looked up and said, "Play him tight?"

My answer just seemed to make him angrier. "We've been preparing for this and *preparing* for this, but you just don't listen. You don't give a damn what happens, Alford, and it makes me sick." He stomped into an alcove and kicked the Zemi machine, a shaved-ice dispenser. Several bottles of colored flavoring shattered, spilling glass and sticky liquid everywhere. Managers scurried around with mops and towels, cleaning up the mess.

19

I felt as if I had been slapped hard in the face. Oh, boy, I told myself, you're at Indiana now.

It was the seventh game of my freshman season, a home game against Illinois State of the Missouri Valley Conference. Coach had assigned me to cover Brad Duncan, a very good outside shooter. Duncan was one of those players you couldn't play off of; you had to stay in his face and deny him the ball or he would kill you with jump shots and quick moves to the basket. My notebook was full of reminders: "Stay with man! No help responsibilities! No weak-side responsibilities!"

So what happened? With a few seconds left in the first half, I made the mistake of picking up a penetrating guard (normally a good defensive move), who dished the ball off to Duncan. Duncan scored on a jump shot from the left wing just before the buzzer.

Coach was on his feet and screaming my name even before the shot fell through the net. *"Alford!"* I risked a quick glance in his direction, and what I saw made my heart sink. His face was purple and he was staring at me as if I had borrowed his car and wrecked it.

One of Coach's cardinal rules was that you never, *ever* let the other team go in at halftime on an emotional upswing. My defensive lapse had broken that rule. The Redbirds were giving Duncan high fives on the way to the locker room, while we trudged in, heads bowed, for a tongue-lashing.

How long is a halftime? Fifteen minutes, according to the rule book. An eternity if you are the sole object of Coach Knight's wrath. The upperclassmen probably enjoyed seeing me get it, although they weren't going to risk a smile right then. My sudden fall from grace meant that their own mistakes were being overlooked by Coach, if only temporarily.

Coach yelled at me for the whole fifteen minutes, his rage undiminished. "What's your reason?" he kept asking. "What's your *reason?*"

I didn't have a reason.

When we took the floor for the second half, I wandered

around in a daze, shell-shocked. To this day, the remainder of that game is a blank page in my memory. I know that we won—the score, 54–44, is written in my notebook.

I do remember that Coach called me over after the game, when I was still wet from the shower. He said, "Do you understand why I was so upset with you at halftime?"

"Yes, Coach."

He gave me a steady look. "Well, that's all I wanted to know. I just wanted to make sure you understood why I was upset."

And with that, he turned and walked away.

"War stories," we called them. Every Indiana basketball player could tell several on himself.

The basketball team ate every night after practice in a private dining room at the Indiana University Student Union. It was a pretty formal setting: oak ceiling beams, a chandelier, china cabinets with lighted shelves. White-coated servers filled our plates from behind a long steam table. We ate at two round tables, six or seven players to a table.

War stories often provided the entertainment at these meals. "Hey, Dan," someone would say, "tell the freshmen about Kitchel's hair."

Dan Dakich, who was a junior, would grin. "That happened my freshman year, when Kitchel and Wittman were juniors. We'd just lost to Alabama-Birmingham in the second round of the NCAAs, but it was a pretty good year and Coach said we could leave for spring break. Ted and Randy decided to go to Florida, and Ted, like he did every year, went out and got a curly perm."

Those of us who didn't know the story would begin to smile.

"The same day, Coach calls us in for a team photo session. We're all lined up in our uniforms, the photographer's all set. And suddenly Coach looks down and sees Kitchel." Dan's grin would widen. "I mean, Coach's jaw drops. Ted's got little curls and ringlets. And you know Coach, he just goes crazy. The photographer's ready to take the picture, and here's Kitchel looking like Shirley Temple."

By this time, everybody would be laughing so hard that the table would be shaking.

"So what did Coach do?"

"Well, you know Coach. He canceled the picture."

When the laughter had died down, a freshman might pipe up: "Is Coach always late to meetings?"

The answer, of course, would be yes. If a meeting was set for four-thirty, Coach would come in at ten to five, or five to five, or five. But that didn't mean you could leave. Winston Morgan, another junior, would offer the unfortunate example of Isiah Thomas, the great point guard who plays now for the Detroit Pistons of the NBA.

"One time we're in the locker room and we're waiting... and waiting... and waiting. No Coach. And finally Isiah can't take it anymore. He jumps up and says, 'This is *enough*. I'm leavin'.' We all say, 'Yeah, great,' and get up to go. And he's leading us around that little wall, when all of a sudden we hear the door opening."

"Uh oh!"

"There's this mad scramble. Coach walks in and practically bumps into Isiah on his way out, and Isiah looks around... and he's *all alone*. Every other guy is sitting in his chair."

Whistles and groans.

Dakich: "One second Isiah's leading the charge... then he turns around and he's got no troops!"

"So if you're asking how long to wait for Coach to show up"—this after the laughter had died down—"I'd say till you read in the paper that he's taken another job."

Sometimes, a story might be triggered by something that had happened at practice. Maybe the freshmen saw Coach punt a basketball in anger, one of those fifty-yard jobs he was famous for. Chuck Franz, the team's only senior, might say, "Two years ago he did that same thing, and the ball came down in a garbage can. That was incredible."

"Yeah, and remember the time he punted the ball up in the stands and it hit that hunting buddy of his on the head?"

More laughter.

Often, the war stories were instructive. Chuck: "Everybody talks about when Dan was a freshman and guarded Coach in practice. We were up at Minnesota the day before the game and Coach wasn't happy with somebody, so he took the ball away from the red-team guard and put himself in on offense. Dan's playing for the white team, see, and he thinks Coach will want him to play defense as hard as he can, even if the guy he's covering is Coach. So on the first play, Dan steals the ball from Coach, and when he gives the ball back, Coach calls him a name and throws the ball at Dan. Hits him right in the face."

Groans and laughter.

"Dan shakes his head to clear the stars away, but he's tough, right? So he gets back into his stance and Coach makes another move, and this time Dan dives for the ball and hacks Coach on the wrist. *Wham!* Coach slaps the ball in his face again and screams, 'Don't you *ever* foul me!' "

More groans.

Dan, listening to this oft-repeated tale, would shake his head ruefully. "My nose is about the size of a pineapple by this time, and I don't know whether to cry or punch Coach in the face."

"So what happened?"

"I may be slow, but I'm not hopelessly stupid. He made his next move and I let him go."

We freshmen got the point: if Coach took the ball to demonstrate something, we would be wise not to show him up.

There were dozens of these tales, and over time you realized that they made up the Indiana basketball tradition in the Bob Knight era. I listened in awe and retained much of what I heard. In my bed back at the dorm, I would fall asleep thinking of Kitchel's hair and Dakich's nose and Isiah's charge.

It was well into the season before it struck me that the

"war" was still going on, and that someday the seniors would be telling war stories about Coach and *me*.

I became an actor in the Indiana basketball morality play on October 15, 1983: my first practice as an Indiana Hoosier.

That was an exciting moment for me, when I put on an Indiana practice jersey for the first time. It was red on one side and white when turned inside out, with the words "Indiana Basketball" and my number, 12, on both sides. I didn't have to be told to wear mine with the white facing out. Red was reserved for the first team.

None of the players required introductions in the locker room. We'd been lifting weights, running, and playing pickup games on our own for a month, but without Coach Knight—NCAA rules. Some colleges—Kentucky, Kansas, and a few others—celebrated October 15 with midnight scrimmages open to the public, but Coach Knight was a traditionalist. Practice meant work, not show biz.

Coach Knight's practices, I was told, usually began without Coach Knight, so I wasn't surprised that he was missing when we took the court. The assistant coaches put us to work on our individual moves. At one basket, the big men practiced their power moves, pivots, and hook shots. At another, the forwards practiced shot fakes and drives.

I fell in with the guards—or, at any rate, the players I assumed were guards. Coach Knight didn't identify his players by position. There were no forwards, guards, or centers. There was no "strong forward" or "off-guard" or "five-man." Any Indiana player, starting at any point in Coach Knight's motion offense, was expected to know where to run, who to screen for, and when to cut.

This came as no surprise. In June, I had received a form letter at home from Coach Crews. "Make sure you understand the terminology of basketball," the letter warned—terms like "post," "baseline," "downscreen," "one step ball-side," and "passing lane." Most of the terms seemed very basic to me because I was a coach's son, but Dad reminded me that some high school coaches didn't use those terms.

Coach Knight, it turned out, didn't use some of those terms either, but he expected his recruits to know them. When I first started working out with the IU players in August, they told me that he frequently just pointed and said, "Stand here" or "Go there."

Puzzled, I asked Dakich about Coach's system. "What kinds of terms does he use?"

Dan smiled. "You'll know soon enough the terminology of Coach Knight!"

At that first practice, I noticed that the upperclassmen had a habit of looking over their shoulders from time to time, always in the direction of a small doorway at the south end of the floor. A black curtain covered this door, which led to the service concourse. This was the door, I was told, through which Coach Knight always appeared.

My eyes drifted elsewhere. When I wasn't executing a drill, I found myself looking up at the stands, trying to pick out the seats that Dad; Mom; my brother, Sean; and I had sat in for years. Or I gazed down at the floor, thinking, This is the very floor that Quinn Buckner played on...that Scott May played on...Isiah Thomas, Kent Benson, Bobby Wilkerson, Mike Woodson...

That's how I missed Coach Knight's entrance. Suddenly, everyone was running down the far end toward the locker room. I wheeled around and saw Coach walking across the floor dressed in navy-blue slacks, a gray shirt, and a red coaching jacket. I ran and fell in behind the older players. They knew the routine.

In the locker room, the upperclassmen went straight to their stalls and picked up their notebooks and pens, so I did the same. The notebooks had red covers, and every player found one in his locker on the first day of practice. You quickly learned the importance of that book. You didn't go into the film room without it. The night before a game, you took the book home with you to study. If you left it in your locker overnight and Coach Knight spotted it, you were in trouble.

Coach didn't tell you this. You picked it up from the older players.

We sat down in our plastic chairs and faced the chalkboard. The assistant coaches filed in and stood against the wall. We opened our books and looked up expectantly. It was time for class to begin.

Make no mistake, it was a classroom. Coach Knight worked at the board sometimes, but mostly he lectured. On that first day, he introduced us to his ideas about training and hard work. "I have no curfews," he said. "Common sense should be your training guide. In everything we do, *thinking* is our base."

Obediently, I copied down the key words and phrases: "Common sense...Thinking is our base." But, like most students, I let my mind wander after a few minutes. While Coach talked, I wrote, "My dream is finally coming true. It's no longer Isiah or Buckner that I'm watching out there. It's actually me."

After ten minutes or so with the notebooks, Coach led us back onto the court for drills: four-corner passing drills, shooting drills, zigzags, lay-up drills, three or four different kinds of shotgun passing drills. Each drill had two purposes: perfecting technique, and conditioning. The pace was punishing, and loafing was not allowed.

Coach Knight did not teach these drills. Nobody did. Freshmen were expected to learn by observing the older players. That was Coach's way of testing you, of seeing how quick you were mentally. "Just get in line behind us," the juniors and seniors said. "Do what we do."

We watched, and when we got to the front of the line, we copied the moves—tentatively at first, then more confidently as we caught on.

Next on the agenda: breakdown drills—so called because they isolated some move or technique. The assistant coaches supervised these drills, working with three or four players at one basket. Coach would walk from group to group, observing. After a few minutes, he would call us back to the main floor and introduce the drill into a four-on-four situation. For instance, if we were working on downscreens and backscreens with the assistants, he would suddenly yell, "All right, four-on-four! You can only downscreen or backscreen. You cannot dribble!" After about ten minutes of intense work, he would shout, "Okay, let's work on the cross-screen!" We would go back to our assistant coach and start a new breakdown drill.

That was the pattern: breakdown drills followed by game simulation.

Mostly we worked on screens, which are the foundation of Coach Knight's motion offense. He taught us three screens that first day: the backscreen, where a player runs up from the low post and sets a pick behind a defensive man; the cross-screen, where the screener comes across the lane; and the downscreen, which is set by a player moving from the high post down toward the basket.

Coach was very precise about screening technique. (Some NBA coaches call certain types of screens "Indiana screens.") He wanted your back to the ball when you made a downscreen, for instance, and he always wanted you to go to the opponent's body rather than let the opponent come to you. He emphasized movement without the ball by the player being screened for, because that player was responsible for setting up his man and bringing him back to the screen. We always had to be in motion, making V-cuts, in and out, before breaking for the ball.

Much of this was new to me. In high school, I had played point guard—my teammates threw the ball in to me and I brought it upcourt alone, looking for the shot or a clear pass. Now I had to learn how to move without the ball and how to "read" screens.

The way Coach taught it, the player being screened for was to keep his eyes on his defensive man at all times—*not* the ball, as many coaches taught. When you got to the screener's shoulder, the defensive man's position told you whether you were to make a "tight cut" (around the screen and hard to the basket) or a "flare cut" (jumping away from the screen to catch the pass and shoot a jump shot). If the defender tried to chase you around the screen, you made a tight cut, curling around the pick and streaking for the basket. If he tried to "cheat" and go around the screen on the high side, that always called for the flare cut, where you faded to the baseline for the jump shot. Nothing irritated Coach more than to see someone set a perfect pick, only to have the cutter not read the defensive man properly and have his defender follow him out.

"The passer is the shooter's best friend," Coach said, and it wasn't an empty cliché at Indiana. Since you weren't watching the ball when you used a screen, it was the passer's job to put the ball in the right place at the right time. The passer, too, had to be watching the defensive man to read the cutter's move. In drills, a misread by either player resulted in an errant pass, and I suddenly understood why Indiana players sometimes threw passes to empty spots on the floor, to the consternation of the fans.

It was hard work, but I loved it. I didn't realize that Coach would keep teaching us those three basic screens nearly every practice day for the rest of my time at Indiana.

When we reached the point where he thought we needed a rest, Coach had us shoot free throws. That first day, I was shooting at a side bucket, still panting from the frantic pace of the drills, when he walked by and slapped me on the back.

"You know," he said, "you're going to have to put up with me for four years. Think you're up to that?"

He walked away before I could answer.

There were three other freshmen. All were bigger than I was.

Todd Meier was a six-foot-eight, 210-pound forward

from Oshkosh, Wisconsin, a *Parade Magazine* prep all-America. Daryl Thomas was a six-foot-seven, 210-pound swingman from Westchester, Illinois, and he too was a *Parade* all-America. Marty Simmons was a six-foot-five, 215-pound forward from Lawrenceville, Illinois. He was his state's "Mr. Basketball" and had scored 1,087 points in high school, the second-best in Illinois history. His team had gone undefeated two straight years, with an incredible 68–0 record.

All three were outstanding guys, and we quickly became close friends, both on and off the court.

I knew Todd already. We had been teammates that summer at the B/C All-Star basketball camp in Rensselaer, Indiana. In some ways, he was practically a taller clone of me; his hair, although lighter, was cut just like mine, right down to the part in the middle. In other ways, he was unlike anybody. He was, for example, the world's skinniest shot-put champion. He had won the Wisconsin Class B shot-put competition his senior year in high school.

Todd was also a snake handler, which I wasn't crazy about. He kept a long red rat snake in a foil-covered terrarium in his dorm room. Sometimes he would cross the hall to my room with the snake draped over his arm or around his neck. I practically jumped out the window when he did that. I was intrigued by snakes, but their quickness bothered me. I told Todd that I had seen a poisonous snake at the St. Louis zoo when I was little. The sign read: QUICKEST SNAKE IN THE WORLD. IT WILL STRIKE YOU SIX TIMES BEFORE YOU REACT TO THE FIRST BITE.

"That is incredibly quick," I told Todd.

He said not to worry, his snake wasn't that quick.

One morning, Todd woke up and the snake wasn't there. The foil was off the terrarium and Todd's pet was AWOL. Todd searched the dormitory for days, going through people's closets, looking in boots, peering into toilet tanks. He was worried for his pet. The rest of us were worried for our lives. I didn't sleep for three nights. Every time I turned the lights off I thought I heard something slithering around the room.

Todd finally found his snake on the fourth day, coiled up in a stairwell. If we'd had a vote, Todd would have been chosen "Most likely not to have a roommate as a sophomore."

Actually, Marty was Todd's roommate, and he didn't seem to mind the snake or Todd's other peculiarities. Marty had a little "country" in his personality, and we got on him all the time about his cowboy boots and clothes. (He was wearing bell-bottoms long after they had gone out of style.) Marty was the only one of us with a car, and he drove home almost every weekend to see his girl and visit his family.

I remember Marty's car because it had bumper stickers all over the back end celebrating the two Illinois state championships his Lawrenceville team had won. Marty usually drove Todd and me to practice, and one day we passed Coach Knight as we turned in to Assembly Hall. The first time Marty messed up that day, Coach stopped play and told him to get rid of the stickers on his car. "I don't care what you did in high school," Coach said. "I don't care that you were Mr. Basketball. This is a different level."

Daryl lived in a different dorm way across campus, so we didn't see as much of him off the court, but he was a delightful guy, too. Coming from the Chicago area, he had a few big-city mannerisms—clothes and accent, mostly—but he struck everyone as a very quiet, laid-back kid. Coach Knight's gripe with Daryl was that he was *too* nice. Once, when chewing Daryl out, Coach said, "Daryl, if I had a daughter, you're exactly the kind of kid I'd want her to date. But I *don't* have a daughter, so I don't *need* you to have this personality right now."

I'm sure my teammates thought I had a few idiosyncrasies myself. Dakich pegged me as a Beaver Cleaver type, naive about campus life and full of questions. If the other guys were talking about a party they had been to, I always wanted to know how late everybody had stayed up and whether anybody underage had been caught drinking.

I was just curious. I didn't drink and I didn't smoke, and I didn't have a lot of social skills. Todd was amazed that I would go to a fraternity party and leave thirty minutes later. He said, "I never met anybody before who worried about getting a good night's sleep so he'd look his best in practice the next day."

The other thing I got kidded about was my hair, which I parted in the middle and combed neatly. My hair never looked messy, and for some reason people thought that was funny. Sportswriters mentioned my hair in their stories, making it a symbol of a sort of bland perfectionism. ("If Steve Alford were a flavor," one guy wrote, "he'd be vanilla.") I never knew how to respond to questions about my hair. I'd just shrug and say, "I guess other guys just don't know how to comb theirs."

Peculiarities aside, the three other freshmen and I were in the Indiana University mold: clean-cut, soft-spoken, polite, and from close-knit families. Except for Todd, who was listed as "undecided," we even had the same line at the end of our biographies in the IU basketball yearbook: "...plans to major in business."

There's a story behind that. When Dad and I paid our visit to Coach Knight's office to make my verbal commitment to IU, Coach sat me down and said, "What do you plan to major in?"

I had been an A student in high school, but my career goal was pretty simple: I wanted to play professional basketball. "I don't know," I said with a shrug. "Physical education, I guess, or recreation."

"No, you're not." Coach's voice practically dripped with disdain. "You're majoring in business."

So I majored in business.

Everybody expected 1984 to be a rebuilding year at Indiana. We were the defending Big Ten Conference champions, but Randy Wittman, Ted Kitchel, Jim Thomas, Steve

Bouchie, and Tony Brown had graduated. Those guys had won three Big Ten titles and the 1981 NCAA championship. Wittman was the conference MVP; Kitchel was a two-time all–Big Ten player.

That left only one returning player with a scoring average better than 3 points a game—our seven-foot-two redhead from Munich, West Germany, Uwe Blab. BLAB THE VETERAN NOW, proclaimed a headline in the *Bloomington Herald-Telephone*.

That was stretching it a little. Uwe was an imposing physical presence in the middle, the tallest player in IU history, but he had played very little basketball in his life. He owed his presence in America to a high school basketball coach in Effingham, Illinois, who had spotted him on a touring Munich all-star team. Coming from another country, Uwe didn't understand American competitiveness, and he certainly didn't understand Coach Knight. Coach treated him like somebody the gypsies had dropped on his doorstep in the night.

Uwe's real passion was computer science, and like most computer scientists he had "stone hands"—he couldn't catch the ball in a crowd. Coach had tried everything to improve Uwe's hands. He made Uwe field tennis balls thrown at him. He lobbed basketballs for Uwe to catch while our managers battered him with football pads. Nothing seemed to help.

It was partly because of Uwe that I figured I had a good chance to be a starter as a freshman. Coach Knight wanted to build his offense around Uwe, who had developed an excellent hook shot and was an effective inside scorer. To do that, Coach had to keep our opponents from swarming around the big man to exploit those bad hands.

Solution: good outside shooting to draw defenses away from Uwe.

Or maybe it was the other way around: maybe Coach wanted to establish Uwe as a low-post center to open up the floor for his good young shooters.

However you looked at it, the departure of so many great players left an opening I thought I could fill.

Why I was so confident, I don't know. I had played very poorly in that summer's National Sports Festival in Colorado Springs. I had played even worse during our preseason scrimmages. I had shot badly, passed badly, and defended badly. I was eager for the real basketball to begin, for October 15 to roll around. I wanted discipline and organization.

Sure enough, as soon as Coach Knight took over the team I began to improve. Like a kid in a toy store, I got excited over each new technique I learned—setting picks, reading screens, learning to move effectively without the ball. My shooting eye returned, my defense tightened up, and my floor sense heightened.

Coach noticed. "I'm very, very pleased with your progress," he told me one day at practice. "After the Sports Festival and seeing you in the preseason, I was ready to send you back home."

If Coach had changed his mind about me, I had not changed my mind about him—I knew I was in the hands of a truly great basketball coach. I was less certain, however, of what kind of person he was. I couldn't understand his need to intimidate people. Everybody around him—players, assistant coaches, faculty, sportswriters—seemed uncomfortable in his presence.

Coach did nothing to discourage that feeling. He had a funny way with people. If you said the weather was beautiful, he said it was too hot or too cold. If you liked Notre Dame in the football game with USC, Coach took USC. Sportswriters hid their own opinions when interviewing Coach, fearing his ridicule.

Sometimes his intimidating ways produced comical results. I remember walking into Assembly Hall one afternoon, lost in thought, only to be brought up short by a hissing sound from behind a pillar. "Pssssst! Steve!"

It was Dan Dakich, lurking underneath the ramp to the

upper concourse. He pointed upstairs, but I practically had to read his lips to understand what he was whispering: "Is Coach up there?"

I looked upstairs. The ramp was empty.

"No," I said.

Dan grinned and hurried past me to the doors. "Thanks," he said. "I owe you one."

It wasn't quite as comical when Coach Knight gave a player a tongue-lashing. His face got red, his eyebrows went down and in, and the veins stood out in his neck. He sometimes got right up in your face and yelled so loud you flinched.

The worst part of it, for me, was the profanity. I knew all the words—I hadn't led *that* sheltered a life—but I had never heard them in such abundance and with so much fury behind them. To a young man of my background and religious beliefs, Coach's vulgarity was like a punch in the stomach.

The trick, according to the upperclassmen, was to understand that Coach used profanity to teach, as strange as that sounds. I think Dakich explained it best: "When Coach calls you an ———, you shouldn't take it as you *being* an ———. You should just try to figure out why he is calling you that."

Coach didn't cuss out everybody; he had a pecking order. Freshmen he treated relatively gently. If I made a bad pass, say, or if Daryl broke the wrong way in a drill, Coach usually said nothing. We were new; he didn't expect us to know it all. He also seemed to spare the feelings of nonstarting seniors, who got yelled at only if they loafed. (*Nobody* got away with loafing.)

Coach directed most of his anger, instead, at the upperclassmen who played the most, the team leaders. My freshman year, that meant Blab, Chuck Franz, and Dakich. Above all Dakich.

It was astonishing the way Coach got on Dan. If a practice was going badly, everything was Dan's fault. Sloppy drills? Coach yelled at Dan. No intensity? He yelled at Dan. Coach might spot a freshman out of position—Steve Alford, for example—and he'd stop play by yelling, "Dakich!"

Everyone would freeze.

"You see that Alford's out of position, don't you?"

"Yes, sir." Dan would always look Coach in the eye—no staring at his feet or looking dreamily at the ceiling.

Coach would then blister Dan for not moving me to the right spot. "That's *your* responsibility, Dakich! If Alford's not where he's supposed to be, get on him!"

While yelling at Dan, Coach was really making a point to me. And not just to me, but to the whole team. Everybody listened intently when Coach chewed out a player because, number one, we knew the slightest smirk would put us on the hot seat, and two, we knew his lectures were not meant for the individual alone.

You couldn't help feeling sorry for Dan, but the older players said he didn't need our sympathy. Dan was Coach's favorite target not because Coach disliked him but because Dan responded to the yelling the way Coach wanted. When play resumed, Dan usually did correctly whatever Coach wanted him to do. That helped hammer the lesson home.

The players to feel sorry for, I soon learned, were the players that Coach *didn't* scream at and swear at.

For the record, I don't approve of profanity and don't use it casually myself. There will be no more of it in these pages. I won't even employ the usual dashes and euphemisms, which the littlest kid can figure out. The reader will understand that when I say Coach was "irate," I mean he was tearing into us with language that would make a Marine drill sergeant gulp.

The truth is, after the initial shock I grew accustomed to Coach's language and pretty much ignored it. If nothing else, he taught me that I'm not made of glass.

I remember the first time he booted me: I was having the practice of my life. I scored on anybody he assigned to cover me, I handled the ball beautifully, I hustled on defense. And suddenly he screamed, "Alford!"

I wheeled around, surprised.

He jerked his head toward the dressing room. "Go take a shower!"

I couldn't believe it. I went to the locker room, slumped down in my chair, and waited. You were supposed to wait, even if he told you to get out of his sight forever.

Coach came in a few minutes later and sat down beside me. "You know," he said calmly, "I just don't want you to get complacent. It's too early in your career to think you're superior to people. You don't have the athletic ability to dominate, and we don't have the talent here yet to put around you. You're going to have to work hard every day."

I followed him back out to the floor, and practice resumed.

Dakich told me later that my getting thrown out was practically a compliment from Coach. "When I was a freshman, only Randy Wittman and Ted Kitchel got thrown out of practices. If Coach respects you and knows you can handle it, he'll do that."

I thought that was a pretty strange way for Coach to show his respect.

There was no confusing his meaning, though, when he stopped practice one afternoon in mid-November and jumped on Chuck Franz for some screwup. Coach gave his little lecture and then turned away with these words: "Chuck, you put on a white shirt. Alford, you put on a red shirt."

That's always how Coach demoted a player: if you messed up, your name came first.

I was so excited I could hardly get my jersey off to turn it inside out. For the first time since high school, I could see real evidence of progress. I was on the first team at Indiana University! No freshman had ever started a season opener for Coach Knight, but I had a chance.

As hyper as I was, I still noticed how Chuck handled the embarrassment of being replaced by a freshman. He didn't pout or get down on himself. He just changed his shirt around, joined the white team, and fought like crazy to get playing time. And as the days went by, Chuck showed no resentment toward me for taking his place, but helped me every way he could, with encouragement, advice, or a ready smile. As a senior, he knew that no demotion was permanent, no promotion was safe, and the team always came first with Coach Knight.

I learned a lot from Chuck. He showed a lot of character.

We played the Italian national team in an exhibition at Assembly Hall in mid-November. Stew Robinson hit a twenty-foot shot with one second left and we won, 73–72. That got the crowd excited, because the Italians were undefeated on their American tour and earlier in the week Coach had told reporters he thought they were probably the best team in the world.

After we beat them, Coach said the Italians were "tired."

We had a full week to prepare for our home opener against Miami of Ohio, a team we figured to beat handily. Coach spent part of the week making speeches to various civic groups, an annual ritual. On Tuesday he lunched with the Bloomington Rotary Club and dined with the Kiwanians. Wednesday he spoke to the IU Men's Club of Indianapolis. Friday he lunched with the Bloomington Varsity Club.

He told these groups, perhaps not as bluntly, the same thing he told us: the win over the Italians meant nothing. "I will be interested to see how we play Saturday," he said. "They've been around people patting them on the back all week for how well they played."

We had a good week of practice. Coach was perhaps a little sharper in his criticisms. One afternoon, Marty fired up a very long jump shot, and Coach yelled as if he had been stabbed. Not only was the shot too long; Marty had also violated Coach's rule of "four passes before a shot."

Coach's version, printed in the next day's newspaper, went

like this: "Simmons has to learn to count to four. I just called him over and asked if he *could* count to four. And he said, 'Yes, I can handle that.'

"That's roughly the way the conversation went."

The game was Saturday afternoon, and 14,527 came out to watch us tune up for Notre Dame, our next opponent. Some tune-up! Uwe controlled the center jump, but one of the Miami guards cut in, stole the tap, and passed to a teammate for a lay-up. The whole game was like that. Miami beat us on the boards, scrambled for the loose balls, and beat us up and down the court. Marty and I both got plenty of minutes off the bench, and Marty was incredible—15 points, 9 rebounds, and 7 assists. But the final score was Miami of Ohio 63, Indiana 57. We were the first Knight-coached Indiana team ever to lose its home opener.

Coach was furious in the locker room. He yanked the top off his marker and wrote the score on the board: 63–57. He jammed the top back on the marker and slammed it down. We didn't know it then, but the Miami score would stay posted on that board for the next two years as a constant reminder of what happens to complacent basketball teams.

It was my first experience with Coach after a tough loss. The language was strong and I had to force myself to look up while he scalded us. I glanced over at Marty, who had played so well, and he looked pretty low. Of course, he had just seen a personal seventy-game winning streak broken; Marty hadn't been in a losing locker room in almost three years.

Coach didn't yell at the freshmen. He heaped his scorn on the upperclassmen, particularly Blab and Dakich. In fact, he blamed *them* for our mistakes. "You haven't learned much about leadership in two years, have you, Dakich? You're testing my patience. Uwe, I'm not going to hold your hand for another season. You've got to grow up, son, and take charge."

Finally, Coach ran out of steam. "You've got an hour and a half. Go get something to eat and then come back. We've got work to do." He left to meet the press.

Todd's face fell. His family was in town, down from Wisconsin, and he had counted on spending some time with them. He swore softly and threw his towel down.

The gym was clear of people by the time we took the floor. Custodians with brooms and plastic bags were cleaning debris from the stands. The assistants started us off with some basic drills, but the tone changed the minute Coach broke through the curtain. "Let's work!" he barked. "Loose-ball drills!"

The upperclassmen groaned quietly.

Coach put us in lines and then rolled a ball across the floor. "Go for it!" he yelled, and two players threw themselves on the floor and wrestled for possession. Coach grabbed another ball and rolled it. Two more players hit the hardwood.

When my turn came, I made sure I had a clear shot at the ball before diving. Otherwise, I let the other guy get it and piled on top of him. That's how you avoided a collision. All of us remembered the war story about Rick Rowray, who broke his arm in '82 diving for a ball in practice.

After the loose-ball drills, Coach Knight put us through some punishing defensive and rebounding drills: one-on-one games, defensive slides, three-man rebounding, line sprints. When we looked too dead to move, Coach led us back to a cluttered dressing room that he used for tape sessions. He put the game on the VCR and started punching the remote control—fast-forward, reverse, fast-forward—stopping and replaying the tape whenever he saw a play he didn't like. "Dakich, you're out of position defensively. . . . Morgan, you've got a shooter on one side of the floor and you've reversed the ball too quickly. . . . Look at that crap! That downscreen doesn't develop. . . ."

He'd lead us back out to the court and drill us on execution until we got that play right. Then we'd go back to the VCR room and watch more tape. "That's *horrible!*" he'd say, contemptuous of our weak-side defense. "Look at that conversion to defense. You're not sprinting down the floor...."

Over and over he ran the play, until we were sick of it. Then he took us back out on the floor to get it right.

The tape session lasted for hours. When I got back to my dorm room that night, I fell on my bed and went right to sleep. Todd's snake could have crawled over me and I wouldn't have noticed.

Coach brought us back in the next morning, Sunday, at six o'clock. We picked up right where we had left off. Drills, videotape, more drills.

The floor work wasn't the hardest part. I enjoyed being on the basketball court, even when the coaching atmosphere was less than congenial. But I was beginning to dread the tape sessions. It was no fun being in a dark room with a scary individual who was very upset with your play. And there was this about film—you had no defense. Out on the court, if you screwed up you could sort of defend yourself— make a case, muddle things up with questions and explanations. But in the dark, with Coach Knight wielding the remote control, you were easy prey. Your screwup repeated itself over and over in full view of your teammates—forward, backward, forward again—with Coach's sarcastic comments as narration.

Finally, he was through with us, and we stumbled out into the cold, ready to pick up the threads of life outside Assembly Hall, if we could find them.

The whole experience was a pretty good illustration of one of Coach's favorite lines: "There are really only two words you need to know to play basketball in this program: 'Yes, sir.'"

Our next game was against Notre Dame, and Coach leaked word to the media: Simmons and Alford might start against the Irish. Tuesday night, when we took the floor, Coach had another surprise up his sleeve: Todd started, too. Uwe and Stew Robinson opened the game on the bench.

Lineup juggling is a Bob Knight tradition. By playing everybody in the first weeks of a season Coach gets to check out the new players under game conditions and test various combinations for the proper "chemistry." On top of that, he gets more effort from his veterans by making them sweat their starting roles.

Against the Irish, it worked. I scored 14 in my first start, and Marty was even better than he was against Miami—22 points, 5 rebounds, 2 assists, and 3 steals. Uwe and Stew came off the bench (the crowd greeting Stew with "Stew! Stew! Stew!" and Uwe with "Ooo-vay! Ooo-vay! Ooo-vay!") and had good games, scoring 27 points between them. We won, 80–72.

Friday we flew to Lexington, Kentucky, for our first road game of the year, against number-one-ranked Kentucky on national TV. The Wildcats were led by two terrific big men, Sam Bowie and Mel Turpin. Marty and I were just as worried about NBC's two big men, Gary Bender and Billy Packer.

The Kentucky trip was my first exposure to the Indiana road routine, which Coach Knight had carved into stone tablets years ago, never to be changed. We had a full practice at Assembly Hall on Friday afternoon, and then showered and got dressed in coats and ties. We boarded a bus outside Assembly Hall and were driven to the Monroe County Airport, where one of the university's two private planes waited in a hangar. We flew to Lexington, boarded another bus, and made it to the hotel in time for dinner. After dinner, we gathered in a conference room for a VCR session with Coach. Then we went to our rooms to study our basketball notebooks and to sleep.

In the morning, we met as a team for a light breakfast, then took the bus to the arena for a walk-through in practice gear. After that, we returned to the hotel for an afternoon of rest. Without exception, we ate our pregame meal three and a half hours before tip-off.

The pregame meal, from the standpoint of staging, resembled the Last Supper, but was not as much fun. You were expected to be on time, wearing a coat and tie. There was always a five-by-seven-inch card on your plate—a poem, maybe, or a pertinent quotation. (For Kentucky, the cards bore nothing but a score: "Miami of Ohio 63, Indiana 57.") Then the meal: spaghetti, pancakes, hamburger patties, scrambled eggs, and vanilla ice cream. In my four years at Indiana, the menu never varied, although the quality of the food did. The spaghetti at the Student Union was usually good, but the stuff we got on the road was a little shaky. Everyone dreaded the pregame meal when we played a noon game; nobody wanted road spaghetti at eight in the morning.

We always ate in total silence, like fighter pilots facing death at dawn. The only sounds were those of knives and forks on plates, or the occasional whispered "Salt, please."

Coach's chair usually sat empty till we got to dessert. That's when he came in for a dish of butter pecan ice cream, which only he was allowed to have. When he was through with his ice cream, he stood beside his chair and talked to us. He often brought in guest speakers to inspire us, but he always had the last word before we left the table. Those last words usually carried us to the arena, where we suited up, warmed up on the court, and returned to the locker room for a final briefing.

Unlike many coaches, he did not lead us in prayer before sending us out to play. "God couldn't care less if we win or not," he once told me. "He is not going to parachute in through the roof of this building and score when we need points."

We weren't supposed to *have* a prayer against Kentucky, but we gave them a good game. The crowd at Rupp Arena took our breath away: 23,864 screaming Wildcat fans. Marty and I both started and scored 36 points between us. Uwe outrebounded Turpin, 12 to 5, and we played such tight team defense that Bowie scored only 3 points. We led by a point at halftime, and lost the game by just 5. Coach praised us in the locker room and on the flight home.

Marty and I were flying high even without the plane. Starting was great. Scoring in double figures was greater still. Playing well against the nation's number-one team on national TV...well, what freshman wouldn't get a big head?

Three nights later, we played Tennessee Tech at home and won easily. Marty scored 13 and I scored 26, my career high—if you call four games a career. Suddenly, our names were appearing in the newspaper the way Isiah's and Buckner's had in the past. Marty and I didn't go around bragging or anything, but it was hard not to dwell on our success.

Everything was great, except one thing: I was disappointed that Coach Knight hadn't singled me out for praise.

He must have read my mind. The next day, Coach put his arm around me as we walked off the floor after practice. "You know," he said, "I'm not going to say anything to you when you're doing well. I'll just get on your butt when you aren't."

He didn't have to wait long. We traveled to El Paso, Texas, to play UTEP, and the Miners showed what they thought of headline-hunting freshmen. Marty scored 5 points, I scored 4, and we lost, 65–61.

The next day, Coach called Marty and me into his office for a little talk. He wasn't loud. He sat in his chair and talked to us like a doctor giving a diagnosis. We had gotten complacent, he said. Carried away by our headlines. We had to understand this about headlines: the El Paso players could read, too.

"You come off a good game," he said, "you've got to forget about that game. Your next opponent will just come at you harder."

Having made that point, Coach slapped us both on the back and dismissed us.

"That wasn't so bad," I told Marty. "I expected something worse."

A few days later, we got something worse: Coach dropped Marty and me from the starting lineup.

This might be a good place to mention something: at Indiana, basketball players go to class.

That's easy enough in the fall, which is beautiful at IU. When the leaves turn red and gold and the sun is out, a walk across campus is enchanting, even to a gym rat like me. But come November, the leaves fall off the trees, the sky turns gray, and the sun sleeps late.

As a freshman, I was stuck with eight-o'clock classes. That meant getting up in darkness in the winter. It meant walking half a mile to my first class through bone-chilling cold. It meant skipping breakfast for an extra hour of sleep.

The typical student, hearing the alarm go off on one of those cold mornings, could roll back over and go to sleep. I could not. If I did, I knew that Buzz would find out and I would be in big trouble.

"Buzz" was Elizabeth Kurpius, who ran the athletic department's academic counseling program. Her job was to monitor the academic progress of every scholarship athlete at IU and to report any problems to the head coaches. She counseled us, signed our class cards, found tutors for us, and negotiated with professors when we had to miss assignments due to travel. Buzz was our first contact with the academic world, and she stayed on our cases right up till the moment when the college president, in cap and gown, handed us our diplomas.

There was no "give" in Coach Knight when it came to classroom attendance. "We have the best graduation rate in the country," he liked to say, "and we haven't done it with a roster full of Rhodes scholars. We're doing it with kids who come here told they will go to class or they'll go home."

He wasn't bluffing, either. My freshman year, one of our sophomores, Mike Giomi, began missing classes for a little extra shut-eye. Coach blew his top when the absent slips came back from Mike's professors. He benched Mike as an example to the rest of us and gave Mike an ultimatum: any more cuts and he was off the team for good. At the end of the season, he withdrew Mike's scholarship and made him come back as a walk-on. And Mike was one of our best players.

Coach took so much pride in our graduation rate that he often let academics influence his recruiting. Coach always took the prospect with good high school grades over a slightly more skilled player with lower grades. He figured a kid who couldn't cut it in the classroom wouldn't learn much on the basketball floor either.

For a while, though, it looked as if Coach were recruiting a College Bowl team. I was an A student in high school. Joe Hillman, who committed to IU when I was a freshman, was fourth in his class of four hundred and had made only one B since the seventh grade. Delray Brooks was the 1983 governor of Indiana Boys' State. Todd Jadlow had a 4.0 grade average at Barton County (Kansas) Community College. And we already had Uwe, who was an A student and an academic all–Big Ten selection. Uwe could say with a straight face that he was not at Indiana to play basketball for Bobby Knight; he was there because IU's mathematics and computer science programs were among the nation's best.

I can't say, though, that basketball helped our academic lives. Our practices were physically draining and packed with pressure. When I got back to the dorm after dinner, I usually just wanted to lie down, watch TV, grab a bite to eat, and fall asleep. It was difficult to open a book and make sense of it with Coach Knight's voice still ringing in your ears. It was hard to go to the library and switch from athlete to student in the time it took to find a book in that maze of open stacks.

After a game, it was more than difficult; it was impossible. I don't care what you are—an athlete, a singer, an actor—if you perform in front of large crowds you need time to wind down after a performance. For several hours you are so keyed up you can't concentrate on anything else. I could never sleep well after a game. I was usually dehydrated, and that does strange things to your body and brain chemistry. I'd stay up till two o'clock, replaying the game in my mind, worrying about mistakes, cherishing the memory of some great move I thought I had made. I've replayed games in that dreamlike way since I was a kid.

Obviously, if I found it hard to study after practices and after games—and I haven't even mentioned the twenty or so days a semester lost to travel—I had to cram most of my classwork into smaller pockets of time. I could never keep up with the reading, so I took extra-good class notes to compensate. When I had to miss class, I borrowed notes from reliable friends. With diligent cramming and careful scheduling, I found I could manage a 2.98 GPA.

Still, my most important class was the one being conducted down at Assembly Hall by one very large, loud instructor.

Among the lessons I learned there was this one: "You don't lose a Classic." That was another of those absolute *don'ts* the upperclassmen laid on us.

There were two Classics, actually. The Indiana Classic was played every year at Assembly Hall, a week or two before Christmas. The Hoosier Classic was played at Market Square Arena in Indianapolis between Christmas and New Year's. Both Classics were four-team invitational tournaments along the lines of most holiday tournaments: a favored host team and three "lesser" opponents. We had never lost a game in either Classic. Ten championships in ten tries.

That's what made it so strange coming into the Indiana Classic with a 2–3 record. We were the only sub-.500 team in the tournament.

Our first-round game was with Texas A&M, and we

pounded them, 73–48. Marty and I didn't start, but we both played pretty well off the bench. The next night, we beat Illinois State for the Classic trophy. Marty started and played great—19 points and 10 rebounds. He even made the all-tournament team along with Uwe, who was MVP.

That's the game where I made the bonehead play to end the first half and wound up getting yelled at for the whole fifteen minutes of halftime. It was not the first time I had seen Coach with his eyebrows down and in, screaming at someone, but it was the first time the someone had been me.

That was probably the most scared I've ever been.

With Christmas coming up, we had the campus pretty much to ourselves. There was a four-week break for the holidays, which left the streets of Bloomington relatively deserted. The town's population is about eighty thousand with students, but just forty thousand when they go home. With no classes, we had a lot of time on our hands and little to do.

So Coach scheduled two-a-days.

If he thought two-a-days would keep his basketball players out of trouble, he was wrong. We began to have nightly snowball fights. *Awesome* snowball fights.

Every night at training table we taunted each other and conspired and broke down into little armies. Then we acted out this little charade. There were three ways to leave the Union. We said good night, went out these different doors, and then ran like crazy. Seconds later, all of us were in front of the Union and the snowballs were airborne.

Uwe drew a lot of fire because he made a big and slow-moving target. On the other hand, he had a Germanic gift for strategy and sometimes ambushed impetuous attackers.

Even more than each other, we aimed at each other's cars. A favorite strategy was to rain snowballs on a player when he opened his car door, in hopes of filling his car with snow.

The snowball wars lasted for days. There was always snow.

We played Kansas State at home the night of the 23rd. Uwe and Dan told the freshmen that the last game before

Christmas was very important. If you played well, you got maybe one extra day off from practice.

No such luck. We played K State poorly, escaping with a 56–53 overtime win. To no one's surprise, Coach Knight scheduled a practice for three o'clock Christmas afternoon.

At least I got to go home for Christmas. Mom and Dad and Sean were waiting in the parking lot after the game, and we drove straight to New Castle.

It was wonderful to be home, if only for thirty hours or so. I appreciated the tree and the decorations and Mom's ornaments more than I ever had before—all the greens and reds, the smells of candles, pine needles, and holly. There was eggnog and fruitcake and Christmas turkey. On Christmas eve, I stayed up late helping Mom make Christmas cookies.

Sunday morning, we all went to church together. A big storm had swept down during the night, but the streets were passable and it just made Christmas seem cheerier. It was with great reluctance that I got into the car at noon so Dad could drive me back to Bloomington.

That Christmas practice was one of the most difficult ever. Coach did very little yelling. He wandered around the gym, watching with cold intensity while his assistants put us through drills.

To start with, we played one-on-one. Not conventional one-on-one—not "get the ball and dribble-dribble-dribble." At Indiana, you play one-on-one with two players and an assistant coach. The coach holds the ball and the offensive player has to make three cuts to get open before the assistant will throw him the ball.

They didn't *tell* you that, of course. But if Stew Robinson and I were going at it and I made a hard cut to get open, I'd be standing there wanting to shoot, and the assistant would just fake at me and hold the ball. "No, no!" he'd yell. "Cut again!"

So I'd have to make another cut and come back, and it was "No, no, cut again!" You had to get open two or three times. They would finally throw you the ball, and *then* you played one-on-one. You did that continually until one of you made five buckets.

Believe me, you were exhausted after one game. To score five baskets you had to make at least fifteen cuts. You also had to *defend* at least fifteen cuts. And since you weren't going to hit every shot, you were really making at least twenty cuts in a single game. Never mind the energy you expended after receiving the ball, which was considerable.

That was our Christmas present from Coach: we played one-on-one for a whole hour. After each game, the winner stayed on and the loser ran punishment sprints before changing buckets.

After that, we ran two more hours of drills—full-court zigzags, four-on-four, five-on-four, six-on-four. There was no resting, either. We had only ten players, because Daryl, Dan, and Todd had been stranded at home by the icy conditions on Interstate 65.

The guys who suffered most were the players who didn't get much game time. They stood bent over between drills, gasping for air. Sweat poured off their faces. When we finally left the floor at six, some of them were almost too tired to shower.

"Those guys missed a good one," someone said wearily, referring to Dan, Todd, and Daryl.

We got to tell them to their faces an hour later. Coach had invited the team over to his house for Christmas dinner, and we were playing pinball and pool in his downstairs rec room when the Three Wise Men turned up at the door.

"Where the heck were you guys?" We tried to make them feel as guilty as possible, and they did look pretty sheepish, standing there in their overcoats and scarves. When we told them what they had missed—in whispers, of course—they shook their heads and rolled their eyes.

"Glad I missed that," Todd said with a grin, reaching for a plate of turkey and mashed potatoes.

No way. The next day, the 26th, Coach put us through a

practice almost as tough, this time with the whole squad. Afterward, Dakich collapsed in his plastic chair, arms limp at his side. "And you say yesterday was *worse?*"

Market Square Arena was sold out for both nights of the Hoosier Classic. I did not start against Ball State and scored a career-low 2 points, but we won the game easily behind Uwe's 28 points and 11 rebounds. Coach wasn't satisfied, though, not even with a 43-point victory. He thought we had loafed on defense and played undisciplined basketball on offense. Before we left the locker room, he told us we would practice the next morning—"Taped!"

"Taped" meant it wouldn't be a walk-through practice. We always checked the chalkboard at home to see if a practice was "taped" or "no tape." A taped practice meant we needed to get our ankles taped for a hard workout.

I was shocked. We had to play Boston College the next evening, and BC was not your typical Classic cream puff; they had Michael Adams, the great little point guard, and they played in the Big East Conference, which many people considered the dominant conference in basketball. In high school, I had been used to a light practice the day before a game and no practice at all on game day.

I was reminded, again, that this wasn't high school.

The next morning, we bused over to Indiana University/ Purdue University at Indianapolis and practiced hard for an hour and a half. Every time I ran a drill or made a hard cut, I wondered if it would take something away from my performance that night. But I never thought of coasting. Coach Knight watched us intently and barked at every miscue.

He must have known what he was doing. We beat Boston College, 72–66, and carried home another Classic trophy. Marty and I both started. I scored 19, which lifted my spirits, but Marty lifted the whole team, dropping in rainbow jumpers from all over the court and rebounding like a man possessed. He not only joined Uwe on the all-tournament team, he was also voted MVP, the first freshman to be so honored in a Classic.

This time, Coach sent us home for New Year's with a stern message: "Boys, go home and relax. But remember— now we've got the conference to contend with. If you want to play in March, you'll have to prove yourselves in the Big Ten."

Dakich translated for the freshmen: "That means now it gets intense."

We opened the Big Ten season at Columbus, Ohio, on January 7. I was unbelievably excited when I walked into St. John's Arena for the first time. I knew its history. Jerry Lucas had played there, John Havlicek had played there—and, of course, Bob Knight had played there. Coach was the sixth man on the team that won the NCAA title in 1960. He wasn't a starter, because he was a step slow on defense, but as he put it, "When I got beat, I made sure the guy felt my presence."

My performance against Boston College had earned me a start against the Buckeyes, and I made the most of it, scoring 24. We won, 73–62. Four days later, I scored 29 and we beat Illinois in overtime... although there wouldn't have been an overtime if I hadn't lost the ball near the end of regulation, when we had a 1-point lead. The biggest mystery of the Illinois game was Marty, who had been playing so well. He had his worst game ever—no points, no rebounds. Still, it was our seventh straight win.

We played Purdue at home on Saturday afternoon, and everybody stank. We lost, 74–65, after leading at halftime by 5. At one point, we let Purdue score 22 straight points.

Coach was predictably disgusted. He told us after the game that we lacked mental toughness, that we just didn't have the character to win. Then he suddenly flared up: "Get the hell out of here in ten minutes, or I'll throw you out with what you have on!"

We took the threat seriously. Some guys tried to catch quick showers, but most of us scrambled into our clothes and rushed out the door before he could lock us out. It wasn't even dark yet, and the parking lots were still jammed with game traffic. People gave us the strangest looks. Todd and I didn't cut the tape off our ankles until we got back to the dorm.

The next day, Coach went public with his discontent. On his Sunday television show he said, "We're a terrible defensive team," and predicted wholesale lineup changes. "It's probably my fault more than anybody's, because I'm supposed to have the team ready, but I didn't have the answer and I don't have an answer today. We will put a lineup on the floor that will compete Thursday night. It won't be made up of the same players, but it will compete."

So began one of the strangest weeks of my basketball life.

Coach had called practice for Sunday afternoon, but we arrived at Assembly Hall to find the locker room empty. I mean *empty*. There were no chairs, no signs on the walls, no managers, no assistant coaches. We milled around in the hallway for a few minutes, unsure of what to do. Then Coach showed up.

"You don't belong in that locker room," he told us bluntly. "A lot of great players have dressed in that locker room, players who earned the right. You aren't in that class."

He then led us down the hall to the visitors' locker room, where he had set up the VCR. For two hours we sat in the darkness, suffering through replays of the Purdue game. Coach was brutal in his criticisms. If anything, he seemed angrier than the day before, when the loss was still fresh.

The next day, Monday, we discovered that we were no longer worthy of even the *visitors'* locker room. All our chairs were lined up in the hallway, our gear and uniforms piled up on top. I found a few teammates in the training room, taping each other's ankles. Again, no managers, no trainers, no assistant coaches.

I dressed in the hallway, but decided not to get taped; I didn't want to risk blisters from inexpert taping. The concrete, I remember, was cold on my bare feet.

Coach arrived at three. Alone.

"The assistant coaches won't be here," he said. "I told them not to come in. You didn't put enough effort into the Purdue game to *deserve* coaches and managers."

He looked strangely distracted, as if he had more important things on his mind than basketball, things like picking up the laundry or returning his library books.

"I'm going to do some things on my own," he went on, "then I'm going home. The assistants might be here tomorrow, they might not. You want to come tomorrow, you can come tomorrow—I really don't care. But I'm not doing anything to prepare for the game. If you can't get fired up to play Purdue, then I've got no interest in you. I've got no interest in coaching players who won't put out the same effort as the coaches."

Having said that, Coach walked to the other end of the building, got on a stationary bicycle, and started pedaling.

Chuck Franz and Dakich were not as stunned as I was. They had seen variations of this hands-washing routine in previous seasons. Coach had walked out of practices before, only to return the next day. On the other hand, he had always left his assistants to coach the team. This time, there were no assistants.

It was totally silent in the gym, except for a nervous dribble or two. Finally, Chuck and Dan took command. Someone said, "Let's get started," and we began our usual drills.

Superficially, it probably looked like a normal practice— basketballs bouncing, feet shuffling and shoes squeaking, players yelling on defense. In reality, it was nonsense work. Without the coaches we couldn't approach our usual level of intensity and concentration.

Down at the far end, Coach pedaled away on his bike. He looked our way from time to time. Finally, he left, stopping just long enough to inform us that there would be no training table after practice. He said we didn't deserve to be fed by the university, either.

Practice limped to a halt at about five o'clock. We dressed in the dark hallway and walked out into the cold and blustery night, wondering what surprises Coach would have for us the next day.

Tuesday's practice turned out to be much like Monday's —no coaches, no managers, no trainers. Coach pedaled away on his exercise bike.

Chuck and Dan thought we should work on the faulty execution Coach had pointed out on the Purdue tape, so we ran some breakdown drills and game simulations. Coach offered no help, except to call Dan over once to say, "If I were running this practice, I'd put Blab in the middle of a circle and have everyone throw the ball at him until he learns to catch it."

This time, on his way out, Coach informed us coldly that the assistants had left a tape of Michigan State for us to watch...if we wanted to. Beyond that, there would be no scouting reports, no game boards, no game plan.

"By the way, Chuck." He turned to our only senior. "The plane is not going up tomorrow. You'll have to get buses. Oh, and you'd better arrange for a hotel for the team in Lansing, and you'll need to schedule court time if you plan on a shoot-around. And you'd better make arrangements for meals."

We were stunned. Apparently, Coach had canceled all the arrangements for our trip.

When Coach was gone, Chuck looked at Dan in disbelief. "Dan, what in the world is going on?"

More than any other player, Dan understood Coach's mind games. "You know as well as I do," he told us, "that the plane's going up tomorrow. No matter what Coach does, the game is gonna be played on Thursday. If we win that game, everything's gonna be back to normal."

His face hardened. "We've *got* to win the next game."

Chuck and Dan brought practice to a quick halt and

rushed off to take care of their new duties. Maybe Coach was bluffing, but they couldn't take a chance that he wasn't.

Chuck found one of our senior managers and got a crash course in travel-agenting. Before the evening was over, he had chartered buses to take us to Lansing, booked motel rooms there, reserved court time for practices, and scheduled banquet rooms for our meals. Dan took charge of the VCR, the Michigan State tapes, the medical supplies, the balls and equipment, and all the other stuff we took on trips.

As a mere freshman, I had no new responsibilities. Marty and Todd and I got something to eat and went back to the dorm, where we sat on our beds and laughed about the day's events. It was the only way to keep our sanity.

The thing that struck us, though, and kept us from panicking, was that the upperclassmen seemed to take everything Coach did in stride. They had been through a lot of strange stuff with him in previous seasons, and they swore that Coach knew what he was doing, even if he seemed totally off the wall. There wasn't a hint of rebellion among the upperclassmen—just the usual bewilderment and awe.

I hadn't been through a full season with Coach Knight, so I was less confident. When I went to my room that night and tried to study, I couldn't concentrate. Was Coach really going to let us travel to Lansing without him? Would he throw away a game against a Big Ten opponent just to make a point?

I pushed away my books. What was I reading, anyway?

For the second night in a row I slept poorly, but I'm sure Chuck Franz slept worse. He was two nights away from coaching his first Big Ten game.

As it turned out, Dan was right. We got word the next afternoon that Coach had changed his mind: we *could* use the plane. The assistants were back, too. But things were hardly back to normal. Coach did not board the bus at Assembly Hall, and he was not waiting for us when the bus pulled up to the plane at the Monroe County Airport. Daryl,

Todd, Marty, and I got out and started carrying the luggage and gear to the plane, traditionally a freshman duty. We expected Coach to drive up any minute, but he didn't.

We all boarded the plane like strangers on a commercial flight. Coach's usual front seat, facing us, remained empty for the entire trip.

We were met on the ground in Lansing by Coach Chuck's bus, which drove us to the motel. He got us checked in with amazing efficiency. The evening meal awaited us, too, along with a motivational talk from Steve Downing, a Hoosier all-America who had played for Knight in the early seventies. Steve evoked the Indiana basketball tradition and tried to explain to us why Coach was so upset, although nobody has ever satisfactorily explained Coach's moods.

After the meal, we gathered around the VCR to watch tapes of Michigan State. The Spartans had lost three straight games since winning their Big Ten opener, but one of their stars, Sam Vincent, had been out of the lineup. He was expected to play. Chuck and Dan, who knew most of their players fairly well, gave the rest of us the benefit of their experience. It was sketchy stuff. "This guy's real quick.... Be sure to block out number 45, Uwe.... Number 20 likes to jump into you to draw the foul...." Never before had an Indiana team faced a major opponent with so little preparation. We had no game plan, no strategy. The defensive matchups were made as if we were playing a pickup game: "Who you wanna cover, Steve?...I'll take number 20, Chuck...."

Of course, we knew that Coach had to have his reasons for letting us play unprepared. "Coach is telling us that our winning or losing here has little to do with Michigan State," Chuck said, "and everything to do with us."

Dan nodded grimly and repeated what he had said the day before: "We *have* to win this game."

The next morning, we had our usual walk-through, but it was a quiet and somber affair. Coach did not attend, and the assistants just watched and offered little advice. We went over the Michigan State offense, based on the previous night's tape session. "It doesn't matter what Michigan State does," Chuck reminded us. "It matters what *we* do."

The bus picked us up at the motel at five-thirty and drove us to the fieldhouse for the game. Coach didn't ride with us. Neither was he with us in the locker room while we dressed and got taped. (Tim Garl, our trainer, was back, thank God.) We watched the clock anxiously. When the time came to take the floor for warm-ups, there was still no sign of Coach. We went out alone.

Back in the locker room, we sat with the assistant coaches and waited. The managers leaned against the walls. Chuck paced nervously. The clock on the wall inched to seven twenty-five. Ten minutes to tip-off.

I looked at Uwe, who stared vacantly across the room. What was he thinking? That America was the land of the insane?

At seven twenty-seven, the door opened and Coach Knight walked in. He immediately gave some perfunctory instructions for the game. He didn't raise his voice. He didn't look anybody in the eye. His posture said, "I'm here because I have to be here." When he was through, he said, "Okay, let's go," and walked out. We followed him to the floor, grim and determined. We were met with rousing boos from the MSU fans.

Chuck and the four freshmen (including me) started the game—a lineup that startled the press at courtside, not to mention our opponents. Michigan State won the tip and scored a basket, drawing a roar from the crowd. We brought the ball down and looked for the good shot... and looked ... and looked. There was no forty-five-second clock in operation that year, so we could be as patient as we wanted. We ran nearly three minutes off the clock before we got the shot we wanted. It was a jump shot from the key, and Chuck buried it.

That set the tone of the game. We controlled the tempo and played for the high-percentage shot. On defense, we scraped and fought for position.

Coach? Legend has it that he sat on the bench and watched, not lifting a finger. Actually, he handled all the time-outs and substitutions as usual. The mind games were over. He wanted to win.

The game was tight from tip-off to horn. Uwe, who had struggled of late and hadn't played much in the game, came in near the end and missed a couple of foul shots. But then he hit two huge free throws that sent the game into over-time. In OT, we grabbed a quick lead and then stalled the game away, hitting our closing free throws for an 8-point victory.

When the final buzzer went off, we celebrated as if we had won the conference, hugging each other and jumping around. For the freshmen, especially, it was a thrilling win. Daryl had 13 points, Todd had 10, Marty 8, and I had 21—we had 52 points out of our team's 70.

Coach was jubilant in the locker room. He told us he was proud of us for overcoming adversity. He thought we had met a great challenge. "This just proves what you can do as a team," he said. "This is what I mean when I talk about mental toughness. Without it, you aren't worth a thing. With it, you can do great things."

He gave us an imploring look. "Why can't you *always* do it?"

After that, he moved among us, joking and slapping backs. He even threw the doors open to the media, which he rarely did on the road. It was a happy, noisy locker room.

It had been a truly weird week, but it had had the effect of pulling us together and bringing out a total effort—just as Coach must have figured it would. It was the first time that I really understood why people called Coach Knight a genius. No matter what he might do the rest of my career, no matter how far-out or wrong he might appear, I would always have to consider the possibility that there was a method to his madness.

Coach was just going out the door when he turned and looked back at Chuck Franz—the senior who had had the whole of Indiana basketball dumped in his lap. "Hey, Chuck!" he yelled. "You did a great job tonight. Do you want to coach the Michigan game?"

Chuck grinned and shook his head. "No, no, Coach. I don't think I want to."

Chuck didn't have to. We had our old coach back.

Our win at Michigan State announced to the conference what Coach had been saying all along: that this was not going to be a rebuilding year after all. We lost to Michigan on the road, but then won seven in a row. We were in first place in the Big Ten.

Let me state the obvious: winning is fun. The petty gripes and jealousies that can tear a team apart disappear. The fans get behind the team. The coach smiles more often and the reporters ask soft questions.

I realize that most people have the impression of Indiana basketball as an endless boot camp with Coach Knight as a sadistic drill instructor. The "war stories" are proof of that, and I'm as guilty as anybody because I tell them myself and laugh at the ones I haven't heard before.

The truth is, most of my memories of Indiana and Coach Knight are happy ones.

First of all, basketball is a gas. By the middle of my freshman season, I was a starter on a winning team in one of the best conferences in the country. It was a childhood dream come true.

Second, Coach Knight's stormy ways did not cover up the fact that he was a brilliant basketball mind. I had chosen Indiana to learn all I could about basketball, and Coach was the man who could teach me. When we prepared for an opponent, he said, "This guy's gonna go here, this guy's gonna be here...." Then we played the game and I saw those individuals making the exact same cuts and moves Coach had prepared us for. He was incredible.

Third, I had my teammates, friends, and family for moral support. I wasn't as social as most college students, but I spent lots of time with Todd and Marty, who were nothing but fun to be around. I went out on dates with Tanya, my high school sweetheart. Mom, Dad, and my brother, Sean, drove down from New Castle for all our home games; they even caught some road games, like Purdue and Notre Dame.

And believe it or not, the drill sergeant himself had his humorous side, which he showed us at least as often as he showed his rage. He has an affectionate way of needling players that is as welcome as outright praise. Marty he would tease about his weight (until it became very unfunny our sophomore year). Todd got wisecracks about being a Lutheran minister's son. Uwe got an earful for being a computer whiz and for his European ways.

With me it was usually some jab about my defense, but Coach's teasing revealed that he knew something about me as a person, too. Once, he wanted me to make a phone call for him, and I said, "I'd love to, if I can do it around nine tonight. I've got an FCA meeting." Coach, whose familiarity with the Fellowship of Christian Athletes probably didn't go beyond the initials, said, "Fine." As he walked away, he turned with a smirk and said, "Hey, Alford. Send up a prayer for me." I grinned and we both walked off in different directions, but Coach turned again. "Hey, Alford! Just don't put me at the top of your list!"

He didn't mind a little teasing himself. One time we were in the locker room after warming up and Coach asked me to stand and tell the team what we should work on in practice. I stood up and said something brilliant like "I think we should work on our defense."

He turned to Dakich. "Dan, you've been here a few years. Why don't you tell these guys what we're gonna do?"

Dakich jumped up. "Can I start over there?" He pointed

at the cinder-block alcove that hid the door that Coach always came through.

Coach raised an eyebrow, but nodded his okay. Dan disappeared behind the wall and returned an instant later, transformed: head cocked to one side, eyes down, shoulders kind of hunched. We laughed in immediate recognition, the assistant coaches louder than anybody. Dan frowned, scuffed his heel. He spit on the floor and worked the stain around with the toe of his shoe. He even picked up the marker the way Coach did.

"Boys," he began, and he launched into a crazy parody of Coach, profanity and all. He roasted Uwe; he got on me about my defense; he attacked everyone's manhood; and he finished up by staring down at his own empty chair and barking, "Isn't that ———— right, Dakich?"

Coach laughed so hard he was doubled over.

(Dakich said later, "I'm not so brave. I kept looking over my shoulder to see if he was still laughing.")

It's a myth, you see, that every day is a nightmare at Indiana. It's only every third day or so.

It is also a myth that every Indiana practice is an endurance test. Yes, there were times when Coach worked us to death. But those practices usually came early in the season, when he needed to work conditioning into the mix. Once we got into the Big Ten schedule, Coach was more concerned with keeping us mentally sharp. I remember practices where we came out—taped—and ran maybe four drills, and if we ran them sharp, that was it. Practice over.

Take Iowa. The Hawkeyes always pressed us, and naturally we prepared for them by trying to beat the press in practice. The starters always wore red, and if we beat the white team on the press five or six straight times, Coach yelled, "That's it!" and sent us home. He always wanted to end on a crisp, positive note, and the sooner you could do that, the shorter the practices.

Another myth: Coach Knight does nothing but tear players down.

Coach would take time out every couple of weeks to go around the locker room and critique each player individually. He'd tell you the good things you were doing, as well as the bad, and tell you what you needed to work on. Coach often pointed out my defensive shortcomings or the way I "looped" on my cuts. With Uwe, it was always those "bad hands," or his inconsistency, or his lack of a "killer instinct." Whatever your failing, Coach always had ideas on how you could correct it: a new drill, a different mental image, modified footwork.

Above all, he insisted that we grow in our understanding of the game. In film sessions he might suddenly say, "Alford, where should Thomas be at this point?" or "Where should Robinson throw the ball here?" You were supposed to answer without hesitation and be right.

If the fans and media didn't always give us credit for knowing what we were doing, it was partly because Coach had such a reputation as a motivator. When we played good defense, people said it was because we were "inspired" or "superaggressive"—as if we were mindless animals scrapping for a piece of meat. Actually, we always took the floor with our heads full of instructions from Coach: "This guy doesn't pass the ball off the dribble well.... This guy can't go to his left.... This guy can't see the floor when he's dribbling; you can attack the ball.... This guy brings the ball down before he shoots in the lane—sneak in and tie him up...." He critiqued the films so carefully that we knew the tendencies and weaknesses of every player on the other team.

Of course, outsiders never got to see that side of Coach, the teacher. What they saw at games was a man who yelled at his players, glared at officials, and sat fuming on the bench when things went wrong, a man who seemed unable to accept mistakes.

Another myth? Uhhh...no.

I remember a game against Wisconsin that February, during the winning streak. We had built up a 16-point lead, and suddenly we went brain-dead. In one stretch, we fouled the Badgers' Scott Roth, and he sank both free throws. Then we threw the ball away and fouled Rick Olson as he made a lay-up. Olson then made his free throw, completing a 5-point giveaway that took only eighteen seconds. When we went to the sideline for a TV time-out, the lead was 7 and Coach wouldn't even talk to us. "Hold your own time-out!" he yelled, and turned away.

Afterward, when asked if breakdowns weren't to be expected on the best of teams, he answered, "I don't see why. I don't believe in the law of averages."

That pretty much said it. Coach's Holy Grail was the mistake-free game.

Coach *did* believe in the law of averages when it came to shooting. "Shooting is the most important skill a player can have," he said. "I didn't used to think that, but I do now. If you can shoot it and you're an athlete, we can teach you how to pass and how to block out and how to play defense."

I was the most obvious beneficiary of that belief. Although I had been a point guard in high school, Coach used me more as a "forward shooter" in his motion offense. My role was to come off a screen without the ball, take the pass, and shoot the baseline jumper. I was the first player of my size to do that for Coach. The guys who had played that role for Indiana in the past—Wittman, Kitchel, Scott May, Steve Green—had been big, strong forwards.

If you were a good enough shooter, Coach sometimes waived his rule about waiting four passes to shoot. "Kitchel could shoot it well enough," Coach said, "that I would sometimes skip a little—zero, one, four, 'Good shot, Ted!'"

Coach never actually *gave* me that license, but I noticed early in my freshman year that he didn't say anything when I broke the four-pass rule. (It wasn't until my junior year that he flat out told the team, "The only player I want to shoot the ball without four passes is Steve.") But Coach's silence often spoke louder than his words. I knew by the start of the

Big Ten season that I was supposed to take the jump shot when I was open.

One reason Coach wanted me shooting jump shots, obviously, was that he thought I could hit them. A second reason was that he wanted me to get fouled so that I could go to the foul line. Early in the season I had a couple of games where I scored big at the line—13 out of 14 in one game, 15 out of 16 in another. The crowds at Assembly Hall, catching on to my foul-shooting routine—which included wiping my sweaty hands on my socks and shorts and dribbling three times—had begun chanting in time to my movements: "Socks, shorts, one-two-three...*swish!*"

My ability to hit 90 percent of my free throws provided me another role in Coach Knight's strategy. If we had a lead late in the game and our opponents had to foul, Coach wanted the ball in my hands instead of, say, Uwe's, because Uwe was about a 55 percent foul-shooter. Many of my free throws came on one-and-one opportunities set up by desperation fouls.

By letting me shoot almost at will and by giving me the ball in crunch time, Coach made me a more dangerous offensive player. Defenses could not collapse on Uwe without leaving me open, and if they pressured me away from the basket, we dumped the ball inside to Uwe. During the Big Ten season, I averaged ten or twelve shots a game, which is about as much as any one player shoots on most Knight-coached teams.

While I was shooting more, Marty was shooting—and playing—less. He had played brilliantly during the nonconference part of the schedule, but he fell off somewhat after the first of the year, when we started playing taller, more physical Big Ten teams. Those rainbow shots of his began hitting the rim more often and bouncing away. He turned the ball over more and forced bad shots. ("Shooting when he should be faking," Dakich said, "faking when he should be shooting.") Coach got on him a lot in practice and yanked him quicker in games.

Coach blamed Marty's slump on his weight. "I think right now he is too heavy," he told the newspapers. "That strength was great in high school, but the bigger guys he's going against now are quicker than he played against before."

Marty's weight, according to the media guide, was 215, but he was really about 220. Coach decided he should weigh 210. "Get that fat off," he told him.

Reducing was not easy for Marty, who was a big-boned, thickly built kid. He began getting up before dawn to run laps at the IU track. He tried to sweat some of it off in saunas. He experimented with diets and exercised in rubber suits.

The less he played, the more Marty got down on himself. In early February, it got into the newspapers that he was quitting the team. Todd and I knew he wasn't quitting, but we could tell that he was discouraged. "It seems like he doesn't have his mind in the game like he did earlier in the year," Todd said. "I'm his roommate, and I can't see what the problem is, unless he's homesick."

Coach, realizing that Marty was losing his confidence, kept him in the starting lineup. Marty exploded for 30 points against Wisconsin on the road, and things looked better. But then he scored just 8 in our rematch with the Badgers at Assembly Hall. Adding to his woes, he began to suffer from back spasms. Marty scored a total of 6 points in his next two games.

Coach was losing patience.

To be honest, Marty's problems didn't seem that critical at the time. As a group, my fellow freshmen and I were big hits with the fans. Todd had a bad knee, but he was playing without a brace and playing well, mostly off the bench. He started six games, including our overtime win at Michigan State, and Coach seemed pleased with his screens and rebounding. Daryl was averaging only thirteen minutes and about 3 points a game, but he started six games, too, and was certainly no bench-warmer. Daryl had 3 steals in four different games. The media got pretty excited about the four freshmen, calling us one of Coach Knight's best-ever recruiting classes.

The upperclassmen were playing great, too, so morale couldn't have been higher when we flew to Evanston, Illinois, on February 17. We were in first place and riding the crest of a winning wave. If we beat Northwestern—usually the weakest team in the Big Ten—we figured to have the drop on Illinois and Purdue going into the last five games.

Instead, we played horribly and lost, 63–51.

The flight back to Bloomington was the worst forty-minute flight I've ever been on. There was no cardplaying, no whispered conversations to seatmates. Coach Knight had the floor—even if the floor was ten thousand feet in the sky—and he was plenty irate. He walked up and down the aisle, calling us names, picking us to pieces collectively and individually. He'd yell some, sit down. He'd remember a bad play from the game, jump up, and yell some more.

We knew what he was doing: playing the game over and over again in his mind. Coach's recall was amazing. It was as if he had a mental VCR and he was fast-forwarding and stopping until he saw somebody screw up. That's when he yelled, "Giomi, you screwed up that backscreen!" or "Alford, what in the world did you think you were doing on that three-on-one?" His language, of course, was stronger. You just sat there, knowing the images were racing by in his head, praying that he didn't see *you* in his head, screwing up.

When he wasn't remembering screwups, Coach sermonized. The subject of his sermon was "mental toughness." His conclusion: we didn't have any.

We were used to Coach's tendency to get physical in locker rooms—that's why all the inspirational signs and team goals were bolted to the walls. His gestures were a little more frightening in a small plane. Coach always wore his huge championship ring, and now he waved his arms in anger and the ring hit the top of the cabin, ripping a gash in the ceiling. For the rest of the flight, we kept peeking up at the ceiling to see if the rip was getting bigger. We all breathed a sigh of relief when the plane touched down safely.

But Coach wasn't through with us. As always, the trip ended with a bus ride back to Assembly Hall, and Coach yelled at us all the way in from the airport. At the gym, we emptied our bags and put our shoes in our lockers. Then we went upstairs to the I-Men Lounge for Coach's final comments, which took another half hour.

When we added up the time later, we estimated that Coach had yelled at us, virtually nonstop, for two and a half hours.

And why not? The Northwestern game probably cost us the 1984 Big Ten championship. We beat Purdue soundly eleven days later—at their place, no less—but lost to Michigan State and Illinois and had to settle for third place. Illinois and Purdue shared the conference title with fifteen wins each.

Were we devastated? Not at all. As Coach said after we lost to Illinois, "We just got beat. There isn't any sense getting upset when you get beat. You get upset when you lose, not when you get beat."

We had reason to feel good about our season. Uwe had improved, all the freshmen had contributed, and we had won thirteen conference games with only one senior on our roster. The Associated Press ranked us eighteenth in the nation. *Sports Illustrated* honored us with an article titled "Now Appearing: Bobby K and the Four Freshmen." Best of all, we were in the NCAA tournament with a first-round bye, looking forward to playing somebody—probably nineteenth-ranked Auburn—at Charlotte, North Carolina.

On a personal level, I couldn't have been happier with my year. I started twenty-four games, finished third in the conference in scoring average, and set IU records for field-goal percentage and free-throw shooting.

With so many things to feel good about, the NCAA pair-ings were only a little discouraging. We figured to be under-dogs from the word go, because Auburn had Charles Barkley ("the Round Mound of Rebound") and Chuck Person, two future NBA stars. If we got past Auburn, it looked like we would have to play number-one-ranked North Carolina, led by Michael Jordan and Sam Perkins. There wasn't exactly a run on Final Four tickets in Bloomington.

Surprise. Auburn got upset by the Richmond Spiders, 72–71, on Thursday night. That threw our preparations off, because we had spent the whole week thinking of ways to stop Barkley and Person. Coach had only a day and a half to drill us for Richmond, and that worried him. He also feared that we would suffer a letdown playing a weaker opponent —the old "mental toughness" issue.

Fortunately, there were no surprises at Charlotte. Uwe played a strong inside game, I scored 22, and seven other players scored for us in a 75–67 win. We flew back to Bloomington joking about the "rewards of victory"—having to face the best North Carolina team in memory.

We had five days to prepare. "Give Coach a week of prep-aration," Chuck said, "and he can beat anybody."

Even so, we were apprehensive about playing the Tar Heels, who were 28–2 and the tournament's top seed. Coach took care of that the minute he walked into the locker room on Sunday. "We are going to beat North Caro-lina," he said, "and I'm going to show you exactly how we'll do it."

He turned on the VCR and called our attention to high-flying Michael Jordan, everybody's player of the year.

"I don't want you to jump with Jordan," Coach told us. "And I don't want you to deny him the ball. I want you to play way off him—two steps or more—and every time he moves toward the basket, cut him off. No backdoor plays. No alley-oops."

Dan, who was renowned for his woeful twenty-two-inch vertical jump, looked unsure. "I give him the outside shot?"

Coach nodded. He had watched lots of tape of Jordan, and he thought the weakest part of Jordan's game was his jump shooting. "It's a gamble. If he hits four or five in a row..." Coach shrugged off the possibility.

Sam Perkins also had to be contained, but Coach had a different strategy for him. "Perkins likes to get out on the fast break and pull up for the fifteen-foot jumper," he said. "We have to deny him the ball anywhere on the court. If he fills an outside lane on the break and a guard is streaking down the middle with the ball, whoever has Perkins, *stick with him*. Do you understand that?" Giomi and the other forwards nodded. "And he gets a lot of his points by crashing the boards. We've got to block him out. Do you understand that?" They nodded again.

The third element of our game plan was to defeat North Carolina's scramble defense. The Tar Heels forced a lot of turnovers, so Coach told us to beat their traps and get the ball to our best shooters for high-percentage jump shots. *And never mind the four-pass rule*. He looked at me. "Steve, you can beat that defense by putting the ball in the bucket. You can do that, can't you, son?"

What was I supposed to say? "Sure, Coach."

"Fine," he said. "Let's get to work."

The week flew by. We didn't work on defense at all, other than to walk through North Carolina's offense and talk over our stop-Jordan strategy. We concentrated on breaking the Tar Heel pressure. Coach put the red team on the floor against a six- or seven-man white-team defense. "Spread out!" he'd yell. "Split the trap! Get rid of the ball!" The practices were not long, but the pace was furious. Todd, who had had arthroscopic surgery on a knee during the summer, said his legs were as sore as they had been in preseason.

Coach never said who would cover Jordan on Thursday, but Dakich was smart enough to know he would get the assignment...if he played. "I bet Jordan's losing sleep at the thought of facing me," he joked. "They took my vertical jump my sophomore year and it was the all-time low. The only other people who jumped twenty-two inches were pregnant grandmothers."

There was one other key matchup, of course—Bobby Knight vs. Dean Smith. The media hyped the game as a great coaching confrontation, a battle of brains. Coach Smith, like Coach Knight, was an innovator, a tactician, a motivator, and a great floor coach.

We flew to Atlanta on Wednesday afternoon and checked into the hotel. The routine was unchanged: dinner at the hotel, a tape session, bedtime...a Thursday-morning walk-through at the Omni, a pregame meal of spaghetti and pancakes, an inspirational poem on our plates, a guest speaker, a few words from Coach.

He said one thing that I'll never forget: "You guys get me to the Final Four, and I'll win it."

What made the week even more exciting for me was that Dad's New Castle High School team, with my brother, Sean, as sixth man, had just won the Indiana semistate tournament. They would be playing Warsaw in the state semifinals on Saturday morning, and I was pretty wound up about that, too.

"Never mind about Warsaw," Sean told me on the phone. "That's our business. You get ready for North Carolina."

"Hey," I told him. "We're *ready.*"

Sports Illustrated called it a "monster upset."

In Bloomington, students set off firecrackers, honked horns, and created a mob scene around the Showalter Fountain, chanting "Go Big Red!" and "We're number one!"

I remember it as one of the most exciting nights of my life.

From the opening tip, the 16,723 fans at the Omni couldn't believe what they were seeing. Where were the famous Indiana screens? What had happened to the four passes? Every time we came downcourt with the ball, Coach screamed, "Spread out! Spread out!" And we did. Every time the Tar Heels tried to double-team a dribbler, Coach shouted, "Get rid of it!" And we did. Every time one of us had the open shot, he yelled, "Shoot it!" And we did.

Dakich was amazing. He played so far off Jordan that Michael looked confused, uncertain whether to shoot or pass off. When he attacked without the ball, Dan was always there to cut him off. The backdoor passes were intercepted; the alley-oops flew out of Jordan's reach or deflected off his hands. Jordan missed eight of his fourteen shots, pulled down just 1 rebound, and fouled out after playing only twenty-six minutes.

North Carolina never quit. Just when we thought they were beaten, they ran off 10 straight points and our lead shrank to two, 59—57. "Get the ball to Steve!" Coach yelled. "Make them foul Steve!"

The trouble was, the Tar Heels were fouling quickly, before I could get the ball. Marty missed three straight free throws and it looked like we were about to fold. Then North Carolina missed a shot and a bunch of players scrambled for the rebound. I got the ball and came dribbling out of the pile with Joe Wolf on my back. I was shielding the ball with my body, and suddenly I stopped dead in my tracks. Wolf crashed over my back, knocking me to the floor.

I heard the whistle, but I had to look up to be sure. I was flat on my back when the official called the foul on Wolf. I pumped my arms into the air with glee, knowing I was going to the line. Dakich was standing over me, and he gave me the strangest look—a look that said, This kid is eighteen years old and he wants to shoot a one-and-one in the NCAAs with the game on the line!

But that's just how it was. I made both foul shots, and that's as close as North Carolina came. In the last five and a half minutes, we didn't take a single shot from the floor, but I got fouled three times and went 6-for-6 in one-and-one situations.

When the horn went off, we went crazy, mobbing Dakich and hugging each other like NCAA champs. It was almost as wild in the locker room. When Coach let the reporters in, everybody seemed to want to talk to me, because I was a freshman and had scored 27 points, and to Dakich, because he had held down Jordan.

Dan was in rare form. "When I found out I was covering Jordan," he told the writers, "I went back to my room and threw up."

Back at the hotel, I raced for the phone and called home. "This must be the week for the Alfords!"

Dad said he was really proud of me. "And listen—did you know you tied my free-throw record tonight?"

"I *what?*"

My excitement, if possible, grew. Dad had led the nation in free-throw percentage in 1964, when he was a senior at Franklin College. His percentage: .912.

He said, "You were 9-for-10 tonight. I got my calculator out, and I've got you with 135 made in 148 attempts, for .912. Those were my exact numbers in 1964—135-for-148."

I couldn't believe it. I knew I was ranked first or second in the nation in free throws, but I hadn't given much thought to it. But beating Dad...*that* possibility fired me up.

"I'm gonna beat you," I said. "Get used to the idea—I'm gonna beat you Saturday night."

He laughed. "We'll see."

Happiness kept me up most of the night.

Too bad we had to play on Saturday.

Two nights after beating a North Carolina team that Virginia coach Terry Holland had described as "the finest college basketball team ever put together," we lost, 50–48, to Virginia—a team that had tied for fifth in the Atlantic Coast Conference. Two nights after shutting down the finest player in the land, Dakich lost the ball on a crucial play late in the game, when we were in a delay. Two nights after scoring 27 points, I scored 6 and had trouble getting open for shots.

The headline on Sunday's *Herald-Telephone* said it all: IU DREAM TURNS INTO NIGHTMARE.

Once again, we had failed to win big games back-to-back. Coach hardly knew what to say to us in the locker room. He looked bewildered.

He didn't have an explanation for the media, either. "That's the kind of thing that drives you crazy," he told them. "Gosh, we've just tried to answer that question all year long."

Was he angry? During the game, yes. But not in the locker room afterward. We hadn't gotten him to the Final Four, but he knew we had come closer than anybody had a right to expect. He was calm when he went out to face the press, and his eulogy for the Team of '84 was heartfelt. He said, "There were times when these kids played the game as close to as well as they could as any team we've had. From beginning to end, they worked at representing Indiana University as well as they possibly could."

My phone call to Dad on Saturday night was pretty subdued. Not only had *we* lost, but Dad, Sean, and New Castle had lost to Warsaw as well. I couldn't think of anything to crow about, except that I had gone 2-for-2 from the line against Virginia.

"Well...I beat you at free throws, anyway."

Coach Knight went to the Final Four without us. It was held in Seattle that year, and it was a great one: Georgetown and Patrick Ewing beating the Phi Slamma Jamma boys from Houston in the final. I watched the games on television with some friends at home in New Castle. At halftime of one of the games, I looked up, and there was Coach Knight on the screen, talking to Brent Musburger of CBS. And it was weird, because Coach said my name. He looked right into the camera and said, "I know Steve's watching back home. The thing I want him working on all summer is his defense and moving without the ball."

I turned to my buddies and shook my head. "He's two thousand miles away and he's still on me about my defense!"

The next week, back at school, I resumed my individual workouts—a program of basketball drills I follow when I'm not practicing with a team. I also spent a lot of time in the weight room, trying to build up from the 155 pounds I played at as a freshman. The rest of my basketball time was devoted to pickup games at the Hyper Building, a huge stone rec center across the street from the Student Union. Todd and Marty and Daryl were usually there, and the games were very relaxed and fun, simply because there were no coaches watching us.

"I've got the whole summer to get better," I told Todd. "And no Coach Knight on my butt!"

Or so I thought. A few days later, I got a letter at the dormitory. "Dear Mr. Alford," it began. "It is our pleasure to extend you this invitation to participate in the U.S. Olympic Basketball Trials, April 17 through 23...."

The letter was signed "Robert Knight, Olympic Basketball Coach."

CHAPTER TWO

MORE LIKE AN OBSESSION

My favorite gyms are old and dark. A tunnel leads out to a floor yellow with old varnish. Iron pillars support a shadowy roof. The bleachers are wooden slabs bolted to concrete. Empty, the place is quiet as a church. Crowded, the court is a deafening pit. The mascots and cheerleaders are so close you can feel their breath on your neck when you shoot from the corner. At night, with the lights out, moonlight shines on the floor from windows high up on the walls.

Those are the gyms I grew up in.

I was born in Franklin, Indiana, but my earliest memories are of Monroe City, a little corn-and-soybean town in the southwest corner of the state. We moved to Monroe City in 1966, when I was one, because my dad, Sam Alford, had taken the head coaching and athletic director jobs at Monroe City High School. It was a small school, maybe one hundred students. A tall kid came along about every ten years, if you consider six foot three tall.

Dad's Monroe City team won twenty straight games that year and won the Wabash Valley Championship. Monroe City was absorbed the following year by South Knox High, a new consolidated school. Dad got the coaching job there.

I don't know what role fate plays in these things, but I'm sure I was destined to be a basketball player. On my first Christmas, Mom sent out baby pictures of me that she captioned, "Mr. Basketball 1982."

I began going to my dad's games when I was three years old, and I missed only two games in fifteen years. I learned my numbers in the South Knox gym. Mom sat beside me in the row behind the players and helped me with the scoreboard: 2 points for a field goal, 1 point for a free throw. I learned to add by ones and twos and to count backward with the scoreboard clock, which had big black hands and turned red and buzzed when time ran out. When I was old enough to write, Dad gave me a piece of paper and a clipboard, and I wrote down the numbers every time the scoreboard changed. For practice with bigger numbers, Mom had me match the numbers in the program with the numbers on the players' uniforms.

That's probably why I remember the numbers of Dad's old players better than I remember their names. Number 45 had a flattop haircut and a pretty jump shot. Number 34 went to the free-throw line about ten times a game. Number 44 was left-handed and Dad yelled at him a lot. Number 52 was always rolling up a slice of bread and eating it for a snack.

My favorite South Knox player was number 43, who always shot from the corner. I liked him because he always "hung the net" when he scored. His shots would arch high and swish through those old short, snappy nets, and the loops would jump up and hook onto the rim. It was the first thing in basketball I fell in love with. To this day, I don't leave the floor after a workout without hanging the net on a long shot from the wing or corner.

I didn't always sit with Mom at games. Sometimes I sat on the bench next to Dad in an unofficial or official capacity. When I was four, I was the ball boy at homecoming. I wore a Sunday-best suit and a tie with "Blue Jeans" printed on it. (We were called the Blue Jeans because former Indiana governor "Blue Jeans" Williams was from Monroe City.) I didn't need much minding. I was happy to be at the games because the gyms were loud and bright (even the dark ones) and fun. I hung around the cheerleaders a lot because they seemed to be in charge of the yelling and screaming, which I liked. When we won a game and the place went nuts, I always ran to hug the cheerleaders first.

It wasn't just the games. Dad says that whenever he left the house for the gym I would be on his heels like a puppy, all excited and wanting out. I loved to go with him into the dark gym and watch the lights come on one at a time and listen to the echoes of our shoes and voices.

I always had a ball in my hand, not necessarily a basketball. When I was real little, I used to shoot Ping-Pong balls into Tinkertoy cans. I went through a phase with peanut-butter jars. Then it was Nerf balls and wastebaskets. Outdoors, I carried around a Wiffleball and bat. I'd throw the ball up and hit it, throw the ball up and hit it. When I wanted privacy, I closed myself in my closet, turned on the light, and played closet basketball. I would call the game like a radio announcer: "Alford comes down the court and screens for the Big O, gets the ball back on the pick and roll, back to Robertson . . . Robertson *scores!*"

Mom and Dad would sneak up to the door and listen. They'd die laughing.

Sometimes, though, they worried that my interests were too narrow. I never played cowboys and Indians, like a normal kid. I didn't want to be a fireman or ride on spaceships. I had no interest in music, even though Mom was a piano teacher. That bothered Dad. He didn't want me or my younger brother, Sean, to feel pressured to be jocks just because he was a basketball coach.

On the other hand, he could see my enthusiasm for sports, and he didn't want to stifle me, either. "There are kids who love basketball," he would say years later, "but with Steve it's more like an obsession."

I played in my first organized basketball game when I was five years old, a kindergartner. That tells you something about me and maybe more about Indiana. The game was at Vincennes, which is just west of Monroe City. I don't remember much about the game, but I remember the gym—I've always been able to remember gyms. I think it was a YMCA. It was a very small gym with an overhead track, and adults ran laps while we played. The baskets were lowered to eight feet for us, and we must have looked real cute heaving basketballs at a target that was still twice our height. I may have scored some points, but I doubt that I hung the net.

We moved to Martinsville in 1971, when I was six years old. Martinsville (population twelve thousand) was the smallest town in the conference, a three-stoplight slowdown on State Highway 37, midway between Indianapolis and Bloomington. It typified small-town Indiana: a church with a steeple, a movie theater on Main Street, a courthouse and war memorial on the town square, and a Dairy Queen at the edge of town. John Wooden, the legendary UCLA coach, played his high school basketball in Martinsville.

Mom and Dad bought a small brick house a block off the main drag. Dad thought Sean and I had gotten too big for roughhousing in our bedroom, so he set up a basketball goal for us in the basement. Not a toy goal—a regulation-size backboard and hoop. The rim was maybe four feet off the floor, but that was fine with Sean and me. We could slam dunk.

There is a picture of me at age three wearing Dad's Franklin College basketball uniform and holding a basketball.

Both the uniform and the ball look huge on me. I was constantly getting Dad's old stuff out. When I played downstairs or outside, I always had to have a full uniform on. I couldn't imagine playing without real basketball clothes. That set me apart from most kids, who didn't care what they wore, as long as they played.

Fortunately, I got plenty of opportunities to wear basketball suits. At Martinsville, Dad developed a kids' basketball program called the Biddy-Ball League. The teams were named for NBA teams, and I played on the Buffalo Braves. The real Buffalo Braves were led by Bob MacAdoo and Randy Smith, and I still have basketball cards of some of those guys. Their uniform colors were baby blue and orange-and-black.

In Biddy-Ball, we played with small basketballs on eight-foot goals, and we had a blast. Dad was one of the earliest coaches to use short goals with kids. A little boy or girl shooting at a ten-foot goal makes about one shot in fifteen, which isn't much fun. With eight-foot goals, we scored a lot of points and learned to shoot with good fundamentals. In fact, I shot at eight-foot goals until I was in fifth grade, and I think that's why I fell in love with basketball. Any time you have success with something, you have a better chance of falling in love with it.

I went to Dad's practices every day. I got out of elementary school at two-thirty, a half hour before the high school let out, and Mom would pick me up and drive me straight to the high school. I'd go right to Dad's office and then into the gym. I'd be at practice a half hour before the players, and since I stayed until Dad left, which was at least a half hour after practice, I usually practiced an hour longer than the team.

I was always on the floor. Dad would give me a small ball and I'd dribble around the side of the court during practice, or shoot on the side baskets. He'd tell me to hold the ball when he was talking, of course. When there was a lull, he would come over and say, "Dribble with your left hand now," or "Let's try behind our back today," things like that. I loved doing it. I loved being there.

I suppose I was a pest at times. I idolized one of the Martinsville guards, a wonderful kid named Jerry Sichting. Jerry just epitomized the Indiana basketball tradition. He was a great shooter, a scrappy defender, and a second coach on the floor. I imagined myself being just like him, ten years down the road. When he and the other players were working out, I was constantly underfoot, shagging balls for them and begging for a quick game of Horse.

They treated me great, but now and then they couldn't resist playing a prank on the coach's son. One time, Dad was running a practice and suddenly noticed I was missing. "Where's Steve?"

Nobody said anything, so he dispatched a manager to search for me. A few minutes later, the manager returned, very embarrassed. "Uh, Coach? Steve's trapped in a locker. He can't get out."

Jerry and one of his buddies, Bill Kramer, tried to look innocent, but their smirks gave them away. They had stuffed me in the locker just before leaving the locker room, and I had patiently waited to be rescued, peering out the air holes and breathing the aroma of stale sweat socks.

Another time, Dad's team was playing a conference game at Columbus High School in Columbus. I was the water boy. It was a terrific game, but I looked up at the scoreboard during the last time-out and felt sick: two seconds to go, we were behind by a point, and the other team had the ball. I left the floor, very disgusted, and ran into the locker room. I was crying my eyes out in a toilet stall when the players tumbled in a minute later. They were yelling and banging on the lockers, hugging each other, laughing. I didn't know what was going on.

It turned out the other team had made a stupid foul, Jerry had hit two free throws, and we had won the game by a point.

The players teased me for quitting on them so quick, but
that's how much I was into the games. I felt a loss as much
as they felt a loss.

Dad was still young enough to play pickup games with the
guys, and I'd often rebound for him when he practiced. He
was always shooting free throws. It amazed me the way he
could step up cold and drop shot after shot. He didn't have
to shoot in basketball clothes; he could shoot in a jacket or a
sweater or a long-sleeved shirt. The foul shot was one of the
first skills he taught me, because that's where you learn good
form. He had me shoot from twelve feet, not the regulation
fifteen; he didn't want me heaving the ball at the basket
from the side of my head.

In third grade, I entered the Elks Hoop-Shoot, a free-
throw contest open to kids in various age classifications. My
age group shot from twelve feet, and I was already deadly at
that range. I won at the school and town levels, then the
county and state levels, and qualified for the regionals at
Warren, Ohio. Martinsville had a game that day, so Dad
couldn't take me, but Mom found a private pilot to fly the
two of us to Warren in a small plane. The competition was
held at a high school gymnasium, and to advance to the
nationals I had to outshoot nine-year-olds from Michigan,
Illinois, Ohio, Kentucky, and Pennsylvania.

That's what I did. I hit 24 out of 25.

That done, we hurried back to the plane and flew to Martinsville, Indiana, where Martinsville was playing that night.
We got to the gym right before the tip, and Dad wanted to
know if I'd won. I said, "I hit 24. I'm going to Kansas City
for the nationals."

Dad was very excited.

Ironically, the game that night was decided at the foul line.
Jerry Sichting was fouled in the final seconds and sank two
clutch free throws to win the game for us. After the game, a
newspaper reporter asked Dad if he would have wanted anybody but Jerry at the line at that time, and Dad laughed and

said, "The only other guy would be my son, Steve." That made the morning paper, and I guess I swelled up pretty good.

The Martinsville players treated me like a little hero for winning the regional contest. Dad had one player, Dan Rhoden, who was a good, physical player but a terrible free-throw shooter, and he came to me and said, "Steve, I need you to work with me on my foul shots." So we'd shoot free throws together, and I'd give him pointers. I was ten years old.

When I went to the nationals in February, my whole family went with me. It was my first time on a huge plane, and I was impressed. The contest organizers met us at the Kansas City airport with a limousine and delivered us downtown to the Phillips House Hotel. We got the basic Final Four treatment: personalized warm-up suits, an awards banquet, good seats at a college basketball game, and a visit to the Truman Library.

The contest itself was staged at Kansas City's Municipal Auditorium, where many an NCAA basketball final had been played. It was a wonderful old cavern of a place, right out of the 1940s. I dressed with the other regional winners in a locker room under the stands, walked out to the applause of a small crowd, and prepared myself for fame.

Instead, I hit 22 out of 25 and finished fourth.

I still have a photograph of the contestants, taken right after the competition. All the kids in my age group are seated on the floor—the winner, who hit 24; the two guys who tied for second with 23; and all the rest of us from around the country. Every kid has a smile on his face except one—Steve Alford of Martinsville, Indiana. I look disgusted. It's a pitiful, ugly look. I went to Kansas City intending to win, *expecting* to win.

I was the fourth-best in America, and I was frowning.

I dreamed of playing basketball at Indiana University from about the second grade on. Bloomington was just fif-

teen minutes south of Martinsville, and we went to all the
games. The only time I had second thoughts was when
Sichting went to Purdue. For a while, my loyalties were torn.
But that ended when Jerry finished at Purdue. No school but
Indiana was ever in the picture again.

I first met coach Knight a few months after the free-throw
contest. Dad had hired on as a coach at Knight's summer
basketball camp, a week-long program that draws hundreds
of youngsters to Bloomington for coaching and competition.
Fifth grade was the cutoff for admission, but Dad was a
coach, so Knight let me in. I roomed with another coach's
son, Chad Tucker, who later starred for Butler University
and played pro ball in Italy. We became good friends. We
were the youngest kids in the camp, but very good for our
ages.

There was nothing dramatic about meeting the famous
coach. He was talking with Dad at courtside when I walked
by, and Dad simply introduced me. I was still little, of
course, and he struck me as a very large man. Dad was six
feet tall, big enough, but Coach Knight, at six-five and
wearing a bright red jacket, overwhelmed me. He looked
down at me—can he see future Indiana stars in squirts such
as I was?—and gave me some good advice: work hard, pay
attention to the coaches, try to get something out of it. I
said, "Yes, sir," and ran off to practice.

I attended Coach Knight's camp nine straight years, until I
was a senior in high school. You didn't see Coach Knight
much, except at his lectures, which were mostly about the
importance of fundamentals and working hard. The coaching at his camps was done by the IU assistants and high
school coaches like my dad. Coach Knight certainly didn't
yell at us or exhibit his colorful vocabulary.

I do remember an exchange with him the year after he let
Jerry Sichting go to Purdue, which he later admitted was his
one great recruiting mistake. I walked by him and he said,
"Has your dad got you to be a Boilermaker fan yet?"

I just looked down and said, "No, sir. I'm a Jerry Sichting

fan, but I'm not a Purdue fan." He laughed.

I always assumed, of course, that I would play high school ball for my dad at Martinsville. One night he called a family meeting to present some news: he had been offered the coaching job at New Castle Chrysler High School, east of Indianapolis. New Castle was bigger than Martinsville—population twenty thousand—and was a better-paying job in one of the powerhouse basketball conferences in the state. It was a definite step up for Dad, but he wanted our input before accepting the job.

He was most concerned about me. Mom was for the move, and Sean was just a second-grader, but I had become very attached to Martinsville. To test my feelings, he drove the family up to New Castle one afternoon. As we were coming into town, he said, "There's one place I want to take you to first."

Now, most fifth-graders are interested in the location of the nearest McDonald's, the nearest movie theater, the elementary school, what the playground looks like. The first place Dad takes *me*, just out of fourth grade, is the New Castle Chrysler High School Fieldhouse.

He opened the door and I walked in. My jaw must have dropped. We were on the upper concourse of a 9,300-seat arena, staring down on a basketball floor that many colleges would envy. An indoor track surrounded the top seats. A professional-style, four-sided scoreboard hung over the court.

I looked at him and said, "Let's come. I want to play here."

That's all there was to it. Dad took me to the athletic director's house, we drove around town, I saw some schools ...I wasn't interested. I had seen what I wanted to see: an unbelievable arena that would someday be full of people watching me play.

I asked Dad that first afternoon, "Has this place ever been filled?"

He said, "It was full when Kent Benson played here. It hasn't been full since."

I looked down on those thousands of empty seats and nodded. "I want to fill this someday."

The first thing I did when we moved to New Castle was try out for one of the Optimists' Little League basketball teams. It was a fifth-and-sixth-grade league that played on ten-foot goals but used junior-size balls. All the teams were sponsored by local businesses, such as the Rose Bowl bowling lanes and the Citizen State Bank.

That Optimists' League had an interesting draft system. The coaches took turns picking from a player pool, but each coach was allotted just so much "money" to bid on players —a clever way of maintaining competitive balance. I was a real little kid, scrawny-looking, but I was fundamentally sound, shot the ball well, and had good ball-handling skills. I caught the eye of John Fisher, who coached Smith's Jewelers. His team spent more points on me than any team had ever spent on a kid in that league.

John coached me for two years. He was very disciplined, loved hard work, and loved watching me play. Best of all, he was willing to push me. One thing John taught me that I still do today is to find the valve stem with my fingers when I shoot free throws, to get a better grip. He's the only coach who ever pointed that out to me, and I think it helps a lot. But the most important thing was, he made basketball fun and exciting. It was a great league—referees, cheerleaders, the whole bit.

Not that I needed all that stuff. Like most kids—well, maybe more than most kids—I could create the world of big-time basketball in my head. Dad had put up a basketball goal beside the driveway, and I could transform that flat patch of concrete into the parquet floor of Boston Garden or the floor of Madison Square Garden, the Forum, the Omni ...wherever I wanted to be. I'd play games in my driveway where it was Oscar Robertson vs. Jerry West. First, I was Jerry West: "West goes between his legs, pulls up, shoots... misses!" Then I was Robertson: "Robertson grabs his own rebound, goes back up...and draws the foul. He'll go to the line for two." And I'd shoot the free throws. I would play a whole game to 100, and when I got to 98 or 99 I always did the countdown from twenty seconds to end the game. Every game came down to hitting or missing a free throw.

It wasn't always West vs. Robertson. Sometimes I would take on one of those guys myself. Of course, you never lose an imaginary game.

I was still a closet-basketball player, too, although I had moved up to a better closet, one with a sliding door. I had sent off for a basketball board game called Fast Break Basketball, and I preferred to play the game in privacy, so I could concentrate. I put all my shoes and stuff on one side of the closet. That left the other side for the game. It was a roll-of-the-dice game that used cards for all the players in the NBA. I had clipboards and notepads and file cards with all the teams and players, and I kept the stats for every game I played. If Dr. J. was 3-for-8 from the field and 4-for-4 from the line, I put it down. I maintained the league standings and the scoring, rebounding, and assists races. When a season wound down, I even picked an all-star team and a Most Valuable Player.

With all that record-keeping, a single game lasted about two hours, but I didn't mind. In fact, I hauled a tape recorder into the closet and began taping my play-by-play, as well.

If it rained, I would stay in the closet all day, playing the game. I played with the closet door open—for comfort and because I was growing taller—but I kept my room door closed. Mom and Dad were still creeping up to the door to listen, but I didn't know that. I was totally engrossed in my fantasy world.

A couple of kids, Jeff and Greg Geozeff, lived two houses down from us. Jeff and Sean were the same age, and I was a year older than Greg. We always played two-on-two in the driveway. I mean *always*. When it snowed, the four of us would shovel the driveway off as fast as we could. The snow might be a foot high, but we played. I remember playing two-on-two in heavy boots and gloves. We'd cut the finger-tips off the gloves to get a better feel of the ball, and we'd stretch out the frozen net with a broomstick.

It was always Sean and Greg against Jeff and me. Twenty was the first quarter, fifty the second, eighty the third, and one hundred the game. Of course, we'd always count down from twenty seconds. We'd even call time-outs. Mom had put decorative white rock around the trees, and we'd huddle during the time-outs and draw plays on the sidewalk with the white rocks. We were imitating my Dad, who drew up plays with chalk on gym floors, but of course he had a team manager to wipe up the mess with a towel. Mom would get mad because we'd never wash ours off.

Dad was no stranger to the driveway. We played a lot of shooting games together: Horse, 21, Around the World— games in which his size and strength didn't give him as big an advantage. Many of the games with Dad were at the free-throw line. When I was an eighth-grader and using the big ball, I was about a 70 percent shooter. We'd go out in the driveway, and he'd say, "Let's shoot free throws until you miss." He'd always go first, and I would rebound.

Well, he would start shooting and he'd hit forty or fifty in a row.

That used to annoy me. Eighth-graders don't like to stand still much, and I had to just stand there under the bucket, catching the ball and bouncing it back to him. As he was shooting, he might ask me, "How's school going?" or "Did you do what your mother wanted you to today?" Just talk-ing about anything. "How many free throws did you hit today?" He wouldn't concentrate at all, and all these shots were knifing through, net after net after net. If he hit the rim, he'd always say, "I shouldn't really count that, but I'll go ahead and take it." He could be shooting barefoot, wearing long jeans, or bundled up in a coaching jacket—he still made shot after shot after shot. And that, too, upset me, because I was out there in my high-tops, my tank top, basketball trunks... all the gear.

He'd finally miss, and I'd get excited to death. But your first free throw is always your hardest, and a lot of times I'd miss my first free throw. (He would never give me a practice shot. *Never.*) And he'd go right back to the line. In a half hour's time, he would shoot eighty free throws, and I would shoot two.

It used to annoy me no end. And he knew that. As soon as he went into the house, I would spend another half hour practicing free throws.

Dad played his college ball at Franklin College, a small liberal-arts school south of Indianapolis. His high school pictures show him as a bony, scrawny kid, just like me, but he gained a lot of weight in college and was named to the Little All-America team in 1964. In the driveway, he showed me some of the moves he used at Franklin, which were very interesting to me. There's one step-back move that I still employ today. Dad used his body very well and was big into ball fakes, which I also enjoyed. He was a very good shooter and a very clever player.

Of course, everything I know about him as a player is from watching him in pickup games and from hearsay. One time, I'm told, he hit a lay-up on the dead run and wound up in the stands. The other team took the ball and threw it almost the length of the court, but they didn't realize that they were playing five-on-four. They missed a shot, Franklin got the rebound, and Dad raced back out of the stands, caught a length-of-the-court pass, and made another lay-up. (I guess that was clever, but Coach Knight would have wondered what Dad was doing so long in the stands while his teammates were playing defense.)

Franklin College was not exactly a stepping-stone to the NBA, but Dad was offered a tryout with the Chicago Bulls. He chose not to go, because of his size. After graduation, he

worked one year as seventh-grade basketball coach at
Franklin Junior High. He then went into high school coaching.

I didn't need hearsay to recognize that he was an outstanding coach. Dad was voted Indiana District Coach of
the Year in 1975 and 1979, making him the first coach to
receive that award in two different districts. He is also the
only coach to win championships in both the South Central
and North Central conferences. Dad was, and is, an amaz-
ingly hard worker. His high school teams played about
twenty games a year, and he made a point of seeing every
opponent twice. He provided his players with in-depth
scouting reports. He conducted film sessions. Like Coach
Knight, he was convinced that when players fell short of
their goals it was because they lacked commitment and discipline. Dad had that commitment and discipline, and I admired him enormously for it.

Still, I wanted badly to beat him at free throws. As I got
older and a little better, things changed a bit. When I practiced by myself, I began hitting ten in a row, twenty in a row,
thirty in a row. I carried this improvement into my contests
with Dad, and *he* began to tire of the rebounding. So he'd
try disrupting me. "How'd school go today?" he'd ask. "Did
you do that errand for Mom?" All the same questions he
asked when he was shooting that didn't bother him, but now
he was trying to affect *my* concentration. I would bounce the
ball a couple of times, look up at the rim, think, Soft over
the front of the rim, and try to answer his questions, all at
the same time. I would hit two shots and miss the third, and
I would find myself right back under the basket, rebounding,
while his shots went *swish ... swish ... swish. ...*

I was still annoyed.

My seventh-grade year was the year of the Indiana Blizzard. School was closed for at least a week during the height
of the storm, and lesser storms shut down the roads several
other times. We literally had to tunnel out the side door of

the house to go anywhere. Six-foot drifts covered the drive-way.

I hated it. The storms canceled all but eleven of my sev-enth-grade games, and I was upset all winter. I got grumpy. Restless. At school, I went to the windows between classes to see if it was snowing. I went home furious because an-other game was canceled and wouldn't be rescheduled.

Eighth grade was better. I played for Roger Miller, a fine coach, and we went 18–1. Roger taught me a lot about winning and encouraged the self-discipline that John Fisher and Carl Benson, my seventh-grade coach, had instilled in me.

I didn't play ninth-grade ball. I jumped up to the junior varsity instead. All my friends were playing ninth-grade, so that was a big adjustment. Grades ten through twelve were in a different building, and I had to run over there every afternoon for practice. I was still very small and thin. The high school kids were older, bigger, and mostly strangers to me, which made them very intimidating.

The junior varsity practiced in the girls' gym, upstairs from the big arena where the varsity practiced. One after-noon, a manager came in and told the JV coach that Dad wanted me down with the varsity. That happened some-times. Players could bounce back and forth between the two teams. You could even play in both games the same night, as long as you didn't total more than four quarters.

I hustled down the fieldhouse steps, very excited, and joined a shooting drill that was in progress. My shooting partner was Brian Lee, a junior who was a pretty good friend of mine. He asked me a question about Dad, and I replied, "Well, let's ask him." Dad was downcourt, so I turned and yelled, "Dad, come here!"

Dad turned and looked at me. Didn't move.

I said, "Dad!"

He stared at me a little longer and then walked over slowly. In a voice loud enough for everyone to hear, he said, "Look, on this floor I'm Coach. At home, I'm Dad. You'll refer to me on this floor as Coach. If you need me, say Coach, not Dad." And he turned and walked away.

Brian and the other varsity players laughed and grinned. They understood, probably better than I, the point that Dad was making. He didn't want to be accused of father-son favoritism.

People don't believe me when I say this, but Dad kicked me out of practices more often than Coach Knight did. There were times he kicked me out after I'd had a bad day in the classroom, or maybe my attitude wasn't what it should have been, and he'd just tell me to go home. I had a hard time dealing with that when I was younger. I would walk home infuriated, not knowing why Dad had done it. A lot of times, he would never tell me. Other times, he'd listen to me grumble at the dinner table, then say, "Hey, I'm going to kick you out just to show the players that I won't play favorites. I don't want them to see us that way, and I don't want to *be* that way."

I struggled a lot that year, not just with the change in my relationship with Dad, but with the game, too. Dad yo-yoed me back and forth from JV to varsity. I always played well in the JV games—I was one of the best players at that level—but at the varsity level the players were just too strong for me. I weighed only 127 pounds and got pushed around as if I were on skates. I averaged 1 point in seventeen varsity games.

If anything stands out from my freshman year, it is my brief appearance in a sectional tournament game against Richmond at the New Castle Fieldhouse. Our star player that year was Kevin Stephens, a very good shooting guard. With just under a minute left in the third quarter of a close game, Dad thought Kevin needed a breather, so he told me to go in for him. When I ran over to the scorer's table to check in, I got a standing boo from the home crowd.

Oddly enough, I didn't hear it. Or, if I heard it, I didn't make the connection that it was meant for me. But it upset Dad a great deal, and he said so in interviews after the game.

The standing boo notwithstanding, nothing significant happened in my minute-fifty of play. I did no wrong and hurt the team in no way, and Dad took me out at the quarter, as he had planned all along. We won the game.

Dad sat me down that night to talk about what had happened. "People don't want to see the coach's son out there," he said. "They want to see their own son."

I just shrugged it off. "Someday that'll all change, Dad. It doesn't bother me, so don't let it bother you."

I was telling the truth: the booing didn't bother me. But I *was* bothered about my game. I was as frustrated as I had ever been in my life. At the end of the season, I went to Dad and said, "Look, I've been *the* player on every team I've ever played on. I love this game too much to go through another season like this one. Dad, I want to be a *player*. What can we do?"

"You've got to make a decision," he said. "You're going to have to do something different this summer if you want to play against juniors and seniors next year. Otherwise, you have to accept that you'll be just another basketball player, one of the guys who comes through my program every year." He grabbed my shoulder. "Hey, it's fine, whatever you want to do. I won't think any less of you if you want to be an ordinary player coming through. Your mother and I don't love you as a basketball player, we love you as a son."

But he knew what my decision would be.

I said, "You know I want to be the best that's ever come through here."

He nodded. "Then we need to devise a workout program to make you better."

That's how it started. We created the workout together, asking ourselves "What can we do that the guy next-door is not doing?" The workout had to be of reasonable length—forty-five minutes seemed about right—and maximum intensity, combining physical conditioning with drills designed to develop my shooting and ball-handling skills. I had to be able to do it alone and anywhere there was a hoop. Last of all, the workout needed to be measurable in some way. We wanted to chart my progress, see where I was strong and where I needed work. If there was no way to measure a specific workout, we knew that my self-motivation would suffer. I would be tempted to coast.

When we were finished brainstorming, we had a workout that consisted of eight solo drills broken up by "rest periods," during which I shot free throws. We fine-tuned the workout afternoons at the gym, with Dad supervising. By the middle of June I was on my own. I did it religiously, every day. I would go home after a workout and chart my performance: how many free throws I had hit out of a hundred, how I had shot from the field, how my two-ball dribble had been (average, above average, poor).... At the end of the week, I would take a calculator and figure my percentages. By summer's end, I had thousands of repetitions of every drill; thousands of jump shots attempted, thousands made; thousands of free throws attempted, thousands made. I knew my summer percentages for every type of shot, my average daily best-string-without-missing from the foul line (between fifty and seventy)—you name it, I knew it.

When I couldn't do the workout at school, I did it in the driveway. Some days I did the workout both at school *and* in the driveway. The phone would ring in the house, and Mom would call out, "Steve, it's for you!" My answer: "Tell 'em to call back in thirty minutes, when I'm done."

Dinner was ready? "Put mine in the oven!"

Dad watched with interest but didn't interfere unless I asked him to. He held up John Havlicek, the great Boston Celtics forward, as a model for me. "You're not as big as he is," Dad said. "You're never gonna be that big, you're never gonna be that strong...so you're going to have to out*think* the guy across from you, you're going to have to beat him with your head." He told me not to worry about the things I couldn't do—like flashy dunks—and concentrate on the things I could do.

We still had our free-throw contests. I was throwing

strings of thirty or forty in a row at Dad now. He still tried to make small talk while I was shooting, but I wouldn't answer him. I didn't say, "Don't ask me that," or "Don't talk to me." I just ignored him.

One afternoon, he said, "Do you remember when you used to answer my questions?"

I said, "Sure. That's why I used to miss. That's why I did the majority of the rebounding."

He grinned. "Yeah, you're right."

We didn't have as many free-throw contests after that. Dad didn't like standing under the basket for long stretches with nothing to do.

My sophomore year, I averaged 18.9 points a game and New Castle went 12–11. Good numbers for me, not so good for the team. Tom Dalton, our six-foot-seven center, got hurt and missed most of the season. With Tom I'm sure we would have been better than 12–11, but I don't know if we could have challenged for the North Central Conference title. The NCC is a big-time basketball conference, producing more state champions than any other in Indiana. The crowds are the biggest, too. We billed our gym as the "World's Largest High School Fieldhouse," but we weren't much bigger than the schools we played against. Anderson's gym held 8,996, Marion 7,690, Lafayette and Kokomo 7,000 each, Muncie Central 6,950, Logansport 5,820, and Richmond, the smallest, 4,000.

Thanks to Dad's workout program, the fans no longer booed me when I went into the game. I now had three goals. The first was the one I had set for myself the first time I walked into the New Castle Fieldhouse: to fill the place. The second was to become Indiana's Mr. Basketball, the title given every year to the best high school basketball player in the state. The third? To win the state tournament for Dad.

The crowds began to come my junior year. We didn't sell out, but attendance jumped to an average of over five thousand in 1982. I averaged 27 points a game and made myself a serious contender for the next year's Mr. Basketball. (It's like the Heisman Trophy—you need a certain amount of publicity and hype going into your senior year.) Unfortunately, we had personality problems on that team, guys who couldn't get along. Our season ended in the sectionals again when we took two bad shots at the end of the game with us leading. Then I missed a shot at the buzzer that would have won it. We finished 12–10, and I was very upset because I had not yet played on a sectional champion.

Overall, though, the experience of playing for Dad and playing in front of big crowds made me very happy. When I think back to this time, many of my fondest memories are of the Sundays we spent together as a family. Indiana high school teams usually play on Friday nights and sometimes on Saturday nights, but you are not allowed to play or practice on Sundays. So, after church, Mom and Dad and Sean and I usually went to the gym. But not to practice; it was more or less a play day. We might get the floor tennis out, or I'd invite some of my friends over to throw a football around. I was co-president of the school's Fellowship of Christian Athletes chapter; we'd have meetings at the gym and then play Wiffleball on the floor, trying to hit homers into the seats.

Sunday afternoons also gave Dad and me the chance to be together, watching game tapes in his little office. It was a special time for both of us. During the week we had to maintain the coach/player relationship, and during the games we were both too busy to appreciate each other in action. On Sundays we reverted to father and son. I'd laugh if the camera caught him on the bench, waving his towel or kicking in anger. He'd smile with pride when I made a good move or sank a clutch basket. His love was unconditional— I knew that—but on Sunday afternoons I could tell how much he enjoyed coaching me and how much pride he took in my accomplishments.

Mom and I had a wonderful relationship, too. When I speak to young kids today, I jokingly say, "Don't dribble the

ball in the house, because your mom's gonna get on you."
That wasn't quite the case at my house. We had a long hallway, and I used to dribble the ball out of my bedroom and
down the hall when I was getting ready to work out. The
first few times I did it, Mom yelped like a mother: "Steve,
don't dribble the ball in the house! You'll break something."
She said that for maybe a week. Then she noticed how disciplined I was in my dribbling, even when I was on automatic
pilot. She stopped nagging me about it. I was outside in a
flash, anyway.

We did have lamps and vases and things that could be
broken, and I was always spinning a basketball on my
fingers. That would annoy her. She would be in the living
room reading by a table lamp, and I'd walk right up to her,
between the lamp and her chair, and spin the basketball on
my index finger. If it had fallen off it would have probably
broken the lamp. She sometimes gave me a look.

As I grew more skillful, I got to where I could spin the ball
on each of my fingers, hopping it from one to the other, up
and down my hand. Mom could be in the kitchen with all
the plates lined up for dinner, and I would spin the ball over
the plates, fully confident that I wouldn't lose control. When
I finally snatched the ball out of the air and went out to
practice, she would laugh and say, "I'm glad you didn't drop
that."

I did things like that to put pressure on myself.

In retrospect, the most important thing that happened the
summer after my junior year had nothing to do with basketball: I started dating Tanya Frost. We had been friends since
fifth grade, but she wasn't precisely the girl next-door. She
lived a whole block away. I thought she was by far the pret-
tiest girl in my class, but she had more than good looks
going for her. She was a straight-A student and a class of-
ficer and lettered in three sports—tennis, volleyball, and
basketball.

Tanya could have done better than Steve Alford, at least

as far as dating was concerned. It was not uncommon for us to meet on Monday to arrange a Friday-night date—a trip to Muncie for a movie, maybe—only to have me tell her Friday morning, "I can't go to Muncie tonight. I have to work out." Why did I have to work out? Because I was disappointed with Thursday's workout. Maybe I missed eight free throws, or drifted on my jump shots when I went hard left. Whatever it was, I couldn't let a bad workout hang like a cloud over my weekend.

To be honest, at that point in my life my ideal "date" was to take a ball and a jump rope out at about nine at night, open the gym with Dad's keys, and turn on all the lights. It was the ideal practice time, the time I liked best. No people. Both goals up. The lights on full-blast. I would use the whole court, dribbling, shooting, practicing all the moves I'd use in a real game. The police patrolled the parking lot at night, and they used to look down through the doors and see me alone on the floor, a kid playing for the championship.

Dad was always nearby, but he gave me the freedom to discover things on my own. If I went to the gym with him on an afternoon when he had office work, he'd get me started on my workout and then go upstairs. He might not come back for forty-five minutes or so. Sometimes I would sense him watching me from the running track above the arena, and I would yell up, "Go to work! Leave me alone!"

Mom would come to the gym sometimes and say, "When are you coming home for dinner?"

I remember being harsh. "Later! If you're gonna eat, go ahead and eat. I'll be there later." I had to get my workout done first.

They gave me that freedom. Mom and Dad always knew if I had a problem I'd come to them and say, "I need help with something." And I did, lots of times.

Besides, there was always somebody around to put me in my place. Dad remembers passing Sean in the hallway at home one time, and Sean calmly saying, "You know, Dad, Steve's nuts."

If I was a nut, I was a happy nut. It's true, I didn't drink, smoke, or party, and some of the kids at school must have thought I was awfully white-bread about life. But I had an old '72 Chevy that would run, and I got a kick out of that. I was very active in the Methodist Church, too. Sean and I were very close, and I had Mom and Dad and Tanya.

What I had, beyond all that, was a powerful sense of who I was and what I wanted to be. Most teenagers don't have that, and that undoubtedly set me apart. My senior English teacher, Steve Dicken, used to open every class by having us write a paragraph or two on a card about something that had happened to us since our last meeting. We had to put down our name, the date, and our "logo"—some little design or mark that we had created for ourselves. For my logo, I always drew a basketball, and I always wrote something about basketball, like "Twelve days till the start of basketball practice!" or "I shot well in Friday's game, but handled the ball poorly."

Mr. Dicken gave me the impression that he looked forward to reading what I had written. He liked to draw, and he always returned my card with the logo altered in some way. He might draw a cannon shooting the basketball, for instance. Another teacher might have criticized my narrowness or ordered me to write on another subject. Mr. Dicken seemed content that my writing expressed a clearly defined personality.

No one understood that better than Dad. He never pressured me or pushed me, but once I had made the commitment to be the best player I could possibly be, he assisted me in every way.

I remember coming home one night, the summer before my senior year, after a particularly good workout. I was working hard because I saw myself in a two-man race for Mr. Basketball with James Blackmon, who played for Marion High School (and later for the University of Kentucky). I got home at about eleven and Dad was on the couch watching TV with Mom. He looked up and said, "How'd it go?"

"It was a great workout," I said. "I hit ninety-eight out of a hundred free throws, I shot the ball well, I did good things off the dribble, my ball handling was good. It was probably the best workout I've had all week."

Dad's only comment was, "The coach at Marion just called me. Blackmon was just leaving to go to the gym to work out."

He didn't say anything else. But I heard this: *Don't get complacent—you've got a lot of work to do.*

I walked right outside, turned the driveway lights on, and pounded the ball until midnight, doing more drills.

Obviously, Bob Knight did not introduce me to mind games.

I know it sounds corny to say that I was pursuing a dream, but I was. All across Indiana, hundreds of youngsters my age went to bed that summer dreaming of basketball glory. They slept in rooms like mine, decorated with Indiana University pennants and posters of Larry Bird and Isiah Thomas. They fell asleep imagining themselves as Mr. Basketball, scoring the winning bucket in the state tournament, cutting the nets down at Market Square Arena.

In my house, the difference was this: when Mom and Dad crept up to listen at my door—which they still did—they heard a light slapping sound. It was the sound the basketball made when I caught it.

I practiced shooting in bed.

As noted earlier, Dad and I drove to Bloomington in October of my senior year to make a verbal commitment to Indiana University. There was never a recruiting war over me. I received more than a hundred inquiries from various colleges, mostly by mail, but everyone knew I had eyes only for Indiana. I'm sure, too, that my six-foot-two, 160-pound frame convinced some coaches that I was a "project." Others probably looked at my scoring average—and the fact that I was the coach's son—and concluded that I was a pampered player who got to shoot at will.

It didn't matter. Mom cut out the logos and letterheads from Kentucky, Notre Dame, Duke, and the other big-time programs and made a collage for me. It still hangs in my room.

That was as close as anybody came to changing my mind. I made no official visits to any of the colleges—not even Indiana.

People assume that I chose Indiana because I grew up with Indiana-red blood in my veins, or because I loved Bloomington, or because my Dad wanted me to go there. They are wrong. I chose Bloomington for one reason only: Bob Knight.

Sure, I had heard the stories. I knew that Isiah Thomas had left Indiana after his sophomore year because he felt smothered in Knight's disciplined offense. I knew that a dozen or more highly rated recruits had quit the team over the years because they couldn't take Knight's tongue-lashings, or couldn't face the fact that they weren't the hotshots they thought they were. At one all-star game, a highly recruited guard told me that he wouldn't even visit Indiana, because he had heard it was "like a prison."

Those stories didn't scare me. If anything, they attracted me. I was from a disciplined background. When I missed free throws at home, I punished myself with fingertip pushups in the driveway or wind sprints up and down the street. I wanted a coach who would push me and make me better.

Other players said they wanted to go where it would be "fun." Well, their idea of fun was an hour and a half of free-lance basketball—short practices with a minimum of discipline. To me, that was not fun. To me, that wasn't even *basketball.*

I was just different that way. Most players loved all-star games; I hated them and played in very few. All-star games were just screw-off time, playground stuff. A whole season of free-lance basketball? That appealed to me about as much as a week-long alcohol binge.

I have said many times that it takes a certain kind of kid

to play for Bob Knight. I loved my teammates at New Castle, but they weren't driven the way I was. Many of them
didn't want to play every day. None of them wanted to work
as hard as I did to get better. I didn't want to go to a college
program where I would be surrounded by players with that
same recreational attitude. I wanted three things out of college: to be a better player, to get my degree on time, and to
play in the NBA.

If Bob Knight could help me accomplish those three goals
...well, to me *that* sounded like fun. When I left Coach
Knight's office that October afternoon, my only regret was
that I had to wait a year to get started.

But, of course, Dad and I had unfinished business at New
Castle.

The memory that stands out from my senior year is the
weekend that fifth-ranked Marion and top-ranked Indianapolis Cathedral came to New Castle on consecutive nights.
Marion's star was James Blackmon. Cathedral's star was
Scotty Hicks, who was probably third in line for Mr. Basketball. Our arena officially held 9,325, but temporary
bleachers on the track level swelled the capacity. We drew
ten thousand fans each night, twenty thousand for the weekend.

The media attention was impressive. A long press table
was set up, running from one end of the floor to the other,
just as in college. Dad's office was littered with requests for
credentials from publications and television stations, and not
just from Indiana. TV trucks hummed with activity in the
parking lot.

Sean got the full impact of it before I did. He was playing
on the junior varsity, and JV games started at six-thirty.
Normally, the junior varsity came out to the smell of popcorn from the popcorn machine and maybe ten people in the
stands. The night of the Marion game, Sean and his teammates came out of the tunnel for the second half and were
met by about nine thousand noisy fans. "I know three-

fourths of my teammates just wet their pants," Sean told me later.

It was an unbelievable weekend of basketball. Finals lay ahead, but even Tanya, the straight-A student, couldn't study. There were pep rallies, a car caravan past the players' homes, good-luck signs in store windows. The whole town seemed to be in the grip of March Madness—the name Hoosiers give to the state basketball tournament—and it was only January.

The games lived up to the hype. I scored 48 Friday night against Marion, and Blackmon scored 41, but we had a huge second half and won big. The next night, Scotty Hicks played great and Cathedral nipped us in overtime by two points. The Indiana newspapers gave the games banner-headline treatment.

Winning both games would have made everything perfect, but Dad and I saw that weekend as the fulfillment of my vow to fill the New Castle Fieldhouse. We sold out six more times that season. Overall, we averaged close to eight thousand a game, which gave New Castle Chrysler High School the fourth-best average basketball attendance in the state of Indiana, behind Notre Dame, Indiana, and Purdue universities. The Indiana Pacers of the NBA came in fifth.

Everybody knew what to expect from me as a senior: points. In our first game of the season, against Winchester, I had 49 points when Dad took me out with about four minutes left. The crowd booed. (Hadn't I told Dad, when I was a freshman, that we'd turn it around?) The New Castle single-game scoring record was 55, set by Kent Benson in his senior year, and the fans wanted me to go for the record.

Dad wasn't sure. He sent an assistant coach down to the Winchester bench to ask their coach, "Do you care if Sam puts Steve in to get the record? We'll take him out as soon as he gets it."

The Winchester coach had no objections.

Then Dad asked my teammates what they thought about it. They said, "Go for it!"

And then he asked me. I was on the bench, sweaty and breathing hard. "I don't care," I said. "I'll have the opportunity again. It makes no difference to me."

Dad grabbed me by the jersey and nudged me toward the scorer's table, and the crowd let out a roar. It was a strange sensation, taking the floor again with no purpose other than to score 7 points, and with thousands of people concentrating on just that.

My teammates cleared out for me on every play, and I scored the 7 points with a minute to spare. The record-setting basket was from the right wing, a typical jump shot off the dribble. When the ball went in, the crowd roared and my teammates went nuts, swarming all over me. I described it this way in a theme for Mr. Dicken's English class: "Fanswise, the place went hysterical."

There were other records that season. I set the state mark for consecutive free throws made—64—and put together an even longer string at home, 83 straight. I averaged 37.2 points a game, which was a New Castle record.

More important, we played well as a team. At the start of the season Dad had said, "This will be the year that we more or less turn Steve loose," but that didn't mean we were a one-man team. Mike Kovaleski, who was already an all-state football player, made the all-NCC team as our top rebounder and inside scorer. Todd Jarvis, a junior, averaged over 14 points a game. Troy Lundy broke the school record for assists.

It was the kind of season Dad and I had dreamed of. Our 17–5 regular-season record was the best for a New Castle team since 1979, when Dad's guys were 16–4 and NCC champs.

It was a bittersweet season, too, because Dad and I were very conscious that our time together was slipping away. Every game I wanted to surprise him with something, whether it was points or passes or a great defensive play. After one game, he gave a newspaper the neatest quote: "Nothing that Steve does surprises me anymore."

I knew I pleased him. He still guarded against favoring me over the other players, but there was a bond there. I could look through him and he could see through me.

Our Sunday-afternoon sessions in his office became even more special. We still watched the game tapes technically, looking for ways I could improve my game and searching for competitive edges for our team. But the tapes were also video scrapbooks of the most rewarding time in our lives. It was hard to believe that soon a calendar page would flip over, saying, "That's it. You can't share this experience anymore."

For Dad, it must have been particularly difficult. He had made a decision, when Sean and I were little, not to pursue college coaching so that he could coach us in high school. Now his time with us was almost up, and he would have to pass us along to other coaches.

That's probably why, when he's asked what memory in coaching he cherishes the most, he picks the Pendleton Heights game, the last regular-season game of my senior year. That's the night he promoted Sean from the junior varsity, at my urging, so Sean and I could play together just once before I graduated.

The opportunity came in the last two minutes. Dad made the substitution during a time-out, and I remember Sean bouncing off the bench and tearing off his warm-up jacket. When play resumed, I grabbed a rebound and threw a full-court pass to Sean. He went in for a lay-up, but had the ball knocked out of his hands. Our fans groaned, but we still had the ball out-of-bounds. I took the ball out from under the basket left, and before the ref handed me the ball I signaled for Brad Phelps, the other guard, to screen across for Sean.

It couldn't have gone better if God had planned it. Brad set a great pick, Sean came off the screen, and I hit him with the in-bounds pass. He went straight up, fired the jumper . . . *good!*

The fans went wild, and I literally jumped for joy. To this day, it's my favorite memory from high school basketball.

The play ended: Alford—assist; Alford—basket; and Alford—proud Pop.

"My highlight," Dad calls it.

A couple of weeks later, my second major goal was realized. I came home one day after practice and Dad said, "Don Bates called." Mr. Bates was director of the Indiana All-Star Basketball Game.

"What'd he want?"

"Well, you're Mr. Basketball."

I got crazy. I yelled and ran up and down the hallway to my bedroom about eight times.

We were supposed to keep the news under wraps until after the season, which was torture for me. Dad pulled me out of practice one day with some lame excuse, and we drove into Indianapolis for a secret photo session with the newspapers. That's where I got to put on the traditional Mr. Basketball uniform for the first time: "Indiana 1."

I obviously needed help to keep such a big secret. As soon as I got home from Indy, I called Tanya and told her to hurry over, I had something to show her. When she got to the house, Mom stone-faced it and escorted her back to my room. Tanya found me "studying" at my desk, wearing the Mr. Basketball uniform.

"Steve!" She jumped and shrieked. "You did it! You did it!"

For the next two weeks, I was like a little kid. I put on my Mr. Basketball uniform every night just to walk around the house.

One goal remained: getting Dad to the state finals.

The road to the Indiana state basketball championship has about 250 bumps in it. Every high school in the state, big and small, plays in a series of single-elimination tournaments—sectionals, regionals, and semistate—leading to a four-team finish at Market Square Arena in Indianapolis. It is a tough ordeal. Two of the tournaments—regionals and semistate—require the winners of the day games to play

again the same night for the championship. There must be a
hundred good reasons why that's a bad idea, but there's one
good reason why it's still done: tradition.

New Castle hadn't won the state championship since
1932. The championship plaque from that season took up a
lot of space in the school trophy case, but there were few
people still around who remembered that team. Our last regional championship had come in 1971 and our last sectional in 1979.

From our fan support, you would have thought we won
every year. Good crowds turned out for the first two games
of the New Castle Sectional, and when we polished off
Knightstown and Northwestern of Wayne County to advance to the finals, Hoosier Hysteria took hold. The "sold
out" sign went up in the fieldhouse ticket window an hour
before game time. People who couldn't go to the game huddled around radios in stores and restaurants.

When the horn sounded at the end of our 73–64 win over
Richmond, I was so excited that I ran, jumped, and hung on
to the rim. Hundreds of fans spilled onto the floor. Not only
were we sectional champs, but the win gave Dad his first
twenty-victory season at New Castle. For hours after the
game, Broad Street was jammed with cars full of screaming,
delirious, arm-waving fans. And this was in the rain.

The regional was also held at New Castle, and that tournament was special to me in a different way: it was the last
time I would play in the New Castle Fieldhouse. We beat
Muncie South in the day game, and then beat Jay County
that night, 75–54. Fans streamed onto the court again,
shouting, "Sweet sixteen!" and "Semistate!"

Tournament fever totally swept New Castle after that. The
windows on Broad Street were plastered with good wishes
for the team: CLIP 'EM, TROJANS! EAT 'EM UP, TROJANS! TAN
THEIR HIDES, TROJANS! Green-and-white good-luck banners
appeared on Interstate 70 overpasses.

It was as if basketball had suddenly put New Castle on the
map again. To a town battered by unemployment—the

Chrysler plant had laid off over two thousand workers—the
Trojans were a welcome source of community pride. I was
asked if that put unusual pressure on us as a team, and I
admitted that it did. "My stomach has turned inside out
about eighteen hundred times."

The semistate is played every year in Butler University's
wonderful, rusty old Hinkle Field House. If you saw the
movie *Hoosiers,* Hinkle is where they filmed the state championship scenes. It's an old, old gym, the kind I like, but on a
grand scale—balconies and high windows and row after
row of bleacher planks bolted to concrete.

We played Broad Ripple in the late-morning game, which
was televised statewide. Twenty busloads of New Castle
fans rumbled into Indianapolis in one long caravan, and
they started shouting even before they found their seats. It
was the biggest crowd we had ever played for, fifteen thousand or so, and I got a chill at how they roared during the
introductions.

I got a chill of a different kind when the Broad Ripple
players refused to shake hands with us at midcourt. All week
long, Broad Ripple's coach, Bill Smith, had been putting me
down in interviews. Apparently, he wanted his team to treat
the game as some kind of "us-against-them" showdown.

If they wanted a war, a war is what they got. Broad Ripple
was a very athletic, physical team, but we weren't about to
be intimidated. We took a big early lead and then scratched
and clawed to hold on. The second half was a free-for-all.
We saw a 19-point lead shrink to 4 as the Broad Ripple
players hustled, fought, and did everything but tackle us
when we had the ball. Near the end, one of their guys
whacked me in the side of the head with his elbow, a fla-
grant foul, and the fieldhouse shook with boos. I got off the
floor scowling.

We won the game, 79–64. I scored 57—my highest ever
and a state tournament record—and made 25 of 25 free
throws. It was probably my best game as a high school
player, and I'm sure my performance was a direct result of

Broad Ripple's attempts to intimidate me.

Coach Smith crossed the floor after the game, but instead of congratulating me, he said, "You're a good player, but you'll have to work on your attitude."

I couldn't believe my ears. "*I* didn't say anything out there. It was your players who were taking their punches at us!"

We went to the locker room drained, physically and mentally. I was still upset by Coach Smith's comments, and when Dad and I encountered him later in the hallway we got into a shouting match. Coach Smith put his hands on my chest and shoved me, and Dad and some bystanders had to separate us.

We were due back at six in the evening to play Connersville, the easy winners of the early-morning game. We drove back to the Speedway Motel to rest, but who could sleep? Dad insisted that we go to our rooms and lie down for fifteen minutes, just to get off our feet. Then we had lunch. We returned to our rooms to stare at the ceiling for another half hour. A few minutes for a team meeting, and we were right back on the bus to Butler.

Dad was worried, and with cause. Connersville had two terrific players, Chris and Mike Heineman, who went on to play at Davidson and Wisconsin, respectively. They had won their early-morning game with Indian Creek handily. So handily, in fact, that their starters had only played three quarters. They figured to be relatively rested.

And they were. From the opening tip you could tell: we were flat. Connersville opened up a quick lead, controlling the boards and beating us to every loose ball. That spelled trouble, because the Heinemans were great ball handlers. Once you fell behind, they were hard to catch.

We never quit, but we never really challenged, either. Too tired to run the fast break, we tried to be patient on offense, but the Connersville zone stopped our inside game and we didn't shoot well from outside.

Dad left me in till the very end, and I remember chasing

the ball around as the clock wound down. I was exhausted. Angry, too. I had to chase that ball back and forth, back and forth. The cheers of the fifteen thousand were for Connersville, not for New Castle. I was practically in tears, because my one remaining dream was getting Dad to the state finals, and I wasn't going to accomplish that.

At the final buzzer, my shoulders slumped and I walked off the floor beaten, the picture of dejection. Shaking hands with the winners was the hardest thing I ever had to do.

The bus ride home was slow torture. I didn't want to talk to anybody, and nobody wanted to talk to me. I just stared out the window at the headlights going by on I-70, feeling sorry for myself.

It was almost midnight when the bus pulled into the school parking lot. There was a huge welcome at the fieldhouse—bands and pom pons and everything—but I was inconsolable. Dozens of people grabbed my hand and slapped my back, told me what a great season I'd had. I could only mumble thanks. I couldn't force a smile.

Dad handled it better. "We gave it our best shot," he said, "and it just wasn't good enough. But the sun will come up tomorrow."

Dad and I drove home without saying much. We were both too tired for small talk. I went straight to my bedroom and right to bed. I didn't even turn on the light to undress.

The next day, I went to the gym. I was still upset, and the only way I could deal with my disappointment was to practice alone. At some point, Dad came down to the floor from his office. I was aware of him walking around the court, watching me. I kept working: the same ball-handling and shooting drills that had been part of my individual workouts since the summer after my freshman year.

Finally, he came up to me. "What's on your mind now?" he asked.

I held the basketball in my sweaty hands. Words of apology started tumbling out. "I'm sorry I didn't get you what you wanted. I know—" I choked on the words.

Dad interrupted. "Don't you think you ought to be thinking about Indiana?"

I took a deep breath. "Yeah, but I don't want to think about that yet."

He walked to the sideline and came back carrying a folding chair. "You're going to have to learn to play without the ball," he said, setting up the chair at the top of the circle. "You've played point guard for me; you've had the ball in your hands all the time. But Coach Knight uses a lot more movement without the ball. He plays a motion offense."

Dad took the ball out of my hands and put it on the seat of the chair. He walked away from it, made a jab-step toward the sideline, and then whirled back. He grabbed the ball off the chair and went straight up for a jump shot. *Swish*. He retrieved the ball and tossed it to me. "Try that," he said.

I put the ball on the chair, moved away, cut back, grabbed it, and fired.

"Too slow," he said. "Do it again."

I repeated the move.

"*Drive* off that jab-step. Don't walk through it." I did it again. "Don't drift on the shot!... Get your arms up!... Pick up the pace!..."

The sweat rolled off my forehead, and my breath came in quicker and quicker gasps. I felt the rhythm of the drill, and with it the excitement that came with anything that improved my basketball skills.

"Left side now!"

I saw myself in an Indiana basketball uniform—cutting around a teammate's pick, taking the pass, burying the jump shot. I saw it again...and again...and again...*jab-step, cut, ball, shoot!*

"That's good," Dad said. "Better...better..." And then he said nothing at all.

He just stood watching.

CHAPTER THREE

THE BEST TEAM IN THE WORLD

On April 17, 1984—less than a month after the end of my first season with Bob Knight and the Indiana Hoosiers—seventy-two of America's best basketball players traveled by car, bus, train, and plane to try out for the 1984 U.S. Olympic basketball team.

I arrived on foot.

The trials were held at the Indiana University Fieldhouse, just across the parking lot from Assembly Hall. The fieldhouse was a huge, cold place, but it had eight regulation basketball courts under one roof. The assistant Olympic coaches broke us down into teams, assigned us courts, and threw out the basketballs. "Play," they said.

So we played.

The scrimmages were wonderful. All around me were players I had watched on TV: Wayman Tisdale, the Oklahoma all-America, with his post-up moves and baseline jumper; Patrick Ewing, the great Georgetown center, springing out of a defensive crouch to swat away jump shots; Antoine Carr, the silky forward from Wichita State, swooping in for a slam dunk; Johnny Dawkins, the lightning-quick guard from Duke, splitting the defense with a burst into the lane....

Coach Knight, wearing a plaid sports jacket and tie, looked down on us from a steel scaffold, like a football coach. For two years he had been directing the Olympic scouting and player development program. He had put together a staff of nineteen college head coaches to conduct the three-a-day workouts and coach the games. Now there was just one task before him and his basketball advisers: to cut the seventy-two players to twelve—presumably the best twelve.

"The selection of the Olympic team won't be much different from the way we select our team at Indiana," Coach said, "which is: you've got to be able to play, and you've got to be able to play the way I want you to play. There are a lot of organizations that will be formed in the next year on a far more democratic basis than the U.S. Olympic basketball team."

Technically, there was a seven-member Player Selection Committee, and Coach made it clear he would also solicit the opinions of his assistant coaches. But everyone agreed on the principle that the head coach should have great freedom in selecting his team.

Even so, I didn't go into the trials with much hope of making the team. With just one college basketball season under my belt, I knew I couldn't match the all-around skills of veteran guards like Chris Mullin, Michael Jordan, and Alvin Robertson. I took it as an honor just to have been invited. There were only two players younger than I was at the trials: a North Carolina high school sensation named Danny Manning, and Delray Brooks, the reigning Indiana Mr. Basketball, who had already committed to IU.

It took only a couple of days of three-a-day practices, though, for me to realize that I had certain advantages. Having played a year at Indiana, I understood Coach Knight's motion offense. I could move instinctively, while other players had to think their way around the court, making them look unsure or tentative. I also knew the ins and outs of Coach's man-to-man defense, which is a little different from the man-to-man played at most schools. (Many coaches, for example, teach that if the ball is on the wing you should force the dribbler toward the middle. Coach teaches the opposite: he wants his players to force the dribbler toward the baseline and into a trap behind the basket. "A good ball handler or shooter can create too much on the open floor," Coach says. I agree. As an offensive player, I would rather be forced toward the middle.)

It also helped that I was in the best physical shape of my life. Coach had decided to test the emotional and physical stamina of his candidates by making the three-a-days practically a survival test. The daytime practices, which included the conditioning and punishment drills we used at Indiana, were exhausting enough; playing a very physical seventy-minute scrimmage the same night reduced some players to red-faced, gasping helplessness. "There is no way you can prepare for this," said Mark Price, the Georgia Tech guard, "no matter what physical shape you're in."

Sometimes the players who looked the best in the morning, when they were fresh, suddenly couldn't score at night, or were a step slow on defense. "We have to know that about a player," Coach explained. "In Olympic play they might have to play a game at ten o'clock at night and then come back at nine the next morning."

That's why I gained confidence from my showing in the first scrimmages. I went 7-for-7 from the field on Tuesday night and 3-for-5 on Wednesday and handled the ball extremely well in the backcourt. Back in my room, I found it difficult to study for finals, which were the following week. Every time I sat down, I caught myself writing down the names of people I thought I would have to beat out in the trials.

A couple hundred pro scouts and journalists watched every day from the sidelines, trying to guess who would survive the first cut. Everybody had his "can't-miss" list: Ewing, Jordan, Mullin, Tisdale. Dawkins and Carr were big names, too, and both were having outstanding trials.

There was a clear-cut sentimental favorite: Charles Barkley, the flamboyant power forward from Auburn. The "Round Mound of Rebound" was a smiling cannonball on the court, a 284-pound wild man who sent defenders sprawling with his thundering dunks and who raced upcourt pumping his arms in celebration. The NBA people, who knew a crowd-pleaser when they saw one, were especially excited by Barkley's play. Bob Ferry, the general manager of the Washington Bullets, said, "If they cut the Breadtruck, I'm rooting for the Russians."

I knew that Coach Knight, who admired intensity, would be impressed with Barkley's; Charles played as if he were furious even when he was smiling. But I also knew that Coach wouldn't like Charles's attention-getting ways. One time, Charles stole the ball, dribbled behind his back in traffic, and finished the play off with a backboard-shaking dunk. The players and spectators loved it, but Coach turned away, shaking his head.

Charles, by the luck of the draw, shared a room with me on the top floor of the Student Union. I say "by the luck of the draw," but it may have been one of Coach's little jokes, putting me with a guy who looked as if he could eat the furniture. I had to hide my food a lot from Charles. If I had any Cokes or candy bars, I stuffed them away in gym bags.

Fortunately, Charles turned out to be a delightful guy. When our practices were over, you would always see him playing Horse with the ball boys or wrestling with some coach's little boy and pretending to lose. His Auburn teammate Chuck Person visited our room frequently, and those two had an ongoing disagreement about who was stronger.

They had some serious wrestling matches on my bed, and I always worried that it would collapse with Charles jumping up and down on it.

When I think back to the trials, though, one player stands above the rest: Michael Jordan.

It was amazing to watch him perform. Most of us had played against him or seen him on TV, so we knew what Michael could do in Coach Dean Smith's disciplined system at North Carolina. What we didn't know was what he could do when things were looser. Whenever Michael was warming up or just fooling around, we all stopped what we were doing to watch. He could leap from the foul line and stuff the ball with two hands. He could drive the baseline and dunk the ball with 360-degree spins. He had jump hooks, underhand hooks, spin-bank shots, alley-oops, rebound slam dunks...and then the games started, and he played great defense, stole passes, stripped the ball from all-America guards. We had all seen plenty of great shooters, great passers, and great defensive players, but none of us had ever seen a package quite like Michael.

The things he could do in the air! Coach Knight—all coaches, for that matter—warned you, "Never leave the floor with the ball unless you're shooting. Don't get stuck in midair with nothing to do." Those words didn't apply to Michael. He could launch himself into the air above the lane, surrounded by defenders, and seemingly hang there, as the others rose up and fell back down, before making some incredible shot or finding the open man with a pass. Opposing coaches told whoever was covering Jordan, "*Don't* let him leave his feet. Make him stay down."

I watched Michael all the time. He had a habit of wiping the soles of his shoes on a wet towel on the floor, and I was so in awe of him that I found myself going to that towel and doing the same thing. Coach caught me at it once and yelled, "See that, Jordan? You think Alford can leap from the foul line and dunk now?"

There didn't seem to be anything Michael couldn't do. He

and Barkley played 8-ball at the Union poolroom, and neither guy was shy about putting money on the table. Barkley
was good, but Jordan was amazing. He jumped balls, played
spins, and thought two or three shots ahead. He talked a
great game, too—a nonstop rap that put Charles away.

The most pleasing thing about Michael was that as great
as he was, he had no ego problems. He was friendly and
sympathetic, took time to talk to everyone, and worked hard
every day. There was no complacency in his makeup, no
big-shot complex. One day early in the trials, Coach Knight
gave Michael a stern look and said, "I'm not gonna select
you on your reputation. You're gonna have to prove to me
that you can make this team."

Michael didn't need that warning. He was the class of the
trials.

The cut to thirty-two was made Friday morning in a fancy
dining room at the Student Union. Coach Knight made a
little speech, thanking everybody for his effort and explaining how difficult it had been to decide. Then an assistant
coach stood up and read off the names of the thirty-two
guys who were staying.

When I heard my name, I practically jumped out of my
chair. As soon as the meeting was over, I rushed up to my
room and called home. "Dad," I gushed, "I made the cut!"

Dad was surprisingly calm. Mom got a little more excited.

Later, studying the list of surviving players, I reached a
conclusion as to why I was still around: the team needed
shooters. Coach Knight knew that the international teams
played a lot of zone defense and banged around under the
basket. To open up the floor for exciting players like Jordan
and Ewing and Tisdale, he needed some accurate outside
shooters.

I ran my finger down the list, looking for pure shooters. I
found two: Chris Mullin and myself.

The action moved now to Assembly Hall for a weekend of
public scrimmages. The schedule called for doubleheaders—

a game in the afternoon and a game in the evening. Every game was sold out, and the atmosphere was like that of a regular college game. The IU pep band played during time-outs. Our cheerleaders led cheers for both the white and blue teams. The crowd even gave me the usual treatment when I shot free throws: "Socks, shorts, one-two-three...*swish!*"

There was one big difference: the play was rougher. I drove for a lay-up in the Saturday-night game and got smashed in the face with an elbow just as I let go. The message was clear: stay out of the lane, little guy. It was even rougher for the big men, who were smacking each other around with abandon. "I knew it would be physical," said Michigan's Roy Tarpley, "but I didn't think it would be as physical as this."

My closest brush with death probably came at the end of the Saturday-night game, when I stole the ball and raced to the other hoop. Looking quickly back, I saw that my closest pursuer was Barkley, and to avoid being wiped out I pulled up under the basket and double-pumped. He didn't land on me, thank God, but I didn't fool him either, and he stole the ball back. For me, it was an embarrassing end to an otherwise passable performance that included 10 points and 4-for-4 from the line.

Coach Knight no longer watched from a tower; he sat at a table with other members of his advisory board. George Raveling, the University of Iowa coach, sat at his right elbow. Henry Iba, the legendary Oklahoma State University and three-time Olympic coach, sat to his left. Their role was not to coach; it was to choose. At a press conference, I was asked to compare the trials with the way Coach did things at Indiana. I said, "The only difference is that he's not saying anything."

I quickly added: "That's a big difference."

That weekend, rumors began to circulate that Barkley was on the bubble, despite his good performances. The sportswriters speculated that Charles was too flamboyant for Coach Knight, that Coach didn't want a player showboating at the expense of his teammates. What the writers didn't know was that Charles was almost at the point where he didn't want to play in the Olympics. He had decided to leave Auburn with a year of eligibility remaining, and he thought if he turned pro before Jordan did he could make a lot of money from endorsements. I think word of that got back to Coach, who had to wonder whether the Olympics were really Charles's top priority.

The fans, thrilled by Barkley's hustle, knew nothing of this backstage stuff. They cheered his every move.

Another controversy was brewing around the big men. Ewing was a shoo-in, but there were so many other gifted centers and strong forwards: Tisdale, Carr, Sam Perkins of North Carolina, Jeff Turner of Vanderbilt, Tim McCormick of Michigan, John Koncak of SMU, Joe Kleine of Arkansas....

For pure skill and versatility, Antoine Carr deserved to make the team, but Antoine had a $225,000-a-year contract with an Italian-league team, plus a part-time job with a pasta-making company in Milan. He was still an "amateur" by International Olympic Committee standards, but some people thought he belonged on the Italian team, not ours.

Again, Coach had to think of who we were playing. The European teams were very tall and physical and could get away with a lot of roughhousing under international rules. If Coach kept Carr and cut Koncak, that left him with Ewing as his only seven-foot player. He really needed Koncak for height in case Ewing got in foul trouble. Cut Kleine? Joe, although not a seven-footer, was a stocky, physical player like Barkley. If Coach needed somebody to do some bruising, Joe was perfect.

Coach made one thing clear: the U.S. Olympic team wouldn't necessarily be made up of the twelve best athletes. He wanted players who could complement each other, who were unselfish, who could fill roles, and who could play his brand of basketball.

The scouts and media started making up new lists.

On Monday morning, the thirty-two of us filed once again into that big room at the Union and sat down. This time the suspense was worse than before. Practically everybody was good enough to play on the Olympic team; the question was, did Coach Knight think we were *right* for the Olympic team?

When I heard my name called as one of the surviving twenty, I lowered my head, closed my eyes, and thanked God.

Charles made the cut, too. Among the very fine basketball players whose names were not called, one stood out: Antoine Carr.

It was an awkward moment. We all stood up, milled around with the twelve who had just been cut, and exchanged words of congratulations and regret. Then the twelve were gone, and Coach Knight called us into a small group at the front of the room. He was sending us home for a couple of weeks, he said. There would be a five-day minicamp in May; practice sessions would begin on June 15, followed by an exhibition tour against NBA players. He had until July 14 to pick the final twelve-man squad.

While we were away, he said, he wanted us to reflect on what it meant to be an Olympic basketball player. He wanted us to come back to Bloomington physically and mentally ready to represent our country.

"Let me tell you what we have." He looked us over dubiously. "A collection of perhaps the twenty biggest prima donnas in college basketball."

That drew some smiles, and Coach raised his hand. "That's not fair. I know we don't have the twenty greatest, because we've already gotten rid of three or four of the biggest. But how many of you have ever guarded the best player on the other team? How many of you have ever set screens for other guys on the team? How many of you guys dive on the floor after loose balls?"

Several heads turned in my direction.

"Don't look at him," Coach cracked. "I've been watching

him for a year and he hasn't dived on the floor yet."

Everybody laughed, and I turned red.

"My point is this," Coach said. "There are some parts of this game that you guys are totally unfamiliar with. Other guys do those things for you. You've got other guys diving on the floor, blocking out, passing and screening. Now we've got to get some guys doing the things that everybody has been doing for you guys."

A few minutes later, we walked back out into the sunshine—twelve Olympians and eight so-close-to-being-Olympians. The biggest surprise was that Coach had kept ten guards, if you counted Michael Jordan, who also played forward. "Play was so strong, especially among the guards," Coach told the media, "that instead of trying to establish guards through debate, we decided to establish the guards through play."

My main competition, I decided, was Johnny Dawkins.

It was clear from the start that Vern Fleming of Georgia and Alvin Robertson of Arkansas would make the final twelve. Leon Wood, from Cal State–Fullerton, was also impressive. All three of those guys were pressure defenders and quick guards who did most of their scoring by penetrating. None of them, at the time, was a real good shooter.

That made it tough for Johnny, because those guys' strengths were his strengths. It also made it tough for the Player Selection Committee and Coach Knight, who had to decide. Did they need another quick jet? Or did they want an outside shooter?

You couldn't guess the final choice from Coach Knight's comments to the media. My hopes shot up when he said, "The only question I have is the outside shooting of the team. This is not a team of outside shooters." But when asked specifically about my chances of sticking, he said, "Alford was probably the best shooter we had here, but he's not a guy that can manufacture shots for himself. If he can't get open, it will be difficult for him."

How was I to take that? The format of the trials didn't exactly showcase my shooting skills. The scrimmages encouraged one-on-one play, there were no zone defenses to bust, and there was little screening to free up outside shooters.

I had to shrug off his comments and keep playing. After all, Tisdale was practically a shoo-in to make the team, and Coach's assessment of Wayman was: "He does one or two things acceptable by my standards." That was about as encouraging as a ticket home.

We returned to Bloomington on May 10 for the mini-camp. When we got to the locker room, each of us found a notebook and pen in his stall. I smiled in recognition of Coach Knight's methods, but the other guys looked bewildered. A few players started to toss the notebooks aside, until I explained what they were for. There was some good-natured joking about how to use the pens. "Can anybody here spell 'basketball'?" That sort of thing.

There were just twenty of us now, playing on one court. Coach Knight was no longer a silent observer. He coached from the sidelines, warming to his task by running his superstars through drill after drill. We could feel the buildup in pressure. Everything was suddenly magnified. With seventy-two players you didn't feel that your every mistake was being observed, but with twenty, you did. And you were right.

Aside from the pressure and the caliber of the players, it was just like Indiana basketball. The assistant coaches ran us through drills for forty-five minutes, and then Coach Knight came through the curtain and led us to the locker room. We ran the same breakdown drills, the same game simulations. It was all new to the other Olympians, but not to me. I found the practices somewhat monotonous.

What kept me fresh was the lure of an Olympic gold medal and the challenge of playing with and against such great athletes. I never lost faith in my jump shot, but I knew I had to work harder on other areas, especially defense. In

practice, I usually matched up against Leon, Alvin, or Vern
—quick, strong players. I've always been a great believer in
defense, but I wasn't as quick as those guys. Besides, if you
get caught one-on-one with a great offensive player, I don't
care who you are, the chances of your keeping him from
getting a high-percentage shot are minimal. I gave them a
step, concentrated as hard as I could, and used my hands as
much as possible.

Coach was quick to recognize my efforts. "Alford!" he
screamed. "You have to be the worst defensive player in the
history of the world!"

The mini-camp weeded out four more players. Barkley de-
parted, although it was more in the nature of a mutual
agreement with Coach than a cut. ("I'm sure he'll be an
outstanding pro player," Coach said. "No question whatso-
ever.") Coach also cut three more guards: John Stockton of
Gonzaga, Maurice Martin of St. Joseph's, and Terry Porter
of Wisconsin–Stevens Point. Coach then flew off to France
to scout teams at the European basketball championship.

Johnny Dawkins and Steve Alford were still around.

We came back again on June 15. There were only sixteen
of us left, but I no longer saw myself as a dark horse. While
others saw it as a disadvantage that I was the youngest
player still on the team, I saw myself as the veteran of the
lineup in terms of experience with the Knight offense. After
all, when other players were unsure of their responsibilities,
they came to me with their questions. I was brash enough to
tell reporters, "I can run the offense, and that is definitely in
my favor."

The final cuts were made after a week or two of intense
practice, and this time I didn't have to sit in a chair while
somebody read names from a list. Coach came to me first
and told me I had made the team.

"Let me make this clear," he said. "I didn't give you this
spot on the team. You earned it."

That was a tremendous compliment, coming from Coach,
and I thanked him for giving me the opportunity. But as I

walked away, I told myself, He's right, kid—you earned it. I couldn't wait to tell Mom, Dad, Sean, Tanya, grandparents, uncles, aunts, and cousins. Hey, I wanted to call everyone. An Alford was an Olympian!

The final twelve were announced shortly thereafter. The last two players to be cut were Louisville guard Lancaster Gordon and Michigan State center Tim McCormick. Johnny Dawkins and Chuck Person were kept as alternates, to practice with the team and play in exhibitions right up till the Olympics.

Coach Knight took some heat for keeping me, which was predictable. It was also predictable that he would answer the criticism calmly. "Who said Alford didn't belong?" he asked. "Some idiot with a typewriter who doesn't know what he's talking about? We had twenty coaches who voted unanimously to keep him on the team. What am I supposed to do, keep him off because he played at Indiana?"

I felt no resentment from the other players on the team. They knew that we needed another jump shooter to make our inside game work, and they knew I had shot very well in the trials. Besides, Coach yelled at me too much for anyone to feel jealous.

I handled his yelling pretty well. After watching him get all over Dan Dakich and Uwe Blab for a season, I sort of understood how Coach used certain players as designated victims. I didn't *want* that role, but I knew he had to show that he wasn't playing favorites, and I realized that he was using me as a buffer between himself and the Olympians. As tough as he could be on people, Coach found it hard to rip into guys like Jordan and Ewing, who were world-class players and not Indiana recruits. When he needed to get on somebody, he felt more comfortable chewing on one of his own players—me.

He was almost as hard on Tisdale. Coach constantly screamed at Wayman about his defense—for being out of position, for standing around, and for not knowing the fundamentals. Wayman had played his college basketball at

Oklahoma University, where they protected him from foul trouble by playing a lot of zone defense. He needed a lot of coaching.

Coach had taken on such challenges before. Kevin McHale, the former Minnesota star, was a weak defensive player when Coach Knight got hold of him at the 1979 Pan American Games. I think Coach had a lot to do with making Kevin the great defensive player he became for the Boston Celtics.

Wayman lacked the basics, so Coach made him run zig-zags, backup drills, and crab steps until Wayman's tongue was hanging out. He followed him with his eyes on play after play, screaming, "Wayman, fight through the pick!... Weak-side help, Wayman!... Get through, get through, get through!..."

Wayman had never worked so hard in his life, but he appreciated it. He told me several times, "If I had played at Indiana, I bet I would have been an unbelievable defensive player."

It became a game with Wayman and me. At most practices, one or the other of us would get ripped by Coach, and we'd come off the court smiling at each other, wondering if the next time it would be more Steve or more Wayman.

Usually, it was more Steve.

Coach's negative tactics boggled the minds of most of the players. They were stunned by his profanity and amazed at the way he threw us out of practices at the drop of a hat. One day, Vern Fleming asked me, "Is there really anything else that he can do that we haven't seen yet?"

I laughed and said, "You haven't seen anything yet."

When a teammate really seemed bothered by Coach's treatment, I didn't joke about it, but passed on the same advice Dan Dakich had given me as a freshman: "Don't take anything personally. Keep your head on your shoulders, and whatever he tells you, listen, because you won't find too many times when Coach is wrong. As long as he's jumping on your case, he's interested in you. If he's quiet toward you, that means he's lost interest."

I was the expert when it came to Coach Knight, but older players naturally assumed the team leadership roles. Coach named Michael Jordan and Sam Perkins as our captains before taking us out on an exhibition tour. Michael was no surprise. Neither was Sam, really. Coach liked him as a player and as a person. Sam listened very well, spoke only when he had something to say, and tried to help everybody out. He was a strong, steady presence.

Our exhibition schedule began with a trip to Providence, Rhode Island, to play a put-together team of NBA players. We won that game, 128–106, and then beat another NBA team three days later at the Minneapolis Metrodome. In that game, I remember, we were running the clock out when Kevin McHale clotheslined me. I hit the floor as if I had been dropped from the scoreboard. Kevin looked down at me and grinned. "That's an NBA foul," he said.

Our third exhibition game was at Assembly Hall on June 20, and it was almost like playing the portraits in the trophy cases on the west concourse. The opposition was an all-star team of former Indiana greats, including Ted Kitchel, Isiah Thomas, Kent Benson, Tom and Dick Van Arsdale, Randy Wittman, Scott May, Mike Woodson, and Quinn Buckner, plus one current Hoosier: Uwe Blab. The game was televised across Indiana and the hall was packed with enthusiastic fans. The biggest cheers were for Landon Turner, the Hoosier great who was confined to a wheelchair after a 1981 auto accident, and for Coach Knight, whose reputation in Indiana seemed to be soaring with the Olympics fervor.

The game wasn't close. We won, 124–89.

Our next exhibition was even more thrilling. We bused to Indianapolis and played an NBA all-star team at the brand-new Hoosier Dome. And what an all-star team! Larry Bird, Magic Johnson, Isiah Thomas, Kevin McHale...the greatest players in the world.

The sights and sounds that greeted us when we ran out onto the floor of the Hoosier Dome almost took my breath away. There were 67,000 people in the place, screaming their lungs out, waving American flags, and chanting, "U.S.A.! U.S.A.!" The ovations during the introductions were deafening, especially for those of us with Indiana connections—Jerry Sichting, Randy Wittman, Bird, Isiah, Coach Knight, and me. Bands played, color guards marched, balloons floated to the fabric ceiling. President Reagan even spoke to us on a giant TV screen.

The game itself surprised and delighted the crowd. The NBA jumped off to an early lead behind Bird and Isiah. I watched from the bench as Bird buried one of his sweep-away jumpers. A few seconds later, he faked two defenders up in the air and dropped a pass to a teammate for an easy lay-up. I almost buried my head in a towel, thinking, What in the world am I doing here?

I found out midway through the first half, when Coach put me in the game for the first time.

Butterflies in my stomach? Sure. There I was, at one end of the court with guys like Ewing and Jordan...and running toward us were Bird, McHale, Thomas, and Johnson. And I had Isiah! Everybody had been making a big deal of my being the youngest Olympic basketballer, but I hadn't felt a thing...until then.

But it went like a dream. We trailed 20–18, but Mullin hit three straight jumpers, two of them on passes from me. I scored my first points on a baseline jumper, and then Ewing stole the ball and fed me for a driving lay-up. Ewing hit a pair of free throws to close out the scoring, and we went to the locker room leading 30–22. I had been on the court during the surge, so I was truly pumped up.

In the second half, I got an even bigger thrill: matching up against Jerry Sichting, my boyhood idol. The first time he dribbled at me, I flashed back to our years at Martinsville, when he was Dad's star guard. I remembered all the times I had shagged free throws for him, cheered for him in games, and hugged him after big wins, and, of course, I remembered the time he and his buddies had stuck me in the locker. Now we were playing head-to-head in front of the biggest crowd ever to see a basketball game under one roof.

He caught my eye and grinned. It meant something to him, too.

We ended up winning the game, 97–82. In the locker room, Coach Knight cautioned us not to get big heads. The game proved just one thing, he said—the difference between a thrown-together all-star team and a *real* team. We had been practicing together. We had a game plan. We had floor balance and players to fill every role. The NBA guys, he said, had none of that going for them. Most of them were worn-out, physically and mentally, from the long NBA season. Others hadn't played in a month and were out of shape. They had no particular motivation, other than to help us prepare for the Olympics.

"I guarantee you," Coach said, "if you played these guys in December it would be a different story."

We knew he was right, but it was still exciting to have matched up with the greatest players in basketball and won.

The exhibition tour lasted another week, although it wasn't really a tour—we flew back to Bloomington after every game. Our NBA opponents changed with every stop. Instead of Bird and Johnson, we ran into guys like Doc Rivers and Dominique Wilkins.

Not that that made our task any easier. Coach wanted to test our fortitude, so he began urging the pros to play roughhouse basketball against us. "Knock us around a little," he told them when they walked by our bench. "Keep pounding us."

They were only too happy to oblige. The games turned into muscle contests: grabbing, elbowing, undercutting, hand-checking, brutal screens. If there were hockey fans in the stands, they had to love it.

Things got out of control at the Mecca in Milwaukee. Since these were exhibition games, we played with a no-

fouling-out rule. Mickey Johnson of the Golden State Warriors must have liked the sound of that, because he committed thirteen fouls in that game. On one of them, he crashed
into Tisdale, who in turn wiped out Mullin. They both hit
the floor hard, scaring everyone. Later, someone slapped
Alvin Robertson in the face, and before it was over we had
pros and Olympians squaring off all over the floor.

Coach blamed the referees for letting the game get out of
hand. Early in the second half, when Vern Fleming got called
for charging, Coach grabbed the basketball and refused to
hand it over to the officials. That got him a technical, of
course. He finally gave up the ball, but he kept screaming at
the two refs. He swiped at the ball in the first ref's arms and
hit it. Don Donoher, one of our assistant coaches, had to
grab Coach and drag him away, and for a moment there was
a shouting match with another Olympic assistant, C. M.
Newton, the Vanderbilt head coach.

"What do you want me to do?" Coach fumed after the
game. "Sit on my butt and let a million-dollar player's career
be ruined by some jerk with a whistle?"

We won the fight on points, 94–78.

Overall, Coach Knight liked what he saw in the exhibitions. Patrick Ewing was the quickest, most mobile center he
had ever coached. We didn't worry too much about penetrating guards; we just funneled them toward Patrick, who
swatted away their shots or scared them into turnovers. It
was unusual, too, to see a player of Patrick's size run the
court with such speed and agility.

Chris Mullin was just as impressive. I loved watching
Chris because he was an unbelievable shooter from almost
anywhere on the court. Everyone kidded Chris about his
New York accent—Alvin Robertson called him a "shooting
god" instead of a "shooting guard"—but we all admired
how hard he worked.

Coach, being Coach, didn't allow complacency to settle
in. He benched Ewing for all but five minutes of the game at
Iowa City. He demoted Leon Wood to fourth-string guard.

He rushed me back to the bench whenever I screwed up. In fact, I began to wonder if I belonged on the team at all, until I scored 15 points and had 5 assists in an exhibition at Greensboro, North Carolina.

The guy I felt sorry for was Tisdale. Coach was on his case constantly, screaming "Wayman!" so often that some of the players mimicked the cry when he was out of earshot. At a practice in Greensboro, Coach suddenly stopped play and with a pen put a big X on the floor, then the date—marking the spot, he said, "where Wayman Tisdale hustled."

"When I get back to Oklahoma," Wayman joked, "I'm going to hug every mean person I used to think was mean."

Wayman's difficulties were not all his fault. He had been a scoring machine at Oklahoma, catching passes on the low post and getting rich on power moves and short jump shots. The trapezoidal shape of the foul lane in international basketball forced him farther away from the basket. His shooting suffered for it.

Wayman's other problem was that he had never played in a motion offense like Coach Knight's, where you are constantly moving, setting picks, running around screens, and sprinting from one side of the court to the other. "I have to think the game now, not just play it," Wayman said.

To Wayman's credit, he didn't sulk or crawl into a shell. He respected Coach Knight for not pampering him and said he wished he had gotten "basketball lessons" earlier in his career.

We moved to San Diego in mid-July to finish our training, and that's when our enjoyment of the Olympics really began. The hard work was over. We practiced at San Diego State University from ten to twelve every day, just to brush up our execution. That was it.

No more tiny rooms at the Indiana Student Union. The U.S. Olympic Committee put us up at the Town & Country Hotel, a huge place with two or three swimming pools. Each player had his own master suite with two TV sets, a kitchen, and a balcony overlooking the pools. In the afternoons, we lay out at poolside, went shopping at nearby malls, or hit the beaches. There were excursions to La Jolla Cove, the San Diego Zoo, and a San Diego Padres baseball game. A few guys slipped off to Tijuana for some cheap thrills.

One day they bused us to a J. C. Penney warehouse to get fitted for our Olympics uniforms and pick up our credentials. It was a little like registration at IU, with booth after booth and signs pointing this way and that. In other ways it was more like a wholesale club, because they told us to go up and down the aisles and pick out whatever we wanted. They had Olympic T-shirts and jackets, caps, duffel bags, sweat suits, raincoats, shoes, pins, mugs, posters, bumper stickers—umpteen different things.

If our practices were shorter and less intense, Coach Knight still had his way of keeping everybody off balance. Because I had played for him for a year, my teammates looked to me for predictions of Coach's mood. Vern Fleming grabbed me once and asked, "What's gonna happen today?"

I shrugged. "I wouldn't be surprised if we get kicked out in the first twenty minutes of practice."

"You're kidding me! We've been practicing great."

Sure enough, we got off to a sluggish start and Coach threw a fit and sent us back to the hotel. I flashed Vern a smug smile in the locker room. He gave me back what I can describe only as a look of awe.

I wasn't psychic. I had just learned to recognize the warning signs. I knew, for instance, that three or four good practices in a row usually led to a Knight blowup. Why? Because he expected progression every day.

I had also learned to read another motive into his tirades: they were a way to give us a rest without letting us get complacent. "Get out of my sight," he might scream, "and don't come back till you're ready to work!"

You'd find out later that he had already made plans to go hunting.

Of all the players, Leon Wood was probably the most in

awe of Coach Knight. Leon loved to wear hats, and hats were an absolute *don't* with Coach, who was taught by his parents that wearing them indoors was rude. Coach showed up one day for a meeting at the hotel and caught Leon wearing a baseball cap. Coach went crazy. "I told you a hundred times that I do *not* want you wearing that ugly hat, and you're not gonna wear it!" He went at Leon, and Leon instinctively ducked his head and hunched his back. Coach snatched the cap off Leon's head, wadded it up, and stuffed it in a wastebasket.

Leon was so shocked that when the meeting was over he didn't go near the wastebasket.

Naturally, we were getting to know each other as people as well as players. I became close with Jeff Turner, the Vanderbilt forward. Jeff was a wonderful guy, quiet but funny. He loved country music and was always talking about Lee Greenwood. I also spent a lot of time with Joe Kleine and Leon. Joe was a riot, a guy with a gift for making people laugh with his off-the-cuff remarks. Leon was just Leon, a very easygoing guy. Nothing upset him—except for Coach, that is.

Really, all the guys were great to be around. Coach had done a terrific job selecting the team, picking not just good talent but good people.

Ewing probably had the oddest personality. He was a very quiet person and kept mostly to himself. Maybe that was because he was married and had a baby, a closely guarded secret at Georgetown. Mostly, I think, that was just his nature. He was the one guy on the team who did not enjoy signing autographs or having his picture taken.

To tell the truth, as our time in San Diego drew to a close, I began to turn inward a bit myself. I tried to focus more and more on our goal: the gold medal. I wanted to win it for my country, sure. We all did. But I came to understand that I had personal motives as well. My inability to win the Indiana state championship for Dad still ate at me. I thought that winning the gold medal would erase the memory of that failure. As I told Dad on the phone, "I think that's why a gold medal would mean so much to me."

He agreed. "There's a lot of players in Indiana who can say they've won a state championship," he said. "Very few can say they've won an Olympic gold medal."

There was a ramp and a dark tunnel, and we had to wait for the longest time, 589 of us, wearing blue sweat suits with red-and-white trim. There was loud music and crowd noise ahead, but we couldn't see beyond our own flags and banners. Finally, we got the signal to move forward, down the ramp, through the dark tunnel, and we emerged suddenly on the stadium floor. A great roar went up from the crowd, and thousands of tiny American flags began to wave in the setting sun. It was at that moment, as we stepped out of the shadows—the last country to come out on the track—that it hit home that we were truly Olympians.

The floor of the Coliseum was a tossing ocean of flags, balloons, and athletes of all races and nations. As we marched around the track, I searched the stands for my family and finally spotted them—Mom, Dad, Sean, and Tanya, who had flown out for the occasion. They were screaming and waving at me and taking pictures. The most enduring image, of course, was the Olympic flame, set against the sky above the Coliseum colonnade.

From San Diego, we had reported directly to Los Angeles for the summer games. The U.S. basketball team was housed at the Olympic Village on the campus of the University of Southern California. For security reasons, they had put up fences all around the campus, and there were checkpoints outside our living units. To get into our sector, which was about two blocks long, you had to have a tag identifying you as an athlete or staff member. Another gate led to a private commercial district built just for the Olympics—fifty or so stores selling knickknacks and Olympic souvenirs, a post office, even a few night spots.

The security was awesome. I remember going into my dorm on the second day, glancing up, and spotting four SWAT-team members with machine guns on the roof. The precautions were necessary, but it made me feel like a stranger in my own country.

Our living units were arranged as three-room suites, two players to a bedroom. Each suite had a central living room with a comfortable sofa, a few chairs, and a TV set. The guards all roomed in one unit, the forwards in another, and the *real* big guys in yet another. Coach Knight lived upstairs in a suite of his own.

The basketball venue was the Fabulous Forum, home court of the Los Angeles Lakers Our first game in the Pool B round-robin was against China, and we won big, 97–49. The Chinese had neither the size nor the quickness to stay with us, but they did some interesting things, such as passing up lay-ups to kick the ball back out for 3-point attempts.

Game two was against Canada, a good American-style team led by Chris Mullin's college teammate Bill Wennington. Michael Jordan scored 20, and I had 13 off the bench on 6-of-8 shooting, and we won, 89–63. The Canadian coach, Jack Donohue, said we were the best team he had ever seen, but Coach Knight was less complimentary in the locker room. "You play that kind of defense again and I guarantee you we'll come out of here without the gold medal," he said. "You're getting careless out there, boys. You're not chasing down the loose balls."

He must have gotten his message across, because we smothered Uruguay on Wednesday, 104–68. In one stretch we sank fifteen consecutive shots, but Coach just talked about our defense. He told Chris Mullin at the half, "That's the best fifteen minutes of defense you've ever played in your life." Chris was startled by the compliment, but not as much as Wayman was when Coach praised *his* defense. Wayman grinned and said, "I sort of liked it."

Thursday night was special, because they let us out of the

Olympic Village and I got to go out for dinner with my family. Up till then, security had been so tight that they couldn't even contact me.

The funny thing was, they had more stories to tell me than I had to tell them. On Sunday night they'd had dinner with Julius Erving of the Philadelphia 76ers. A couple of days later, they had toured Magic Johnson's house. (Sean said, "Would you believe it cost eight thousand dollars just to wire up his stereo system?") Another night, they had met tennis star Jimmy Connors at a Converse Shoe function. (Al Harden, a family friend, was a Converse executive, and he and Converse set up the celebrity stuff.) Of course, they had gone to Disneyland. They had spent a day at Venice Beach, watching characters juggle firesticks and chainsaws. "We're going to Universal Studios next," Sean said. "We've done all kinds of neat stuff."

I was a little jealous.

Friday night, France played us shorthanded. The French coach, Jean Luent, had suspended three of his players for drinking wine after curfew, and his subs couldn't stop us from scoring. We had our best shooting game of the Olympics and won, 120–62. I was suffering somewhat from a staph infection, for which I was taking antibiotics, but you wouldn't have known it from my shooting. I was 8-for-8 from the field and 2-for-2 from the line in twenty-three minutes. In four games, I was 20-for-27 from the field—as hot a streak as I'd ever had in my life. What was really funny was that I had 15 rebounds, too—4 more than Michael Jordan and 3 more than Sam Perkins. Must have been my shoes.

Next up: Spain, a team our scouts said could upset us. Instead, we won by 33 points, outrebounding them 44–16.

Compared to the drama and intensity of the NCAA tournament, these Olympic routs felt like exhibition games. The crowds at the Los Angeles Forum were big, but not that noisy. Many of the seats were occupied by what we called "festival fans"—people who went from basketball to boxing to gymnastics without knowing or caring much about the sports. There was nothing wrong with that, but most of us missed the rabid, knowledgeable fans we were used to in college.

Maybe it wouldn't have made that big a difference. To be honest, our games were dull. If a team dared to play man-to-man defense against us, coach let Jordan, Fleming, and Robertson shred them with drives. If a team played zone and doubled up on the cutter, he told us to kick it back out for the open jump shot. That's how I got many of my points—not off picks, just waiting for the ball to come back out to me.

ABC, the network telecasting the games in the United States, continually hyped us as the best Olympic basketball team in history, but declined to air our games live, showing only taped highlights. Fans across America called the network to protest, but it didn't do any good. Dan Korb, an Indiana sportswriter, blamed everything on the president of ABC News and Sports, Roone Arledge. "They should collar him as he struts out of his skyscraper office," Korb wrote, "strip him naked, tar and feather him, drag him kicking and screaming through the streets of Los Angeles, and then strap him to the H on the Hollywood sign."

Other Hoosiers were less forgiving.

As a team, we were very loose. We believed we were the best basketball team in the world. We could hit you with speed, we could hit you with strength, we could hit you with jumping ability, we could hit you with shooting, and we could hit you with all-out defensive pressure.

We could also hit you with Michael Jordan, although Michael was not a superstar who played by himself. We all admired him for that. He had to know he was head and shoulders above the rest of us, but he never went crazy, never tried to take the game into his own hands. We were beating teams by 30 and 40 points, but Michael wouldn't pad his stats. He was very unselfish. As good a player as he was, that made him even greater.

Finally, we could hit you with Bob Knight.

I didn't envy Coach his position. The U.S. men's basketball team was 73–1 in Olympic basketball history, and that one loss was the game stolen by the Russians in the disputed finish of the 1972 gold medal game. The Soviets had decided to boycott the L.A. games, so that left us as the overwhelming favorite in men's basketball.

Coach was in a no-win situation. If we won the gold medal, the world would shrug it off. If we didn't, Coach would be second-guessed and criticized for the rest of his life.

Coach tried not to look at it that way, saying, "I want to keep it simple: I want to coach the best team in the world for two weeks."

That was what he kept trying to drum into our heads— that we could be the best. Never did he say, "You have to win." He said, "Let's go out and show the world this is the best basketball team ever put together. Let's show the rest of the teams it's just awfully hard to beat us."

We were finally tested by West Germany, a team with three future NBA players in its lineup—Detlef Schrempf and Christian Welp, who played for the University of Washington, and their center, a tall, red-haired computer scientist from Munich who looked awfully familiar. Their front line went seven-two, seven, and six-eleven.

Michael Jordan had his worst game against the Germans. They sat back in a tight zone and dared us to shoot over them, and for a while we looked flustered. At halftime, Coach Knight got all over the starters and threatened to bench them if they didn't start hustling. A few minutes into the second half, he did yank them, and it was something to see: Michael Jordan, Patrick Ewing, and Sam Perkins sharing the pine, not knowing when, if ever, they'd get out of Coach's doghouse.

We finally hustled enough and made enough outside shots to beat the Germans by 11 points—I scored 17 and Jordan had 14—but Coach was so angry that he wouldn't let the media talk to us after the game. He chewed on us awhile and then sent everybody to the showers, but first he pulled me aside into a little room.

He looked very tired and troubled. "Steve," he said, "what do you think is wrong with this team?"

I was taken aback. "Gosh, Coach, I'm just a freshman, I don't know these guys very well...."

He interrupted me. "I'm not interested in that. I want to know why we're not playing as well as we should."

I took a deep breath and jumped in. "Well, one thing I notice is our pregame routine. We've got guys who are sleeping on the floor, guys who don't pay attention to the notebooks. At Indiana, we sit in front of our lockers before a game and we study what you've made us write down. If you say, 'Force the guy left,' we're reading that. Here they write down everything that you say, but they don't pay any attention to it. They think the notebooks are a novelty."

He nodded. "You know, Steve, if you're not with us tonight, we probably don't win."

I couldn't think of anything to say. He had never paid me such a direct compliment before.

He shook his head. "I'm just *sick* of compromising."

I thought about his words later. I decided Coach just couldn't be happy with a team of superstars—even unselfish superstars like Jordan. He believed that the flashy players, in a pinch, would always revert to playground basketball, and Coach hated playground basketball. He wanted to coach the perfect game.

I think that's what frustrated him. For once in his life he had players who could play the perfect game, but he knew in his heart that we wouldn't.

I saw the results of our private conversation the next day at practice. Coach was all business in the locker room. "Our pregames are gonna change," he said sharply. He grabbed a notebook. "You see this? From now on, you're to have these notebooks with you at all times. I want to see you studying your book when you're getting taped. I want your head in your book at your locker. You'll take your pregame seriously, or you won't play. Do you all understand me?"

Everybody nodded or mumbled, "Yes, sir."

"Okay," he said. "Open your notebooks and let's get to work."

Three teams were supposed to give us a run for the gold: Spain, Italy, and Yugoslavia. Yugoslavia lost to Spain, 74–61, and then Canada pulled off the upset of the Olympics by beating Italy, 78–72. That meant that only two teams stood between us and the gold medal, and we had already beaten them both badly. Canada came first, and we knocked them off in the semifinals, 78–59.

One more for the gold.

We walked into our locker room at the Forum on Friday night, and the walls were covered with inspirational signs. Coach had asked Coach Raveling to put up some slogans that would make us think about what we had to do, but even Coach was stunned by their sheer number and variety. We had poetry, slogans, aphorisms, famous quotations— motivational material of every kind. One particular sign hit most of us like a hard punch: "Each of you has an ancestor who died for this country. The least you can do is give forty minutes for it tonight."

Our opponent was Spain—a team we had already beaten by 33 points. Even so, we were very high-strung, itching to get out on the court. Michael Jordan was so excited that he left the Olympic Village with the wrong color uniform, and it took a police escort to get the right outfit to the Forum by game time. "It was Duke blue," Michael explained. "If it had been Carolina blue, I wouldn't have forgotten it."

It had been a long, hard summer. Everything we had worked for was at hand.

Coach looked pretty keyed up himself. He went over the game plan, as he always does, and then stepped out into the hall for one last consultation with his assistants.

The moment the door closed behind him, Michael jumped up and went to the board. Grim-faced, he picked up the marker and wrote this message, which he signed "The Players":

COACH: DON'T WORRY. WE'VE PUT UP WITH TOO MUCH S——
TO LOSE NOW.

A minute later, Coach came back in to give us our final send-off. He turned as he started to speak and saw Michael's message. He paused for an instant, and then smiled. He looked around the room, his eyes falling on each of us individually. Then, he said just three words: "Let's go play."

We didn't know it till later, but as he walked out on the floor with the other coaches, Coach said, "Boys, just sit down and relax, because this is going to be over in about ten minutes. There isn't any way anybody's going to beat these guys tonight."

It was never a game. The crowd chanted "U.S.A.! U.S.A.!" and waved the red-white-and-blue, and we played for our dead ancestors and for our moms and dads and our neighbors and all fifty states of the Union and for the sheer joy of playing basketball. We led at the half, 52–29.

I started at guard, my third start of the Olympics. Maybe it was Coach's way of rebuking those who had criticized my selection to the team. Whatever the reason, I was thrilled.

One play stands out in my mind. I shot-faked and then jumped, shooting for real. Just as I was about to release the ball, I saw a teammate streaking for the basket. Instinctively, I fired a pass on a line. It was Wayman Tisdale. He caught the ball in the air and reverse-dunked it, all in one motion. The crowd roared, and I couldn't help grinning—it was a glorious moment for Coach's two whipping boys.

Coach was still Coach, never mind our 30-point lead. He screamed at Leon, raged at Wayman, yelled at me to "guard somebody." "Fussin' at us right to the end," as Wayman put it.

It was like music. When the horn went off, the spectators flooded onto the court, and we were swept up in a huge celebration. Somebody hoisted me into the air and handed

me a pair of scissors, and I made a snip or two at one of the
nets before passing the scissors on to a teammate. When we
had it down, we raced around the floor, looking for Coach.
When we found him, we draped the net over his neck and
started to lift him up on our shoulders. Coach waved us off
and pointed across the floor at Coach Iba. Coach wanted
Coach Iba to get that honor because Iba had been cheated
out of the gold in 1972, when Olympic officials kept putting
time back on the clock until the Russians won.

Grinning, we ran across the floor and lifted the startled
Iba on our shoulders. The crowd cheered. Those who could
see Coach Knight's face say he had tears in his eyes for the
coach he so admired.

When we put Coach Iba down, we ran back to Coach
Knight. This time, he let us hoist him up and carry him off
the floor. The crowd chanted, "Bobby! Bobby! Bobby!"

The gold was ours.

We started home the next day by van. It would have been
nice to see the closing ceremonies, but I was more excited
about having time off with my family. The trip was leisurely
—Dad behind the wheel, Sean and I playing cards or talking,
Mom pointing out areas of interest along the highway.

We drove across the desert and stopped in Las Vegas for a
couple of hours. Walked around Caesars Palace. Hopped
into the van and drove back out into the desert.

Mom and Dad tried to catch me up on events back home,
such as the woman in New Castle who had trained her par-
akeet to say, "*Ahhhh!* Go Stevie! Get the gold! Go Stevie!"
Somebody in Wabash had put out a sign that said, THE RUS-
SIANS ARE AFRAID OF STEVE ALFORD!

I couldn't get the Olympic images out of my mind, especially the medal ceremony. You can't stand up there on that
platform with a gold medal around your neck and the national anthem playing without being powerfully moved.
Someone asked me later if I had sung along with the national anthem. I said, "We all did."

As we drove through the Rockies I thought a great deal about my teammates and about Coach Knight. I suspected that Michael and Sam and Chris and all the other guys would look back on the Olympics as the toughest grind they had ever endured. But I also knew they wouldn't trade the experience for anything. As Chris said, "There were days when you wondered if it was worth it—all the yelling and screaming and swearing, the blood, sweat, and tears. But now that I've got a gold medal in my hands, I know it was worth it."

In the end, I think Coach felt as warmly toward us as we did toward him. He even found kind things to say about Tisdale! "One thing I have enjoyed more than anything in coaching this team," he told the media, "is working with Wayman. He's done an excellent job at working to do what we want."

When Wayman heard that, he practically busted with pride.

I slept a lot as we crossed the Great Plains. I was extremely tired, both physically and emotionally. "You were really put through the wringer," Dad said.

That's exactly how I felt. At rest stops, I stood around lethargically while Dad went and made his phone calls, whatever they were about. It wasn't until we hit Illinois that I started to perk up, knowing that we were close to home.

The first sign greeted us on I-70 as we crossed the Illinois-Indiana border: WELCOME HOME, STEVE. CONGRATULATIONS.

"Hey, look at that," Sean said.

Mom was delighted. "Well, isn't that nice?"

Before we hit Indianapolis, we spotted several more signs and a banner or two on overpasses. Dad stopped one last time for gas and went to the phone again, but I didn't make anything of that. I was thinking about how good it would feel to plop down on my own bed in my own room and sleep for about a week.

The first inkling I had that something was afoot came on the other side of Indianapolis. We passed a police car parked on the shoulder, and a pretty girl waved at me from the backseat.

"Hey, Mom!" I couldn't believe my eyes. "That's Tanya! What's Tanya doing in a police car?"

Suddenly, cars were honking and people were waving as they went by. Just past the Greenfield exit, we approached another police car and a caravan of convertibles decorated with banners, bunting, and dozens of American flags. Dad, smiling to himself, pulled over. "Here's where we change vehicles," he said.

Before I knew what was happening, they had loaded me and Tanya into a convertible and Dad was hanging the gold medal around my neck. Mom looked at me critically. "I wish you'd gotten a haircut," she said.

Mom, Dad, and Sean piled into two other convertibles, and the caravan began to roll. Horns honked, streamers and balloons trailed in the wind, helicopters hovered over the motorcade to get good angles for the television cameramen.

Highway 3 into New Castle was even wilder. There were more cars, people waving from the roadside, and signs everywhere, on front lawns, on porches, over the highway, painted on store windows: WELCOME HOME, STEVE ALFORD, THANK YOU! YOU MAKE US PROUD....WE SALUTE THE ALFORD FAMILY: SAM, STEVE, SHARAN, SEAN.... STEVE, OUR GOLDEN BOY....STEVE'S PRIDE IS HENRY COUNTY WIDE. I nearly fell out of the car when I saw the marquee of the Castle Theater: WELCOME HOME, STEVE, YOU'VE GOT US BURSTING OUR BUT-TONS WITH PRIDE.

The parade slowed to a crawl at the intersection of Route 3 and Riley Road, where people clogged the street. They shouted greetings and reached out to shake my hand. We turned down Hickory Lane and I saw hundreds of people lined up on either side of our house. American flags lined our driveway and red-white-and-blue pennants waved from lines stretched between trees and light poles. There was a big sign on the front lawn: STEVE ALFORD'S FAVORITE COLOR IS GOLD.

The crowd cheered as we turned into the driveway, and I was so busy waving to everyone that I didn't notice the backboard until Tanya pointed it out to me. It had been repainted. Over the hoop, Tanya's brother, Scott Frost, had painted the Olympic rings and the letters "U.S.A." In one corner, under a map of Indiana, was "Steve." The other corner had "Sean" and the New Castle Trojans logo.

I looked at Tanya, shaking my head in wonder. Meanwhile, the crowd drew in around the car, filling the driveway and the yard and spilling out into the street.

I stood up to get out of the car, and the crowd suddenly hushed.

"I think you have to say something," Tanya murmured.

What do you say? I was stunned by the welcome, practically in a trance. The first words out of my mouth—"It's good to be home"—were delivered in a hoarse voice.

"As you can tell, I'm losing my voice. I've had to do a lot of instructing for Coach Knight." The people near the car laughed, and I relaxed a little—if you can relax with three television cameras drawing a bead on you.

"It's been a very long summer, a very hectic summer. When you do something like I've done with a group of eleven other young men that I've really grown close to and will be close to for the rest of my life, and when we can get together with the coaching staff we had and accomplish what we did, it was well worth it. When you come from a community like New Castle, it makes it even more special, because I know how good New Castle's been to me. No matter what happens to me and no matter where my career takes me, New Castle will always be number one in my heart because this is where I got my start."

My friends and neighbors cheered again as I got out of the car, and I practically had to wrestle my way into the house. It was the experience of a lifetime, an unforgettable moment.

But it wasn't over. Two nights later, on a day designated Steve Alford Day in New Castle, the fieldhouse filled up with friends and neighbors and thousands of people I didn't know at all, but who felt a part of the basketball gold medal because I was part of New Castle and New Castle was part of me. I sat with my family on the stage, the gold medal around my neck, and squirmed as speaker after speaker said kind things about me and evoked memories of my time at New Castle. It was hot and muggy in the fieldhouse, but I'm sure I would have been sweating had it been December.

Or crying. More than once, I had to lower my head and pinch my nose. I couldn't stop thinking about the dream Dad and I had brought to New Castle, the dream of filling the fieldhouse. Never, in my wildest dreams, had I imagined that we would fill it for such an occasion. Or that the people would all be dressed in red-white-and-blue instead of New Castle green-and-white.

Tanya took the microphone, and I must have swallowed hard a dozen times. "I remember you from your first day in New Castle," she said, "when you were in the fifth grade. The cute, scrawny little kid always had a roundball in his hands, playing pickup games, and always had a new girl-friend every other week. The girls were always bigger and taller than you."

That got a big laugh.

"You're an idol and a hero to us all, but most important, you're a fine and considerate young man. You set a fine ex-ample." Tanya's voice broke. "We all love you and think the world of you."

And then it was my turn to speak, and it was frightening to face those thousands of upturned faces, but thrilling, too. This time, at least, I was prepared.

"There's nothing I will do in this lifetime that will mean more than this night you have given me," I said. "It was a great honor for me to represent my country and to represent this community. In making the Olympic basketball team, I give that gift to New Castle and Henry County and the state of Indiana. Everyone sitting here, each and every one of you, I love you dearly. My Olympic experience, to share it with this community, is a little payback for all you've done for me and all that you continue to do for me throughout my career. To have an opportunity like this is very special to me, like winning a gold medal for my country."

What made it so special? I tried to explain. I told of my disappointment that I had not won a state championship for my father and for New Castle. I recalled my depression the night my dream died in the semistate, and how my religious convictions had helped me regain a healthy perspective. "My faith said, Something is down the road in the near future."

But mostly I talked of my father, saying, "I've wanted so dearly to repay him for what he has done for me and other players around the state."

I turned to Dad. "Dad, would you step up here, please?"

Dad got up and crossed the stage. When he reached me, I leaned into the microphone and said, "There is no greater thing I'd rather do than to present my gold medal to my father."

I took the medal off my neck and put it around his. And then I gave him a huge hug. The crowd rose and gave Dad a long standing ovation, and as I stepped back and grinned at him, I felt a great load lift from my heart.

Sean stood up and grabbed me, because he could tell I was getting emotional. It was his dream, too, winning the state for Dad. He understood how much this meant to me.

Dad stepped to the microphone again to thank the crowd and the whole community. And then we left together, the entire family, up the tunnel behind the stage.

Dad looked over at me, his eyes sparkling, and said, "You gonna get your workout in tonight?"

For once, I didn't rise to the bait. "No, Dad," I said. "I think I'll take the day off."

CHAPTER FOUR

TWO KINDS OF MAD

It was the worst six minutes of basketball I can recall.

The Buckeye fans were going crazy. They were jumping out of their seats, waving their arms, and yelling loud enough to raise the roof.

We could have used their energy. Instead, we lurched around the court as if we were on sedatives. Coach screamed at us from the sideline, but we couldn't hear him over the roaring of the crowd. Our defense had collapsed; nobody was blocking out on the boards. We turned the ball over five times. We gave up 11 points on rebound baskets, including two 3-point plays. The Ohio State guards grabbed 6 rebounds. All in six minutes.

It was a Hoosier meltdown.

Coach was beside himself at halftime. We had allowed 26 points in the last 6:09 and 51 points in the half. No Knight-coached team had ever been scored upon so freely. For it to happen fifteen games into the 1984–85 season was inexplicable to him. We had practiced well all week, we hadn't looked flat at all, and now this.

Winston Morgan and Mike Giomi bent their heads under Coach's tirade. He was fed up with them, sick and tired of their lackadaisical play. They had no guts, they had no brains, they were sissies, they didn't belong on a college basketball team, they belonged on a girls' field hockey team. "You don't care! You don't know how to be good. You don't *want* to be good."

We took the court for the second half determined to shut Coach up. Uwe played tough inside, our defense stiffened, and we slowly chipped away at the OSU lead. Finally, it came down to one shot. With four seconds left, Uwe went up for a high, beautiful hook. The ball hit the front of the rim and bounced off.

Final score: Ohio State 86, Indiana 84.

Maybe—and this is a *big* maybe—maybe if Uwe's last shot had hit the rim, bounced a couple of times, and toppled in... and maybe if we had won that game in overtime... then maybe my sophomore season would not have been the nightmare it turned out to be.

I'm not blaming Uwe. He scored 33 points in the Ohio State game, his career high. Coach praised his effort after the game, telling the media, "There really isn't any more we can expect from him than that. He got no help."

But that was the turning point, the moment when things began to unravel. Coach was so angry in the locker room that he cut his talk short. (That was always a danger sign, when words failed him.) He singled out Winston and Mike again, called them a few choice names, and finished them off with a stinging get-lost: "You're not flying on the same plane with us. Find your own way home."

Out in the hallway, Coach was overheard telling his assistants, "I don't want to go nuts on the plane. I don't want to make this more difficult that it is, so I don't want them on the plane."

In the telling and retelling, this war story has often been

"improved." One version has it that Coach left Mike and Winston in Columbus with no tickets and no money. The truth is, Winston and Mike bused to the airport with us. Coach then assigned them to IU's other airplane, which carries athletic department staff and certain members of the press.

We felt sorry for those two guys, but if you had taken a poll, most of us would have gladly traded places. We had to fly back to Bloomington with Coach fuming in his seat, saying little. No one dared talk or play cards.

When we landed, it was cold and dark. Coach hustled us onto the bus and we pulled away without waiting for Winston and Mike, who were just off the second plane. I remember looking out the bus window and seeing them wandering around the hangar, looking dazed and baffled.

The Ohio State game didn't seem like a season-breaker at the time. It knocked us out of a tie for the Big Ten lead, but we were still 11–4 overall and had beaten Kentucky and Iowa State, two good teams. We opened conference play with a tremendous win, beating Michigan by 25 points at Ann Arbor. (And that Michigan team had Roy Tarpley, Gary Grant, and Antoine Joubert.) Our fans were pumped up, and so were we.

We had entered the season with great expectations. Uwe and I were back from our Olympic successes. Winston, our best defensive player, had recovered from a stress fracture in his right foot that had kept him out most of the '84 season. Todd was a question mark—his painful right knee had required arthroscopic surgery in September and he was still working himself into shape—but Daryl had added about fifteen pounds of muscle and Marty figured to bounce back from his late-season slump. Dakich was still a hero for his play against Michael Jordan in the NCAA tournament. (Dan had these ugly black high-tops with the white swoosh; he now called them "Ground Dakich" as an answer to Michael's "Air Jordan.") Coach had also recruited six very talented freshmen: Delray "Indiana Mr. Basketball" Brooks, Steve Eyl, Joe Hillman, Magnus Pelkowski, Brian "Illinois Mr. Basketball" Sloan, and Kreigh Smith. Most polls had us ranked in the top five.

Not that Coach took the rankings seriously. "We snuck up on a lot of teams last year," he said. "This year, they'll be ready for us."

Were they ever! We played very sloppily and lost another home opener, this time to Louisville on national TV. Coach looked smug after the game. "Now you know," he said. "Now you know you've got to play against a lot of people who can *play*."

I scored 18 against Louisville, but not without a struggle. Four different players guarded me. They were very athletic and did everything they could to deny me the ball—hand-checking, face-guarding, bumping, jump-switching. "Get used to it," Coach told me. "You've got a target on you now. You're an Olympic gold medalist, and every guard you face is going to try to make a name for himself by shutting you down."

A couple of weeks later, that very thing happened. Notre Dame held me to 4 points with a box-and-one. Four men played zone defense while my old high school rival Scotty Hicks hounded me man-to-man. I hadn't faced that defense since high school, and I let my scoring troubles spoil my whole game. I had only 1 assist and 2 rebounds. Meanwhile, a freshman point guard named David Rivers scored 23 for the Irish. They won, 74–63, proving Coach's point: headlines yellowed fast.

Now, when he called me an Olympian, the word dripped with sarcasm. He got all over me in the locker room after the Notre Dame game: "Alford, if you give us *anything* tonight, we win. Maybe you think you can blind people with your gold medal, but they're just eating your lunch. That Hicks kid was practically inside your shorts."

In a quieter moment, he used the Notre Dame fiasco to make an important teaching point. "You don't need to score

20 points to have a good game," he told me. "You've got to distribute the ball, hustle, play defense, get some rebounds." The Olympics, he implied, had spoiled me. I thought I could stand around on the perimeter and wait for teammates to pass me the ball for easy jump shots.

I didn't agree that the Olympics had spoiled me—I felt I had worked very hard and was a better player for it—but I listened and kept my mouth shut.

Coach was particularly impatient with my defense, and I think his public comments gave people the impresson that I dogged it whenever I didn't smell a scoring opportunity. That wasn't really the problem. I could cover my man pretty well and I hustled, but sometimes my concentration was poor and I got out of position.

Coach's concept of man-to-man defense is a team concept. He accepts that no single defender can stop a great offensive player in the open court, so he teaches a "helping" defense in which players move quickly to rescue the beaten defender and steal passes. He doesn't care so much where your man is; you move according to where the ball is.

In preseason, we practiced with a white line of tape down the center of the floor from one rim to the other. Coach taught that we should play every game with that imaginary line in our minds. All our defensive vocabulary was based on that line: "one step man-side," "one step ball-side," and so on. If the ball was above the foul line you were supposed to be in one place, and if the ball was down low you were supposed to be in another, so that you could quickly rotate if a teammate needed help.

My problem was that I would lose concentration and be a step out of position. I would help on defense, but that extra step meant the difference between drawing a charge—which Coach said I never did—and committing a foul myself. Sometimes it meant a basket for the other team, and that's when he yelled, "Alford!"

Coach did most of his defensive coaching off the court, in the film room. If he ran a play on the VCR and you saw yourself in the wrong spot, you died inside because you knew you were about to get it. Sometimes there might be three or four guys out of position, and you'd pray that he wouldn't—

"*Alford!*" (Sound of something breaking in the dark.)

No, he didn't miss much.

The film sessions were bad enough, but Coach also had a staff of forty thousand assistant coaches to stay on my case. Every fall, before the season started, Coach gave a free talk to the students at the IU Auditorium—a sort of State of the Union message—and this year he asked for their help. "If any of you pass Steve Alford on the campus," he said, "I want you to stop him and ask him if he can spell 'defense.' "

Oh, brother. I must have had fifty different people come up to me and say, "Hey, Steve—can you spell 'defense'?"

"Yeah," I'd say, "the first three letters. I haven't got the last four yet."

It was a real pain in the neck. I finally went to Coach and said, "You know, I may never be able to play defense the way you want me to play it, but I'll sure be able to spell it."

He thought that was pretty funny.

Of course, when Coach roasted a player in his talk to the students, it was *meant* to be funny. He knew that the students didn't want the usual head-coach babble—"Alford is the greatest shooter of all time, Blab's hook is unstoppable, blah, blah, blah"—they wanted to hear his intimidating humor. So he gave it to them.

Uwe, for one, didn't understand that kind of humor. At training table one night, he reached into his wallet and pulled out a newspaper clipping, which he unfolded and read aloud. The story quoted Coach: "If you see Blab walking across campus, please tell him that he's not playing for the Germans."

Uwe calmly put the clipping back in his wallet. "It's saying, basically, the Germans are crap."

It was like Uwe to carry around something like that. He was proud to have been co-captain of his national team, and he couldn't believe that Coach would use it as a put-down. "There's this big difference between the European attitude and the American," Uwe said. "We play for fun. For fun and exercise. The American attitude is winning at all cost."

"Come on, Uwe," I said. "We Americans play for fun, too. It's just that we understand there's more fun in winning."

To be honest, though, Coach began to push a few buttons that made me resentful, too. He started yelling at me to hustle more in practice. My surprise and annoyance must have showed—I thought I was working as hard as I possibly could. It's one of his mind games, I told myself.

One afternoon, Coach pulled me off the floor and said, "Do you feel like you're working very hard?"

I figured my heavy breathing and the sweat pouring off my body were answer enough. "Yes, sir. I think I'm working hard."

"I don't think you are."

Bam, just like that. You're loafing, Alford.

It became a constant irritant. Coach questioned my effort in practice and in games, in film sessions and on plane trips. "Alford, you're not working hard! Get after it or get out!" He'd take me aside, privately: "Don't tell me you're working hard. I can show you films. Do you want me to ask the assistants if you're working hard?"

"I don't understand," I'd say. "I think I'm working hard."

Daryl, Todd, and Marty would see me arguing my case, and they worried that I would say something that would set Coach off. I didn't always live up to Dakich's standard as a whipping boy: I avoided Coach's eyes, pressed my lips tightly together, and shook my head in disbelief. I made little noises of exasperation. Actually, I don't think Coach ever threw me out for something I said...just for how I looked.

Coach had really found the way to get under my skin. It didn't bother me when he screamed about my defense—I knew I had to improve in that area. It didn't shake me, either, when he called me a "privileged character" or threw the Olympics in my face. I knew he had to do that to assure my teammates I was their equal (just as Dad had thrown me out of practices to prove he wouldn't play favorites). But when Coach accused me of not working hard, he attacked everything I represented as a player. I told myself, I don't want to hear this. I don't *need* to hear this.

It was ironic. On the Olympic team, I had been the guy who advised all those great players on how to withstand Coach's yelling. "Don't take it personally," I had said. "He's just trying to make you better." Now I was walking around with hurt feelings. I felt sorry for myself. I staged mental arguments with Coach while my teammates told jokes at training meals.

My fellow sophomores were in similar states of shock. Todd didn't get yelled at much, because he was playing on a very painful knee—Coach admired him for that—but Marty and Daryl caught their share of flak. Marty, looking heavier than he had as a freshman despite all his running and saunas, started the season on the bench, but he quickly won his starting job back and made the Indiana Classic all-tournament team along with me, Uwe, and Giomi. Then Marty scored 1 point against Kansas State and 2 against Miami of Ohio. Coach busted him back down to the white team.

Daryl was up and down, too, very inconsistent. Coach expected more of him as a sophomore. He yelled at Daryl constantly to play tougher and meaner inside, to use his body for rebounding and power moves to the basket. When Daryl didn't respond, Coach blistered him with locker-room critiques that questioned his manhood. Daryl just seemed to shrink under Coach's verbal attacks. He didn't quit playing hard, but he lost confidence. In practice, he'd grab a rebound and it would fall out of his hands. You could see he was rattled.

I never knew what provocation Coach would spring on us next. Our very next game after the Notre Dame loss was a nationally televised home game against Kentucky. The day before the game, we were having a pretty normal practice when suddenly Coach started yelling at me every time I touched the ball. "Watch for him left!" he barked. "Watch for him right!...Look behind you!...Look up the floor!... Take the ball left two dribbles instead of right, Alford!"

It was all a loud mumble-jumble, totally confusing. If I made a pass to the right and the guy hit a jump shot, Coach would get all over me. "No, pass it *left!* I don't want you passing to the right!"

I began to get rattled. He kept pumping me, pushing me, harassing me. Ten minutes passed, and I still couldn't do anything right.

Finally, he exploded. "Alford, get off the court! Take a shower and get out of my sight!"

I walked straight off the court and down the hall to the locker room, slammed the door, and slumped down in my plastic chair. I waited. I was near the boiling point myself. Why did I put up with this garbage? The man was nuts!

Five minutes later, Coach Knight came in to get me. He stared at me a minute and then said, "Do you know what I was doing out there?"

I shot him a sullen look. "No, I don't. I thought I was doing things right."

He nodded. "For the most part, you were." He waited for my look to soften before explaining: "I was trying to put as much pressure on you as possible."

"You did," I said. "What's the point?"

"The point is, the pressure will be twice as bad tomorrow when Kentucky gets here."

Neither of us said another thing. Two minutes later, I was back on the floor, dishing out passes left and right. When I made my next mistake, Coach swore and yelled, "Alford, get your head in the game!"

The next day, I was 11-for-14 from the field, with 6 rebounds and 7 assists, and we beat Kentucky, 81–68.

And no, I wasn't prepared to give Coach all the credit.

• • •

Coach had two kinds of mad: one where he didn't say anything and one where he said absolutely everything.

He was so upset after the loss to Ohio State that he went hunting for a couple of days—the first kind of mad. He didn't want to see us. He'd come to practice, say a few words, and leave.

We were surprised; we had expected some hard practices. But Coach said what ailed us couldn't be cured by doing drills. We were good at drills. We were sharp; we had things down. The problem, he said, was in our minds. We didn't know how to win. We didn't *want* to win.

He thought we just didn't care enough. We weren't mentally tougher than our opponents. "And I don't know how to coach those things," he said.

We weren't sure what he was getting at. We wanted to win as much as ever, and we *had* been winning. The Ohio State game just seemed like one of those inevitable letdowns that mark a basketball season.

One night, Coach asked Dan, Uwe, and me out to his house to discuss the situation. He met us at the door and led us to his upstairs room, which was a big room absolutely packed with trophies, photographs, framed letters, and all sorts of basketball memorabilia. We sat on the couch and Coach sat opposite us in his favorite chair.

The tone of the meeting was very positive. Coach took us into his confidence, bounced ideas off of us, asked our opinion on things. "Who do you think should be starting?" he asked Dan.

Dan didn't hesitate. "I would start the three of us, Giomi, and Marty Simmons."

Coach looked at Uwe, and Uwe said, "That's who I'd start."

He looked at me. I said, "Me, too."

The conversation went on in that vein for some time. I don't think Dan or Uwe believed, any more than I did, that Coach needed our input to pick a starting lineup. Coach just wanted us to feel more confident as team leaders, and sharing his thoughts with us had that effect. It was the same strategy he had used with me at the Olympics, when he had asked me what was wrong after the West German scare.

Our next game was Thursday night at Purdue, but we didn't have to wait that long for a crisis. Giomi and Morgan were deep in Coach's doghouse, Mike more than Winston. Coach had yanked Mike's scholarship the year before for cutting classes, and he had put his foot down: no more cuts, *period*. Now he was unhappy with Mike's effort on the basketball floor.

After the debacle in Ohio, Coach had told Mike and Winston that they would not practice that week or play at Purdue. Winston showed up anyway on Wednesday and flew with us to West Lafayette. Giomi did not. He arrived the next night just before game time, carrying his gym bag. He and Winston watched the game in street clothes.

With two of our best players out, we played Purdue tough for about thirty minutes. Then we fizzled, blew an 8-point lead, and lost, 62–52. We got outrebounded 36–19, but Coach told the media it was not the fault of our big men, it was the fault of the guards (meaning Alford and Robinson), whose poor perimeter defense had caused too many defensive switch-offs.

The flight home was predictably grim.

After Purdue, Winston and Mike came back as white-team players, but the crisis wasn't over. For some reason, Mike wasn't working hard in practice. He seemed to be in a dream world—not rebellious, just detached and withdrawn. He was basically an outgoing guy with a fraternity man's sense of fashion—loafers, jeans, cardigan sweaters—but he seemed to be losing the fraternal sense that binds teammates together. He had begun skipping team meals.

The team, to a man, was furious with him. It made all of us crazy, because Mike's lackadaisical play made Coach angry, and when Coach got angry we all paid the price. Dan tried to talk to Mike, but Mike didn't seem to listen. He nodded, but you didn't know it if was a meaningful nod.

Nobody knew what Mike was thinking. Maybe he thought Coach's anger was just another mind game.

If he did, he was wrong. One evening, Coach called a team meeting to watch some tapes. Everybody was in the locker room in street clothes when Coach came in. He fixed his stare on Giomi, and a hush fell over the room. Mike waited nervously.

"Mike, have you missed any classes?"

Coach already knew the answer. He had gotten a call from a professor.

Mike looked very uncomfortable. He hesitated, and then said softly, "Yeah, I missed a couple."

Coach didn't miss a beat. "Well, you know our deal. You're gone."

Mike stared back, his mouth open.

"I told you," Coach said. "I explained to you what the situation was. I just can't have that kind of irresponsibility on my team. We'll have to play without you."

Mike stood in front of his locker, frozen. Nobody else moved.

"We're waiting," Coach said. "Get your stuff and get out so we can get on with things."

No one wanted to meet Mike's eyes. We knew how badly he wanted to stay.

There was no point in arguing. Mike gathered up his things, and without saying a word he went out the door.

Saturday, we were scheduled to fly to Champaign, Illinois, for a Sunday-afternoon game of great importance in the Big Ten race. The Illini, led by Doug Altenberger, were picked by some to win the national championship. NBC would be on hand to televise the game nationally, and since it was Illinois, the game had regional recruiting implications. (All TV games did, of course.)

Imagine the surprise in Bloomington, then, when the Sunday *Herald-Telephone* appeared with this headline: BLAB, 4 FROSH COULD START AGAINST ILLINI.

For my first birthday, I got—what else—my first basketball and hoop set. Note the balance and form, though my aim was a little off.

The finalists for the National Elks Hoop Shoot, where I finished fourth; I'm the disappointed-looking kid in the Martinsville t-shirt up front. [*Anderson Photo Co.*]

The elevation, the extension, and two points for New Castle High.
[*Ron Tower*]

Two happy Alfords—me and Dad—
after we won the Regionals in 1983.
[*Ron Tower*]

Socks, shorts, one-two-three . . .
[*Courtesy Indiana University
Athletic Department*]

When Coach Knight talks—as here in my freshman year—you listen. *Hard*.

Uwe Blab grabs a
rebound while Dan
Dakich and I look on.
[*Courtesy Indiana
University Athletic
Department*]

Storming up court
against Notre Dame:
me, Todd Meier, Blab,
and Stew Robinson.
[*Courtesy Indiana
University Athletic
Department*]

Proudly representing my country (though here it's against former IU greats in our practice game at Assembly Hall).

Sharing a happy moment with Tanya and my friend and roommate Curtis Wright (driving) as New Castle celebrated our Olympic victory. [*Ron Tower*]

They weren't all stationary: here I'm driving the baseline against Iowa State.

Celebrating the title win over Syracuse with fellow seniors Todd Meier and Daryl Thomas. [*Courtesy Indiana University Athletic Department*]

Even Hoosiers take off their basketball clothes sometimes; that's my brother Sean at left, and Mom in the middle.

Thanks, Coach: on the sideline after our NCAA championship
win, at the end of a long, fulfilling four-year run.

We were already in Champaign, so I didn't see the news-paper, but Coach had hinted during the week that most of the regulars wouldn't start. No one had gotten too excited, because Coach often used starting as a carrot to go with his stick. I figured he would make us squirm for five minutes or so, and then send us in to play.

I got the bad news at the hotel, before our morning walk-through. Coach pulled me aside and said, "Steve, I'm going to sit you down today. You're just going to watch. You're not going to play."

I was speechless. I can't describe how shocked I was.

"I want you to watch the freshmen," he went on. "Watch how they play defense. Watch how they move."

Watch the *freshmen?* I couldn't believe my ears.

"I've never had a player who didn't have to sit down and watch a game. Buckner's done it, everyone's done it. I want to see how you're going to respond." He clapped me on the back. "Now get on the bus."

I boarded the bus with tears in my eyes. Everybody I knew back home would be watching the game on television— Mom, Dad, Sean, Tanya, my friends, our neighbors. What would they think if I didn't play? Would they imagine that I had done something illegal or immoral? The possibilities left me numb.

On the way to the fieldhouse I stared gloomily out the window, my mind racing backward for answers. Our trou-bles had started with the Ohio State game, but I thought I had played a pretty decent game there. At Purdue we had played without Winston and Mike, and I hadn't played par-ticularly well, but not badly either; about average. And both those losses had come on the road against good teams. I knew Coach was upset with those losses, but surely he didn't hold me solely responsible... did he?

I was almost sick with disappointment. It was like being in seventh grade again with the snow falling outside and the principal coming on the loudspeaker: "Because of bad weather, the seventh-grade game at Rushville has been canceled." Only this was worse, because Coach Knight said he was benching me because I wasn't playing hard enough.

By game time, my feelings had changed from shock to resentment. I sat on the bench, biting my lip, as the starters took their positions for the tip-off. What a lineup! Uwe and four freshmen—Steve Eyl, Brian Sloan, Delray Brooks, and Joe Hillman. Coach was pleased with Uwe's play of late, which is why he started, but the freshmen were out there just to send a message to the rest of us.

The Illinois players looked confused: this wasn't the Indiana team they had prepared for.

A newspaper writer summed it up pretty well the next day: "It was a basketball event that caused furrowed eyebrows nationwide." Our freshmen gave it everything they had—sprinting back on defense, taking charges, diving for loose balls, crashing into the seats. Coach Knight pumped his arms and cheered them on. Every time one of the freshmen made a gutsy play, he wheeled toward us on the bench. "See what I'm talking about! Why can't you guys give that kind of effort?"

Uwe was just as impressive, battling for rebounds and barking defensive instructions to the rookies. "I've never had a kid playing for me that I've ever been prouder of than Blab," Coach said after the game. "The doggone kid has just come a thousand miles to be a player."

But courage wasn't enough. Our shooting was awful. The freshmen were tight and rushed their shots. Foul shots clanged off the rim. Put-backs rimmed out. At halftime, we had only 12 points, and the Illinois players couldn't believe what was happening. They kept looking over at the bench to see when Coach Knight was going to put his starters in.

Don't ask me what Coach Knight told the freshmen at halftime. I was completely absorbed with my own thoughts. I kept thinking, I'm an Olympian, I was freshman of the year, things have been so good... we'd be winning this game if he'd put the upperclassmen back in....

But Coach would not yield. When a freshman needed a

rest in the second half, he just sent in another freshman, either Kreigh Smith or Magnus Pelkowski. Like a captain, Coach was prepared to go down with his ship.

And down he went. Illinois won, 52–41. For the game we were 3-for-15 at the line and got outrebounded 43–23. I walked off the floor with my uniform dry and the taunts of the Illinois fans ringing in my ears: "Nice game, Alford!"

I was upset after the game. All the veteran players were. In our eyes, Coach Knight had thrown the game to teach us a lesson. It seemed too high a price to pay.

Coach grabbed me again as we left the locker room. "Did you learn anything today? Did you see what I was talking about?"

I tried to hide my unhappiness. "Well, they worked awfully hard. They didn't shoot the ball well, and that's why they lost, but they gave it everything they had."

"That's exactly right." He put his arm around my shoulders. "I'm not concerned if you miss every shot, as long as you're working as hard as you possibly can, as long as you're trying to make your teammates better."

It was a point he had tried to impress on me before: good players just make themselves good. Great players make the players around them better.

He left me, saying, "I don't want you to be satisfied with just being a good player."

But I was still ticked off. Was I loafing? I thought not. Was I complacent? Hardly. Was I satisfied to be just a good player? *Never.*

When we got back to Bloomington, I called home right away. Dad said our phone had been ringing off the hook. Friends were calling to ask why I was being punished or to blame Coach Knight for my benching. Reporters were calling to get Dad's reaction. Did he think Coach Knight was out of line? Was Steve going to quit Indiana? Were the Indiana players on the verge of mutiny? There were even calls from total strangers, asking, "Why Steve?"

That was actually a headline in the Bloomington paper:

WHY ALFORD? Bob Hammel, the sports editor and Coach's best friend, wrote that Coach had called his own mother in Ohio after the game, and even she had asked, "How come you didn't play Alford today?"

Coach tried to answer the questions raised by the Illinois game on his radio show Monday night. I didn't hear the broadcast—we were having dinner at the Union—but I read some of his comments in the next day's paper.

"When somebody talks about Steve Alford," he said, "you almost have to start with me in terms of people who support him and like him and want to see him do as well as he can. I recruited the kid when he weighed about 155 pounds and was six foot one and not a whole lot of people thought he could really be an outstanding player at the major-college level. I never had a doubt about it. I happen to be the guy who picked him to play on the United States Olympic team and got all kinds of criticism all over the country because I picked Steve Alford.

"So the thing with Steve is a very simple one: there are things Steve has to learn about basketball. There's a whole lot more to playing basketball than sticking the ball in the bucket. I think Steve has a great intensity when he's in a position to score. I think he understands his scoring is very important to us. But I want to see Steve Alford be more than a scorer. I want to see him be an outstanding basketball player. I want to see him be a *great* player. A great player is a guy who makes everybody else better.

"If my primary purpose at Indiana is to go out and win ball games, I can probably do that as well as anybody can. I'll just cheat—get some money from a lot of people around Indianapolis who want to run the operation that way, and just go out and get the best basketball players I can, and then we'll beat everybody all the time.

"That's not why I'm coaching basketball at Indiana, and that's not why the people here at the university have me coaching. Basketball is a classroom situation. Basketball is a learning experience for players. And if Steve can learn, in my opinion, by sitting out for a game, then I just right now happen to be the guy who can make that decision.

"I think Steve Alford will come back to be a much better basketball player."

Coach's comments didn't make me feel any better, and I don't think they won over our disappointed fans, either. Todd got around more than I did—fraternity parties and that sort of thing—and he told me that the kids at these parties were all worked up about Coach and the team. "What's wrong with Bobby—has he gone crazy?" they were asking. Our fans were used to unusual behavior from Coach, but they weren't quite ready to accept a virtual forfeit to a Big Ten rival.

And there was the Giomi mess, too. Coach had announced Giomi's dismissal to the media with this brief statement: "I have learned that Giomi has not fulfilled the academic requirements that were placed on him, and therefore I have no choice but to separate him from the team."

To most people, that implied that Giomi had flunked out or was otherwise academically ineligible. That was not the case, and Coach had to go back and make it clear that it was *his* academic requirements that Giomi had violated, not the university's.

Suddenly, Coach began to feel the heat from usually docile IU supporters. Newspaper columnists were blasting him as a tyrant. Callers to radio sports-talk shows asked if Bobby Knight hadn't finally blown his cork.

Uwe Blab, of all people, was the quickest to defend Coach, particularly concerning the Illinois benchings. "I was really supportive of that," he told Bob Hammel. "It was probably one of the first times when I was really, *really* supportive of Coach Knight, because I think something had to be done about the team. As a matter of fact, I was a little disappointed in the fans' reaction. We weren't playing hard. I think people ought to see that."

Most people, though—and that includes some of his fellow coaches—thought that Coach had gone too far. Was it fair to other teams, they asked, to put an inferior team on the floor against Illinois? Wouldn't that affect the Big Ten race? (I don't remember having any thoughts on this issue; I was too wrapped up with what was happening to me personally.)

Coach, predictably, defended himself with sarcasm. "Just as I leave the law business and the grocery business to people who know what they're talking about," he said, "I think I'm capable of handling the coaching business here."

I couldn't escape the questions any more than Coach could. They came from the media, my family, friends, strangers on the street. Everyone kept asking: Why didn't you play? What's going on? Why? Why? Why?

Those were answers I didn't have. Quite frankly, I didn't think being benched helped me any. I didn't understand the move. It wasn't a case where if Coach could shame me I would come back extra-hard the next game. I was already giving my best effort. And I wasn't an idiot; I knew Coach would have to play me if we were going to make anything of the season.

I would have to say now that I respect the move. By benching his leading scorer and three other scorers, Coach certainly proved that winning at all costs was not what he was about. But at the time, I was bothered and angry with him, and I couldn't have cared less about his principles.

It was a move Coach thought would work. But it didn't work.

The crises kept coming. Our next game was at home against Iowa. Winston, Stew, and I returned to the starting lineup, and Todd replaced Giomi, but we fizzled in the second half and lost, 72–59. Some in the Assembly Hall crowd voiced their displeasure by booing.

This time, Coach focused his anger on Marty, who had hardly played in the game and hadn't scored a point. Marty's weight was no longer a teasing issue with Coach, and the first thing Coach did in the locker room after the

Iowa loss was to order Marty onto the scale. He told Todd to get weighed, too, which made it seem like he was fishing for something. Todd stepped on the scale and stepped off. Tim Garl, our trainer, wrote his weight down on the clipboard.

Marty looked very uncomfortable. He stepped on the scale and sort of blocked our view with his body as he fiddled with the weights.

Most of us were puzzled. We had to weigh ourselves before every practice and write the weight down on a chart kept by the trainers. Marty's chart said he weighed 218, the same as his freshman year.

Tim stood by the scale while Marty moved the weights. When the pointer finally balanced out, Marty knew he was in trouble. The scale showed he weighed 238—20 pounds more than he had been writing down on his reports.

Coach was livid.

The next day at practice, Coach came through the curtain with what looked like a harness. He had taken a big rope, strung a twenty-five-pound weight on it, and secured the weight with a knot.

One by one, he made each of us put it on. "That's what twenty-five extra pounds feels like. Imagine what twenty-five pounds of deadweight would do to your game."

He turned and glared at Marty. "That's what you're doing to the rest of us, playing with that weight."

When all of us had tried on the weight, Coach handed it to Marty. "Wear it," he said. "Let's see how you play with it."

Marty put his neck through the rope while Coach started us on a full-court lay-up drill. When Marty's turn came, he stumbled downcourt with the weight dangling between his legs. It would have been comical if we hadn't known how angry Coach was with Marty. More than the weight, what bothered Coach was that Marty had fudged on the charts. Bad play could be forgiven; dishonesty, however minor, was unforgivable.

A great heaviness settled over us. Giomi was gone, we had lost four straight games, the whole team was in the dog-house, and now Marty's future as a Hoosier looked dim. What else could go wrong?

Looking back, I can see that we, the players, didn't handle the adversity well. We blamed everything on Coach or Giomi or whoever was the scapegoat of the day. What we needed was for somebody to say, "Hey, we've lost four games and there's not a thing we can do about it. Let's just go out and try to play better. Let's see if we can reach the NCAAs again." But nobody wanted to stand up, take the cart, and pull.

We looked to Dakich and Blab for leadership, but nei-ther one was equipped to stop our skid. Dan did what he could. He had all the right qualities of mind and character, but he played sparingly as a senior, and it was hard for a nonstarter to be a team leader. As for Uwe, he had made giant strides as a player and had won everyone's respect, but he was too quiet to be a take-charge guy. And Uwe still didn't have a complete grasp and understanding of the game.

Why not Alford?

Good question. I was the team's leading scorer. I was the guy Coach wanted handling the ball at the end of a close game. I was the guy we looked to for free throws in pressure situations. I even had an Olympic gold medal. Didn't that make me a leader?

I didn't think so. I was a sophomore, and I didn't feel comfortable throwing my weight around with older players. And maybe my Olympic experience held me back. I didn't want the guys to think the gold medal had given me a big head.

Whatever my reasons, I didn't step forward. And neither did anyone else.

The six freshmen suffered the most. They showed up for training meals and found empty seats where upperclassmen should have been. They looked for leadership and got excuses. ("I'd like to help, but I've got to get my own game together.") We told them that practices would get shorter during the Big Ten season, and instead practices got longer and harder. The freshmen were thrown into action and asked to produce, but they got little guidance or emotional support. We didn't have time for them; we couldn't get untracked ourselves.

The freshmen must have wondered what they had gotten themselves into. They had chosen Indiana because of its winning tradition, and now Indiana was losing. And not just losing, but losing badly.

Add one more element to this bad mix: the assistant coaches.

Coach had four full-time assistants: Jim Crews, Royce Waltman, Kohn Smith, and Joby Wright. All four were fine coaches and fine people, but they sometimes seemed as confused in their roles as we were in ours. They tended to think of themselves as Coach Knight's eyes and ears. If they saw something or overheard something, they went straight to Coach and spilled the beans.

For example, if Winston Morgan didn't understand the thinking behind a certain move, he might go to one of the assistants for clarification. Instead of giving an answer, the assistant would go straight to Coach and say, "Morgan doesn't understand that weak-side screen." Coach would get angry: "Why the hell doesn't he understand it? We've worked on it for a solid month!" Then he'd go looking for Winston to chew him out.

The assistants were fostering paranoia and secretiveness, even though that wasn't their intention. There was no real mediator between Coach Knight and the players. Anything a player said to an assistant coach got to Coach Knight, and that was like pouring gas on a fire. He got madder and madder. We got scareder and scareder. He couldn't calm his nerves. We couldn't calm ours.

• • •

We beat Minnesota by 23, which ended the losing streak, if nothing else. We squeaked by Wisconsin at their place, and then beat Northwestern, for three in a row. Uwe and I shot very well in those games, and Coach said our second half against Northwestern was probably the best we had played all year.

But then Ohio State came to Assembly Hall and started our cycle of despair all over again. Uwe played brilliantly— 15 rebounds and 28 points—but I went 2-for-7 from the field and contributed nothing. We lost, 72–63.

Uwe summed up our team effort: "We were like a bunch of zombies out there."

Coach's patience was shot. Our practices continued on the long side, two hours and over, and every afternoon was an exercise in uncertainty. If you were on the red team and made a mistake, Coach blew up and demoted you to the white team. You might play well for ten minutes and end up back on the red team, or you might be white all day, the next day, and the day after. None of us knew his role anymore. Nobody knew who would start the next game. The twelfth man on the team was suddenly on the red team, and the star was on the white.

Coach moved us so much that the demotions lost their impact. As a freshman, I had felt humiliated when he put me with the white team. I would get angry and fight to get back with the reds. Now I was on the white team so much that my attitude changed—"Whatever. Let's play." Being on the red team didn't seem special anymore.

Naturally, there were more temper tantrums and flare-ups in practice. Bodies bumped in the lane, and suddenly good friends were throwing elbows at each other or making ugly faces. It wasn't that we couldn't get along as teammates—I don't remember any personality conflicts off the floor—it was just that everybody was frustrated and on edge. If I made a bad pass in practice, I might flare up at whoever was guarding me, claiming I got fouled. Afterward, instead of talking it out, we'd all just shower and leave separately.

Team meals were much quicker; nobody hung around to swap stories. Players spent more time with their girlfriends or with anybody who promised not to talk about basketball.

Of course, that attitude carried over into the games. When we broke from time-outs, it was the same thing: five guys going in separate directions. Winning wasn't our main focus anymore. We were individuals struggling to get our individual games back on track.

And then, as if things weren't bad enough already, I suddenly forgot how to shoot the basketball. I went 3-for-14 in a loss to Illinois, 3-for-12 in a loss to Purdue, 2-for-12 in a loss to Michigan State. Coach benched me with 6:55 left against Illinois and got booed for it, but Bob Hammel had it right when he wrote, "On this night, it was like asking for a sprint from a lame horse. The young Olympian had missed eight shots in a row and obviously was pressing."

That was an understatement. I was upset and disappointed with myself to the point of despair. I remember talking to Dad on the phone and suddenly blurting, "Dad, I don't want to go to practice tomorrow. I'm dreading going in."

It was true. For the first time in my life, I hated going to practice. As freshmen, Todd and Marty and I had always hurried off to Assembly Hall at one forty-five every afternoon, eager to get started. Now we watched TV in our apartments till the last possible minute. All three of us had cars now, and we always seemed to be passing each other leaving the parking lot at quarter past two. We drove in separate cars because we needed a way to get home if Coach threw one of us out of practice.

The atmosphere was poisonous. Players talked about quitting or transferring to other schools. The assistants talked among themselves in whispers. Coach shouted at us until I thought my head was going to burst. On top of that, we had the typical Indiana winter: week after week with no sunshine, the sky an unrelenting gray.

When I had been playing well I had always stayed upbeat,

no matter how much Coach yelled, because I understood that he was a negative teacher and that he got a lot done with negativism. But now his negativism, piled on top of my own, was drowning me. There just weren't any positives to grab on to.

I had long talks on the phone with Dad, and he came down to visit a couple of times. He could feel how upset I was. Mom, too. She wrote me a lot even in good times, but suddenly I began to get cards from her every other day. Mom and Dad were concerned. They could see the love of the game going out of me.

Dad thought it was burnout. "You haven't had a break from basketball since you left home," he said. "You went straight from your freshman season to the Olympic trials, and from there to the Olympics, and from the Olympics right back into another college season. You've had a lot of attention and publicity, and that's added to the pressure. I'm surprised it didn't get to you sooner."

The words made sense, but they couldn't dispel my gloom. There had never been a time when I didn't want to play basketball. I had played every summer and never gotten tired of it. "If only I could get my shot back on track, maybe I'd feel better," I said.

"Hey, you've been through this before," Dad said. "You've had tough years; you've shot the ball poorly." Like Coach Knight, he wanted me to come to the forefront as a leader.

"I'm trying to do that," I said, "but some guys don't want to listen to me. They think I'm trying to fix problems they don't have. And who am I to tell them what to do? I'm telling Kreigh Smith what to do on defense, and I'm not doing it. I tell Joe Hillman how to move without the ball, and I'm not doing it."

Actually, the others on the team weren't resisting my leadership. How could they? I wasn't providing any.

When fatherly advice didn't seem enough, Dad reminded

me that I had another resource to see me through tough times: my faith.

My spiritual life has always been important to me. I've never gotten caught up in doctrinal arguments—I attend Methodist and Baptist churches—but I have always maintained a relationship with God. Church is like a separate classroom to me. I'll grab a piece of paper out of the pew and write down things the minister is saying, so when I get home I can learn from them. (If you don't write things down—I learned this from my basketball workouts—you never see your progress. I approach my spiritual life the same way.)

When I got discouraged, I didn't lack for spiritual resources. I met weekly with the campus chapter of the Fellowship of Christian Athletes. I attended Sunday services at a church in Bloomington. Sometimes I called Kent Benson, the former IU great from New Castle who played for the Detroit Pistons. Kent was a strong Christian and a good friend, and he always had a comforting word. When alone, I prayed or turned to my favorite Bible verse, James 1:12: "Happy the man who remains steadfast under trial."

The pressure, though, wasn't coming from God, and it wasn't coming from my mom or dad. The pressure was coming from Coach Knight. And from myself.

"Talk to him," Dad said.

I finally did, the night of the Iowa loss. After dinner, instead of going back to my apartment, I drove over to Assembly Hall. I found Coach Knight in his downstairs office, where he was studying film.

"Coach?"

He looked up.

"Do you have a minute? I need to talk to you."

He stopped what he was doing and told me to sit down.

Once I started talking, I couldn't stop. I told him how upset I was. I didn't know why I was playing so poorly—I didn't know what to do. I told him how much pressure I felt.

"I feel I have to shoot well for us to win."

Coach patiently went over some old ground, telling me that I didn't have to shoot well for us to win. "I want you to do the other things—get the ball into the right position, be a leader, play better defense...."

Tears welled up in my eyes. "I...I just don't know what's going on."

There were other people in the room—an assistant or two, I think—and Coach saw I needed some privacy. He stood up and touched my shoulder. "Let's go for a walk."

We walked through the curtain and out on the floor of Assembly Hall, which was still brightly lit. I spilled my guts to him as we stood together on the court. I told him I thought I was playing awfully hard. I told him how difficult it was for me to be a leader because I wasn't playing well and couldn't lead by example.

He listened patiently. He reassured me. "A lot of times, Steve, I'm getting on you to make a point to another player. Do you understand that?"

I nodded. "I try to."

When I was sufficiently calm again, he took me back to his office and ran some tape of our most recent game. He showed me things I had done wrong that had nothing to do with shooting: defensive mistakes, missed opportunities, lapses of concentration. "Those concern me more than your shooting," he said. "Work harder. Make the other guys better. Be a threat every time you catch it. Think what you're doing. Anticipate every play."

Finally, he turned off the VCR and turned to me. "Steve, you ask what I expect from you in the way of leadership. It's this: work with me, work with your teammates. Let's get the guys in here, feel them out, and see if they really want to be a good ball club. Let's get to work."

He looked around the room, strewn with the tools of his trade: videotapes, clipboards, books. "As you can see, I'm still here and I'm trying everything I can to make this team better."

I left his office feeling much, much better.

• • •

Whenever I think back to that meeting, I remember his words: "I'm still here...."

To those of us close to him, Coach Knight seemed almost exhausted. He would deny it, but the Olympics had clearly taken a toll. The pressure and strain of the national effort, on top of his Indiana responsibilities, had consumed his energies for almost three years. Now, as his team crumbled before his eyes, he didn't give up, but he was all out of energy.

What could he do that he hadn't already tried? He'd benched me, he'd benched the other starters, he'd canned Giomi, all to no avail. He dusted off every pep talk, pulled every trick out of his bag of tricks, played every mind game —and we still lost. We simply didn't respond.

Coach had never had a team with a personality like ours. Great kids, every one, but how to motivate us? You had kids like Daryl, who responded to tongue-lashings by losing confidence and crawling into a shell. But if you praised Daryl, he got complacent and didn't play the rough, physical game that went with his build.

Coach was confused, and what came out was anger. In practice, he expressed his frustration through verbal abuse and longer workouts. At games, he raged at his players and provoked referees into giving him technical fouls. He got so angry during the second Illinois game that he put his foot through a chair at courtside.

But that's not the chair that got him in trouble.

That came two days later, when we played Purdue at Assembly Hall. The game wasn't even five minutes old when Coach was on his feet, screaming at the officials. We had a full house—17,279—and most of the fans seemed as frustrated as Coach. They roared whenever he roared, and booed the refs on every questionable call.

The trouble started when one of our guys poked the ball loose on defense. There was a scramble for the ball. Marty Simmons and Purdue's Mark Atkinson ended up wrestling for it. One ref signaled a jump ball, but the other called a foul—he said Marty had hit Mark's hand.

Coach screamed and threw his hands up in the jump-ball signal. The refs ignored him, but the crowd roared at the gesture and rained boos on the refs.

Purdue got the ball out-of-bounds on the side, but the whistle blew immediately: Daryl was called for a foul on the pass-in.

Coach howled again, and the booing got louder. He argued with one of the refs, and then, as he was sitting down, made one last remark that caused the ref to turn toward the table with his hands upraised in a T. Coach jumped to his feet, purple with rage, and shouted a string of oaths that were lost in the roar of the crowd.

I didn't actually see what happened next. I was at midcourt with the other players, watching Steve Reid step to the line to shoot the technicals. Suddenly, a red plastic chair came spinning across the court, and the crowd let out a mighty cheer. I turned around, and our bench was bedlam. Our assistants were trying to hold back Coach Knight, and the referee was holding up his hands in another T, which meant that Coach was out of the game.

"What happened?" I asked.

"Coach threw the chair," somebody said.

This may sound strange, but I wasn't shocked that he had thrown a chair, not even surprised. In less than two years, I had seen Coach draw about a dozen technicals. In locker rooms and practices, I had seen him do things that would have gotten him a hundred more if refs had been around.

It took some time to restore order. Reid went to the line to shoot six straight free throws. With seventeen thousand people booing, the best he could do was make three. Still, that gave Purdue a 14–6 lead and the ball, and we never recovered. Jim Crews coached us the rest of the game, a 72–63 loss.

Coach apologized publicly the next day. "I am certain that

what I did in tossing the chair was an embarrassment to Indiana University. That was not my intention, and for that reason I'm deeply sorry for it. . . . While I certainly take exception to criticism on who I start or play in any game, I feel a criticism of my action in throwing the chair is justifiable. It's something that I will not let happen again."

The national reaction was harshly critical. There were demands for his resignation, demands that IU fire him, demands that the Big Ten do more than slap him on the wrist. "Here in Bloomington, we have a tough time putting the coach in perspective," confessed an editorial writer for the *Herald-Telephone,* "because the man is often misunderstood and treated unfairly by the news media." But this, the writer went on, was not one of those times. "Knight has always stressed defense, but hurling a chair across a basketball floor was indefensible."

Two weeks later, the Big Ten suspended Coach for one game and put him on "probationary status" for two years. He did not appeal.

The Indiana House got in the act, too, with an official "admonishment." This last penalty was funny, because the state representative who introduced the resolution said he had prepared it a month before and was just waiting for Coach Knight to do something crazy so he could file it. "I knew I wouldn't have to wait long," he said.

I still think, to this day, that Coach threw the chair with a purpose. I think it was his way of trying to shake the bush one last time. He wanted to wake up his team, to wake up the crowd—*anything* to pump some life into that disaster of a basketball season. I don't think he would want to throw a chair again, and I don't think he will.

If I may add a postscript to the chair incident: on the Friday between the Illinois and Purdue losses, Uwe Blab got a letter informing him that he had been elected to Phi Beta Kappa. He was the first IU basketball player in thirty-two years to be so honored.

I mention it now because Uwe didn't get the attention

then that he deserved. His parade, like everybody else's, got rained on by the dark cloud that hovered over Assembly Hall.

We sank like a stone in the Big Ten, losing six of our last seven games.

It was obvious we were hurt by the absence of Giomi. He had been our leading rebounder, a six-foot-eight kid who ran the floor extremely well and could shoot. With him gone, teams began putting their big people on me. Michigan State's Larry Polec guarded me, and he was six-eight. Purdue's Mark Atkinson guarded me, and he was six-seven. If we'd had Mike, those guys would have guarded him and I would have been covered by a guard. Without him, we seemed unable to match up against some teams, no matter how hard we played. As Uwe put it after one of the losses, "We were intense and we were hungry again, and we played like crap."

Our last conference game was at home against Michigan, the Big Ten champs. We played very well for a change, but Gary Grant recovered a deflected in-bounds pass and sank a game-winning jump shot at the buzzer. Michigan led for only one second of the entire game, but it was the last second.

After the game, we stayed on the court to honor our seniors, Dan and Uwe. It was a bittersweet moment. We were tired of losing, tired of playing badly, tired of bad press... and now, for the first time in the Knight era, our seniors had lost their final home game.

For Dan, the season had been a big disappointment personally, and I'm not sure the ovation he got at the end made up for it. Uwe, at least, went out having proved himself—all–Big Ten, honorable mention all-America, a probable first-round NBA draft choice. The Indiana fans had always loved Uwe, and it brought tears to many an eye when they chanted "Ooo-vay! Ooo-vay! Ooo-vay!" for the last time and he waved in acknowledgment.

We weren't going to the NCAA tournament, of course —seventh-place teams rarely do. In the locker room after the Michigan loss, Coach told us he was going to refuse a bid from the National Invitational Tournament. "Season's over," he said.

We understood how he felt. When he had been the coach at Army, before coming to Indiana, the NIT had been the scene of Coach Knight's greatest triumphs. But now, with the expansion of the NCAA field to sixty-four teams, the NIT was seen as a tournament for losers and also-rans. Coach respected the NIT, and he thought that the bids should go to smaller schools that had earned their way, not to big schools like ours that had not.

We expected him to change his mind, though, and he did. There were financial considerations, for one. But more than that, the NIT represented a chance to start anew, to make something positive out of a dreary season.

And that's what happened. Coach suddenly stopped being negative. He showed flashes of his old humor and praised us unexpectedly. "You can still get something out of this season," he told us. "And we can build something for next year."

The whole team responded to the change in atmosphere. We played Butler to open the tournament, and I set an NIT record with 8 steals, in a 79–57 win. Uwe continued to play well and my shooting slump ended, which gave us back our inside-outside balance on offense. We beat Richmond and then Marquette in overtime, after Uwe tied the game with a pressure free throw with no time left on the clock. That got us to New York and Madison Square Garden, where we beat Tennessee in the semifinals and then lost by 3 to UCLA in the finals.

Coach saw improvement, both in the team and in Steve Alford. I sat beside him on the bench during the NIT awards ceremony, and he turned to me and said, "You've done a much better job the last three weeks." He talked about the opportunities for improvement on the around-the-world basketball tour he had booked for us that summer. "It'll help us come together. We need to get closer as a team." He seemed very happy at the prospect.

Still, the season ended on a sour note, another loss. Back at school, we picked through the rubble of the program and found little that was encouraging. Giomi was gone. Todd couldn't even walk without pain; he faced knee surgery. Uwe's graduation left us with a huge hole at center, and Coach needed Daryl, who was just six-seven and played facing the basket, to learn how to post-up and guard giants. Coach Crews was leaving to take the head coaching job at the University of Evansville. The players and assistants were barely talking to each other.

And then Marty decided to leave.

I can't say we were surprised. We knew he was thinking about it with three or four games left. Coach hardly played Marty anymore, and it was pathetic to see a player of his ability sitting on the bench game after game. Marty went and talked to Coach, and they reached an understanding: Marty would follow Coach Crews to Evansville, where he was sure to play more.

There was no goodbye ceremony, no announcement to the team. Marty didn't attend the postseason basketball banquet, and suddenly everybody realized he was gone.

One day, his dad came up from Lawrenceville and they packed Marty's things with help from Todd. It was hard to find the right words for such a parting. "Keep in touch...." "Hey, good luck down there...." "I'll be thinking of you guys...." And then the car was loaded and there was nothing left for Marty to do but to get in it and drive away.

School let out in April, and I went straight home to New Castle. There was no motorcade to meet me this time, there were no parades and speeches—which was fine with me. I desperately needed a rest.

Most days, I went mushroom hunting. The mushroom season in Indiana is in early May, when the grass and weeds start popping up. You drive down a gravel road after school and you'll see seven or eight cars parked along the fencerow. I worked out every morning at the school and then went into the woods from noon till three, waiting for Mom and Dad to get out of school.

My grandpa had started me hunting mushrooms when I was four or five years old. Dad would take Sean and me to visit Grandpa in southern Indiana, and they would give us bread sacks and lead us out into the woods. If Sean and I found a couple of toadstools we were thrilled, but Grandpa and Dad would always bring back a big bag of mushrooms for Mom and Grandmother to dip in batter and fry. They're delicious.

Hoosiers tell their mushroom stories—"how big" and "how many"—the way fishermen tell fish stories. But the real appeal of mushroom hunting is the serenity of the woods. It was nice just to get away and forget about everything, to enjoy the fresh air and notice the way the light filtered down through the trees. Even if I didn't find any mushrooms, I'd always spot a raccoon or a possum or something. Dad said, "That's one thing about mushroom hunting —you always come home with a story to tell."

There's one thing wrong with the mushroom season: it doesn't last very long.

CHAPTER FIVE

AROUND
THE WORLD

That was a vicious tour.

Today, if you came to me and said, "Steve, how would you like to go on an around-the-world basketball tour and play seventeen basketball games in thirty-five days and visit eighteen international cities and stay in twenty hotels and ride on twenty-one airplanes, twelve trains, eight ferries, three passenger boats, and three dozen buses?" I might say, "That sounds like fun."

As the summer of 1985 drew near, it sounded more like punishment.

We were still uptight from our nightmare season. Coach Knight had sent us home with the bluntest of warnings: "This is going to be a key summer for a lot of you, because if you don't improve you're going to be gone. I'm going to replace you with other kids. I refuse to go through another season like this, and if you can't understand that, if you're not ready to improve, I'll take your scholarships away and give them to somebody else."

That got a lot of us whispering among ourselves: "Can he do that?"

Answer: *Who wants to find out?*

I thought the scholarship threat was just Coach Knight's way of putting a scare in us to make us play harder. But you didn't know. He had already signed a couple of junior-college transfers, Andre Harris and Todd Jadlow, and that was a huge departure for Coach, who didn't like to recruit juco players. Neither Harris nor Jadlow was eligible for the world tour under NCAA rules, but we understood what their signing meant.

We practiced three days in Bloomington before we left, and Coach continued to give us mixed messages about the tour. On the one hand, he said he planned to relax on the trip; he wouldn't even coach from the sidelines. On the other hand, he told us he expected dramatic improvement. "We're going to redefine roles on this trip. It's going to be a great experience for you guys, but more than for the experience, we're going over there to be a better basketball team. I want us to grow together as a team."

Then he put us on a plane to Canada and said, "See you in San Francisco."

I flat out didn't want to go. Everybody told me it was the trip of a lifetime, my chance to see the world at somebody else's expense. "That's great," I said, "but when do I get a chance to see my family?" My sophomore struggles had convinced me I needed a rest from competition and from Coach Knight. I boarded the airliner to Toronto with a big grin and a camera bag slung over my shoulder, but I would much rather have been home in New Castle, working out alone in the gym.

The Canada leg of the trip was brief: three days and two nights in Toronto with a little sightseeing wrapped around two games against the Canadian national team. From Toronto we flew to San Francisco, where we ate shrimp cocktails and clam chowder at Fisherman's Wharf and watched the fog roll through the Golden Gate.

Coach Knight joined us in San Francisco for the flight to Tokyo. The atmosphere was tense at the airport, and the security was tighter than usual. The newspaper headlines and TV news shows were all afire with the hijacking of TWA Flight 847, which had been held by terrorists on the ground in Lebanon. It didn't seem like an auspicious time to be flying abroad.

We chased the sun for eleven hours, but when we landed in Tokyo it was all fog and rain. We cleared customs, collected our baggage, and took a chartered bus to the Prince Hotel, speeding along busy freeways with a convoy of Toyotas, Hondas, and Nissans. We couldn't see much beyond the roadway because of the gloom. At the hotel, we grabbed a quick American meal and went right up to our rooms to sleep off the jet lag.

It was still raining the following morning when we came down. There were posters everywhere advertising the tournament. They were in Japanese, of course, but they had my picture on them, shooting a jump shot, and one line of English: KIRIN WORLD BASKETBALL TOUR. The format called for us to represent the United States in Tokyo against the national teams from Russia, Japan, and the Netherlands, and then head out for an exhibition tour to five Japanese cities.

We practiced at the 1964 Olympics Basketball Center, and right off the bat we were in Coach's doghouse. We were sluggish from the long plane ride, and Coach got mad and kicked Kreigh Smith and Stew Robinson out of practice. Already I was thinking, the fun trip starts.

More depressing still, another idea began creeping into my thoughts: We are a bad basketball team.

I had promised Mom that I would keep a journal of the trip. I did so, but without wasting words:

JUNE 28, TOKYO

- Went to Pearl Shop downtown, got pearl earrings; very nice store (expensive, though).
- Tokyo is a huge city, I've never seen so much industry. Big downtown, lots of neon lights. A lot like L.A., but majority of Tokyo is industry.
- Rained all day, very muggy.
- Reception tonight. Japan has one guy 7'7" tall (huge). Saw Soviet team (3 guys over 7'2") (men).
- Attended press conference.
- Watching American TV channel (CNN).
- Still feeling jet lag (sleeping 12 hours).

We played our first game the following day against the Japanese national team, and it was a bizarre experience. Coach Knight sat with some friends, twenty rows up in the stands, but he shouted at us all through the game. "Downscreen!" he'd yell. "Find your man!" The Japanese were turning around in their seats to see who was making all the noise, but that didn't bother Coach. "Who's *Sloan* covering? ... Move your feet! ..." Some of the things he yelled made us hope that the Japanese didn't understand English as well as they seemed to.

Maybe we were still tired from the flight, but we played very badly. I was dead on my feet and not into the game at all, and on one trip downcourt I heard Coach yell, "Get Alford out of there!" When Coach Walton didn't do anything, Coach Knight sent a boy down with a message, and before I knew it I was on the bench. I didn't play at all in the second half.

We ended up winning by 13, but it was a sorry performance. Coach got on us good afterward. "The Russians beat the Dutch team 130 to 60," he said. "I'm not sure you guys can hold the Russians to 130 points. You sure as hell can't *score* 60 points against them." He kept us up most of the night watching film.

My journal entry: "Great fun."

JUNE 30, TOKYO

- Play Russians at 3:30.
- Walked through Russian stuff in morning.

- Typhoon warnings all day.
- Russians brought their national team, very good team. Sabonis is the best white 7-footer I've ever seen. Great mobility. Good shooter (hit two 3-pointers against us). We lost 74–54. We held the ball for the first 15 seconds before looking for a shot (my kind of offense).
- Played better as a team. We still are very poor on offense.
- Went to Japanese restaurant. Pretty good food. We had to take off our shoes and sit on pillows, and the food was cooked right before us.
- Japanese eat odd things totally. Example: shrimp head & tail with shell.
- Typhoon hits hard during the night.

The typhoon didn't hit us any harder than Coach did. We continued to play poorly, and he couldn't figure out why. We flew to Hiroshima to play the Japanese again and lost, 68–59. He was so angry at one point that he stormed down from his seat and coached from the bench. The assistant coaches walked the streets of Hiroshima that night, wondering if they were about to lose their jobs. They had never seen Coach so worked up.

"You ever been in a five-by-five cage with a wounded tiger," Joby Wright said later, "who has just had salt poured on the wound and is very hungry, too? Think about that and then think about someone rolling a live grenade in there, and that's what it was like."

The players were no happier. Coach was making all kinds of wild statements. He threatened to fly home and leave us in Japan. He said he was quitting coaching. (We had heard that before.) The weather showed no improvement either, and the gray skies reminded us of Bloomington in winter. I told Todd, "If we've got three more weeks of this, I don't think I'm gonna make it."

JULY 3, NAGASAKI (VIA BULLET TRAIN)

- Dad's B-day. Thinking and wishing I could be there.
- Japanese are very nice people, will not cheat you.

    Leave merchandise out in open, no thieves.
- Never see a policeman or police car.
- Fast-paced people—intelligent.
- Played Japan again and lost. Court and refs were horrible. Coach took us off the floor with 8 minutes to go, but we returned.
- Nagasaki—did not see much. However, it is obvious they have not recovered from A-bomb as well as Hiroshima.
- At this point I would eat a tomato to be home.

It wasn't pleasant, but I guess you could say Coach Knight kept it from being dull. It was more interesting to see him get upset on foreign ground than it was back home, because there was always the possibility of an international incident.

People were fascinated with him. One night I was sitting with some teammates at a food bar in a Tokyo cafeteria when some players from the Russian national team sat down across the bar. One of the Russians, trying to cross the language barrier, spotted us and yelled, "Your coach...Bobby Knight..." And with a finger next to his head, he made the internationally known gesture signifying "screwball."

From Nagasaki it was just forty-five minutes by ferry to Kumamoto, and the ride was beautiful. The rolling hills all around us reminded me of San Francisco. Once there, however, we celebrated the Fourth of July by losing to a very ordinary Netherlands team by 20 points. Coach did not play me at all. He said he wanted to see what would happen without me.

"Not a fun trip so far," I wrote in my journal. "We need a win bad."

No letup from Coach. No matter how many shrines and temples we visited, or how many snapshots we took, he couldn't seem to get his mind off basketball. He took it personally when we didn't play well. The basketball team was always a potential embarrassment to him. "That's a tremendous burden to carry," I told Delray. "Can you imagine tying your own feelings of self-worth to twelve young people you can't really control?"

Sometimes Coach was like a man picking at a scab till it bled again. At one practice he caught us by surprise and started quizzing us on our "team goals." This was a list of performance goals that was permanently mounted on the locker-room wall back at school, things like "58% of all rebounds," "Hold opponent to 65 points per game," and "Get 12 more shots per game than opponent."

Coach started going around the room: "What field-goal percentage do we aim for? How many turnovers do we want to force? What do we hold the other team's field-goal percentage to?" The numbers he got back were completely wrong, and he just went crazy because we didn't even know the goals he had in mind.

It didn't take a genius to see that he was drowning in anger and frustration, and taking us down with him.

JULY 6, KOBE

- Waited and rested all day for Russian game.
- We lost again 90–70. I played pretty well (against box & 1 again). Coach threatens that when we get back home we have 2 days then back to Bloomington (HA, HA, HA, HA).
- Time is like a turtle right now.
- Doing a lot of Scripture reading. It's the only thing getting me through. Then again, it always gets me through —what a friend I have.
- Miss home dearly.
- Do I sound homesick? (I am.)

We were always bumping into the assistant coaches in hotel lobbies and hallways, and I began to buttonhole them individually to pass on the players' concerns. If things didn't get more relaxed, I said, it would be disastrous. "We aren't even thinking about playing anymore, just about what's going to happen next. We were told Coach was going to sit back and evaluate us, but he's treating the tour like it's the Olympics again. Everybody's real jumpy and tense. We need some space."

All three assistants—Waltman, Wright, and Smith— seemed sympathetic. They could see how tight everyone had become and how the situation was affecting our play. The question was, what could they do?

JULY 7, SAPPORO

- Traveled to Sapporo today, on northernmost island of Japan.
- Saw the site of the 1972 Winter Olympics.
- Played at 2:20 p.m., beat the Dutch by 13 this time. Played good, 16 points.
- Played Pachinko, which is a kind of slot machine, lost 100 yen. But that's only 45 cents.

Our last full day in Japan was another cloudy, drizzly day. We returned to Tokyo for a reception in the evening, and then went up to the hotel ballroom for a farewell dinner with the other national teams. For entertainment, the tournament director had come up with a novel idea. He wanted a player or players from each team to get up and sing a song that the other countries could relate to. To get the ball rolling, the Japanese team stood up and sang the title song from Footloose, an American rock movie that was a big hit in Japan.

We didn't have anything prepared, but Coach Knight looked us over like a platoon leader picking someone for a suicide mission. Finally, he said, "Stew Robinson—get up there and sing for us."

Stew drew back. "Oh no . . . no, no, no, no!"

Coach asked him again, and this time he made it sound like an order. Stew was stuck. He got to his feet and cleared his throat. The Russian, Japanese, and Dutch players looked up expectantly. And then Stew began to sing "Old MacDonald Had a Farm."

Some of our guys lowered their heads and clenched their jaws tight to keep from laughing, but everybody lost it when he got to the "Here-a-chick, there-a-chick" part. Stew changed the words to "Here-a-Jap, there-a-Jap, everywhere a Jap-Jap," and the room erupted in laughter. If Coach had sung it, people would have been offended, but it was funny coming from Stew. The Japanese players thought it was a riot.

Coach slapped Stew on the back as he returned to his chair, which was Coach's way of saying, "You did okay."

After dinner, we got together with the Russians. Todd and Joe bought them all beer. In return, the Russians gave us little bottles of whiskey. I didn't drink mine, but I kept it for a friend back home. Todd traded a lot of stuff with the Russians—shirts, hats, that sort of thing. I almost gave them an Olympic shirt, just for laughs, but thought better of it. Coach Knight had been very outspoken in saying that our 1984 Olympic team would have beaten the Russians easily. I thought it best to steer the conversation away from that subject.

It was a good party, but I was very tired when I got back to my room. The last entry for Japan in my journal summed up the whole Japanese experience: "Coach is still Coach."

I could have added, "Team is still team—bad."

The morning we left Japan, the sun came out, both literally and figuratively. I can't explain it, but it was a definite turning point. We had lost five of our seven games in Japan, but we won ten in a row once we got out from under the clouds.

The moment we landed in Beijing, China, it hit us that we were in a very different country from Japan. The runway was a narrow concrete strip in the middle of a dirt field, and the terminal was primitive for a city of ten million people. It was midday when we stepped off the plane, and the heat and humidity were smothering.

Beijing's technology was a hundred years behind ours. Cars and televisions were scarce, and the only high rises were hotels and apartments. Our guide said that by the year 2000 they would have enough apartments to house eighteen million people—three and a half Indianas—but we had to wonder.

What impressed us most was the bicycles. At the hotel, we all pressed against the windows to look down at the rush-hour traffic, and it was just like New York except it was mostly bicycles, thousands and thousands of bicycles. The cars, we were told, belonged to government officials.

China seemed to revive Coach Knight's interest in the trip. He has always been a student of history, and China's history was much more accessible than that of Japan, which is an industrial country like ours. You could tell he was awed and inspired by the spectacular sites we visited, and that he was moved, as we all were, by the poverty. Everywhere we went, there were homes with dirt floors and no doors. I saw a woman doing laundry in the dirtiest pond I'd ever seen.

The contrasts were amazing. On our second day in Beijing we went to the Forbidden City, where twenty-seven em-perors had ruled during the Ming and Ching dynasties. The entrance to the Forbidden City was through Tiananmen Square, an enormous courtyard with thousands of people crossing back and forth. There was a huge picture of Mao Zedong over the gate and more pictures of the Communist leader across the street, where he is buried. Inside the wall, we found a vast complex of gardens and palaces, all a kind of orangish color. We took tons of pictures and stayed close to Coach, who seemed to know the right questions to ask the tour guides.

The next morning we visited the Great Wall of China, about an hour north of Beijing, and everybody agreed it was the highlight of the trip. We posed for a team picture on one of the lookout towers, and it was unbelievable to see the wall climbing the mountains in either direction as far as the eye could see. We peppered the guides with questions: How was it built? Where did the stones come from? Did it keep out the invaders? Even Coach Iba, who had seen a lot in his lifetime, seemed in awe of the wall.

JULY 11, NANJING

- Similar to Beijing.
- Arrived 7:00 p.m.
- Ate dinner & about died (squid).
- They reuse Coke bottles and caps.
- Filth.
- Hotel room bed is a board. Very dirty.
- This is interesting, but get me out of here!

JULY 12, NANJING

- Ate breakfast—eggs taste like fish because they save the fish oil to fry them (this is great).
- 97 degrees, extreme heat (sticks to you).
- Saw some temples and parks.
- Went to zoo, saw pandas.
- Played Nanjing Prou team & won 79–59. Played pretty well, played 21 minutes, 7–12 FG, 5 assists, 1 RB, 1 TO, 1 steal.
- Dinner was terrible—served us chicken with his head still on (didn't touch it).

We left Nanjing by train early the next morning for Shanghai. It was a four-hour trip, and I managed to win ten dollars playing gin. We'd interrupt the game every so often to stare out the windows at the passing scene—mile after mile of rice fields. Women hoed in ankle-deep water while men loaded things onto donkey carts. To a bunch of kids from Indiana, the land looked very unpromising. We didn't see how they could even grow rice on it. We were also in awe of the farmhouses, which looked like huge grass bee-hives. Was it possible that people were living in them?

Shanghai was huge, a city of twelve million people. The heat was, if anything, more oppressive than Beijing's—ninety-eight degrees and humid—and the continued scenes of poverty and squalor were depressing. The people looked happy, but I felt very fortunate that I lived in the United States and shared its many blessings.

We played the Shanghai team in a gym that looked like a Salvation Army, and of course I loved it, and I shot very well there (12-for-18). We were tied at halftime, 45–45. Coach took us back to the locker room and calmly offered some suggestions for improvement, and we went on to win, 104–76.

The hotel in Shanghai was comfortable, except for the beds, which had the thin mattresses common in China, but the air-conditioning went off at sundown. Delray climbed up on a chair to see what was wrong with the vent, but could find no problems. "It's open," he said. "It's just hot air." It turned out the hotel turned off the air-conditioning every day at sundown and turned it back on again at dawn. We opened the windows, but that didn't help. The temperature never fell below eighty-eight degrees that night, and it was very humid. I got up twice during the night and walked up and down the halls to get some air. It was probably the worst night of sleep I ever had.

I couldn't believe Delray. He slept right through.

Our last stop in China was Canton, a three-and-a-half-hour flight from Shanghai. Canton was little more than a stopover for us on the way to Hong Kong, but a bunch of us had time to go out for a walk. We were aimlessly strolling down a street when we came upon some young Chinese men playing full-court basketball. It was an asphalt court such as you'd find in a park back home, surrounded by a chain fence. A big crowd of Chinese were watching. There were old men squatting, young men leaning on the fence and smoking, children running around.

We hesitated a moment before going through the gate, because we didn't know if we would be welcome. The Chinese stared. The game broke up after a few minutes, and the players stood around catching their breath. One of the Chinese put down the ball.

That was like an invitation to Brian Sloan and Kreigh Smith, who were the most outgoing and adventurous guys on the team. They grabbed the ball and started racing up and down the court, passing to each other for slam dunks. The Chinese immediately began to smile and yell their approval, and the more they laughed, the more Brian and Kreigh got a charge out of it. We had to practically drag Brian away. He wanted to keep dunking.

When we left, the Chinese all clapped for us and smiled in appreciation, and we waved back. We couldn't speak each other's language, but we had found a way to communicate through basketball.

After so much dirt and poverty, Hong Kong looked to us like all the great cities of the world combined. There were soaring skyscrapers, luxurious stores, and beautiful hotels, and best of all, we had nothing to do but enjoy them all. There were no games scheduled, and Coach decided to give us a vacation from practice, too.

We did what you do in Hong Kong—we went shopping. A Hong Kong tailor named George pulled Todd and me right off the street. He was an old man with light gray hair, not Chinese-looking at all. "Would you like a suit?" he asked.

"Yeah," I said.

We followed him down some stairs to his little shop, where he asked us to sit down. "Let's not talk business," he said. "Let's have a drink first." He brought out some soft drinks for us, and he lit a cigar, and we visited for a while. After we got to be friends, I got myself fitted for one of those famous Hong Kong suits, with a silk shirt and a couple of ties thrown in.

It was fun to bargain with people. On Stanley Island I picked up some polos at seven dollars each, a sweat suit for twenty dollars, and a jacket for five. The bigger guys on the team were upset, though, because they didn't carry many things in extra-large.

Joe Hillman and I looked over some electronics stuff, too, but didn't buy. The shopkeepers wouldn't bargain.

Our second day in Hong Kong proved to be one of the most significant in my whole Indiana career. One of the assistant coaches knew that Tom Wisman, the brother of former IU player Jimmy Wisman, worked in Hong Kong. Tom had access to a luxury yacht, and he invited us out on the boat for a day of skiing and swimming in Hong Kong Harbor. Coach Knight—and this is significant—had other plans. "You guys go have fun," he said.

We messed around on the boat all morning, just the players, the assistant coaches, and Dr. Bomba. The setting was magnificent: the skyscrapers of downtown Hong Kong against a ring of mountains, white clouds drifting across a blue sky. It was a hot day, but the sea breeze made it comfortable. Brown-sailed junks bobbed in the distance, and big freighters lumbered across the horizon.

Everybody swam, and some of us tried to ski, although the water was a little rough for that. I gave it three tries, but I just made a fool of myself. I kept letting go of the towrope and falling clumsily into the ocean. Stew tried it and actually got up, but in a crouch. (He pulled a groin muscle, which he tried to hide the rest of our time in Hong Kong for fear that Coach Knight would find out how he got it.) Joe and Brian got up and skied around like it was nothing, but they had done it before.

When we weren't scaring the fish, we sat out on the deck with the assistants and talked. Not about basketball, though. There seemed to be a sense that this was an opportunity, a chance to fulfill the promises we had made to each other in Japan. It was the first time we had really seen the assistants as people and not just as extensions of Coach Knight. Instead of Coach Wright, it was suddenly *Joby* Wright, the former Indiana star and NBA veteran, who had lots of good stories to tell. It wasn't Coach Waltman, but *Royce* Waltman, the former high school teacher. It wasn't Coach Smith anymore, but *Kohn* Smith, who told us of his playing days in Utah.

It was a revelation. As players, we thought *we* had it rough trying to please Coach Knight from three to six every afternoon. The assistants had to do it, some days, from dawn till midnight. And their situation was more precarious than ours, because basketball was their livelihood.

Nobody actually said, "We've got to find a way to protect each other," but there was the definite feeling that our relationship had abruptly changed. The coaches wanted to build trust among us. They wanted to create a situation where nobody was alone and everybody had someone he could talk to.

Around noon, we dropped anchor about a hundred yards offshore and swam in for lunch at a Chinese restaurant on the beach. There was a beach house with a patio and gardens, where we could eat in our bathing suits. Everybody was happy and relaxed.

The only thing that marred the afternoon was that Delray almost drowned when we swam back out to the boat. Delray didn't have much swimming experience, and he started weakening about eighty yards out. He was with Dr. Bomba and I was right behind them, so he was in no real danger, but with fifteen yards to go he looked as if he would hit the ocean floor before he touched the boat. It took all of Dr. Bomba's coaching to get Delray over that last fifteen yards, and we practically had to haul him over the rail like a gaffed fish.

Delray went below and slept the rest of the afternoon. "I should have taken swimming lessons before the trip," he said.

When we got back to the hotel, I picked up my notebook and pen, stretched out on the bed, and wrote, "Best day of the trip!"

• • •

It took all night to fly to Holland, what with stops at Bangkok and Dubai. At Bangkok we got off the plane to stretch our legs, and everywhere we looked there were guards and soldiers with machine guns. We knew we had to fly over Iran, and some of the guys were nervous about that.

We landed in Amsterdam at eight-thirty in the morning and made a frantic tour of the city. We saw the famous windmills, of course, and there were flowers everywhere. Most of the houses had greenhouses in back, which made me think of Mom. (She's a flower nut.) We even took a stroll through the red-light district. It was Sunday, so everything was closed, but we peppered the guide with questions. He told us that on a normal day the picture windows we were passing had live girls beckoning at men to come inside.

We went right back to the airport and boarded a flight to Belgrade, Yugoslavia.

I hated Yugoslavia. Dad had been there before and loved it, but he had visited the towns along the Mediterranean. Belgrade is inland. The first morning, I got up early and left the hotel for a long walk along the Danube River. I saw some fishermen and people going to work, but it was a dirty river and most everything was ugly. "Did a lot of thinking," I wrote. "Thought mostly of telling God how much I appreciate home and family."

The view indoors was even worse. Everybody in Yugoslavia seemed to be a smoker, and there was smoke everywhere. We walked into one restaurant and there was smoke from waist level up to the ceiling. It made my eyes burn and had half the team coughing.

After lunch, we rode a bus fifty miles to Pozarevac, where we beat the Yugoslavian national team, 76–72. I missed my first four shots, but then went 13-for-15 the rest of the way, and crowed about it in my journal: "Simply filled the Yugos up!"

It was a beautiful evening in Velika Plana, where we spent the night. I saw the stars for the first time in a long time.

We beat the Yugoslavians again the next day, but this time

I got poked in the eye and played only two minutes. The eye swelled up so much that it was almost closed, and Dr. Bomba gave me a patch to wear over it during the night. "You scratched the iris," he said.

"I just hope I can play tomorrow," I said. "I've really been shooting the ball well."

JULY 21, OBERNOVAC

- Eye looks a lot better today. An eye isn't much of an injury to mess with, so I did not play in tonight's game. Although I really wanted to. There was a bench-clearing fight at halftime: the police were called in for the second half. Coach was unbelievable, in great form.

Actually, the fight took place the night I got poked in the eye. There was some question about whether my injury was an accident, and Coach was arguing with the officials when I went back to the locker room with Dr. Bomba. He was working on the eye when we heard a big racket outside. I said, "Why don't we see what's going on?"

We went to the doorway and looked through the little windows, and there were guys flying everywhere, a real brawl. Winston had one Yugoslavian wrapped up. Stew was on somebody's shoulders. And Coach was right in the middle of it, trying to play the peacemaker.

The fight came on the last play of the half, and Coach had the whole halftime to cool everybody down. "I like your aggressiveness," he said, "but we're not here to cause any trouble. Let's try to keep our cool."

I don't remember what the fight was about.

JULY 23, FINLAND

- Arrived Helsinki, Finland, 10 p.m. Still daylight.
- Took bus to Kotka 1 ½ hours.
- Saw many lakes on way in. Finland has 60,000 lakes.
- Very pretty country.

- Capitalistic society with some social control.
- Everybody is outside during the summer because of 20 hours of daylight. We were told that during the winter they may only see the sun a couple of times if lucky.
- A very bitter country toward Russia.

We played the Finns at Kotka and won by 11, and although I didn't shoot well I was proud of my 7 assists, 7 rebounds, and 3 steals. We played the Finns again at Salo, an hour up the coast from Helsinki, and won by 9. This time, though, Coach took off on me at halftime about my defense.

"Alford," he shouted, "I'm telling you this, here and now. Come October 15, you're on the white team, I promise you. You may think you have this team made, but the next Indiana basketball team is going to be made up of the best five defensive players, and believe me, *you* aren't one of them."

I was seething when I took the court for the second half, and I took it out on the Finns. I allowed only 2 points the rest of the way, made 3 steals, and wound up with 21 points. I was named MVP after the game and got a tennis racket as a trophy. I didn't exactly toss the racket at Coach's feet and say, "There!" But I was thinking, *Face,* Coach.

Of course, the joke was on me, because that's precisely the response Coach wanted. There were many times when I'd give him an ugly look or a look of disgust, and other times when I'd say to myself, He's crazy—why doesn't he get off my back? But deep down I knew he was doing it to make me better. His tongue-lashings just seemed to bring out the best in me as a basketball player. As I told Delray on the bus back to the hotel, "I guess I've got Coach to thank for this tennis racket."

In my notebook I had begun to count the days—"6 days to go," "5 days only"—and finally it was "1 day, 1 night." We were like soldiers at the front, counting the hours. It made us a little lazy, and seven or eight of us skipped shaving and walked around with light mustaches. At the walk-through before the final game, Coach got us all in a huddle, looked at our faces, and said, "If you need razors, you can come up to my room. But I want them off *tonight*."

We beat the Finns one last time in Helsinki, and everybody went disco-hopping afterward to celebrate. Every third or fourth song was Finnish, but most of the music was American rock, which made home seem that much closer. We walked back to the hotel at midnight, and it was so strange, because it was still light out.

It was hard to get to sleep that night. I was both tired and wired—tired from too much travel, wired because I was so excited about going home. "Need Mom's cooking bad," I wrote in my journal. "I've lost ten pounds."

As tired as I was, I felt my enthusiasm for basketball returning. From China on, we had showed considerable improvement, beating national teams as good as the ones that had routed us earlier in the tour. Daryl seemed to be making the adjustment to playing center. Winston Morgan and Stew Robinson were happy that we were running more. Kreigh Smith, Brian Sloan, Steve Eyl, and Joe Hillman had gotten valuable playing time.

Best of all, we seemed to have gotten over some psychological hump. By sharing so many unique experiences, we all felt a stronger bond. Even Coach Knight appeared to have mellowed with the miles.

JULY 29, COPENHAGEN TO AMSTERDAM TO CHICAGO TO INDY TO NEW CASTLE

- Very excited to get home.
- Can't wait to see everyone.

I wasn't the only one. Most of the guys cheered when the pilot of our transatlantic flight came on the intercom to say that we had passed into American airspace. When we got off the plane in Chicago, Stew Robinson got down on his hands and knees and kissed the ground.

Chicago didn't do it for me. I didn't feel close to home

until my connecting flight touched down in Indianapolis. I felt closer still when I walked off the plane and into a blizzard of hugs from Mom and Dad and Tanya and Sean and my aunts and uncles and everybody else who had turned up for my surprise reception.

We all went to a Steak and Shake on the east side of Indianapolis, and I wolfed down a double cheese steakburger with steak fries and a chocolate milk shake.

That did it. I was home.

CHAPTER SIX

THE INVISIBLE MAN

Coach Knight brought a stranger into the locker room at the beginning of my junior year. The stranger was short and wore a tweed jacket over a sports shirt. He was pretty young—thirty, I guessed. He carried a reporter's notebook and a pencil.

Coach introduced the stranger as John Feinstein, a college-basketball writer for the *Washington Post*. "John's going to be around a lot this year," Coach said. "He's writing a book about Indiana basketball." It was okay to talk to him, because Coach Krzyzewski at Duke knew him and said he was a good guy, somebody we could trust. "John will probably want to talk to you for the book. The interviews will be set up by the sports information office. Please give him your cooperation."

Turning to the board, Coach picked up his marker. "Now, on those downscreens..."

We opened our notebooks and began writing. The stranger, too.

He rarely missed a practice. He usually sat by himself in the stands, watching and listening. Sometimes when a player did something wrong or said something stupid, Coach would turn and yell to Feinstein, "Did you get that, John?" or "Take Meier out of the book—he's history!"

John would smile.

Mostly he made himself invisible. If we were watching tapes, he was there in the dark. In the locker room at half-time he stood in back, arms folded, watching. We didn't know where he lived in Bloomington or what he did in his free time. He was just there.

As players, we were surprised at the access Coach granted John. Our practices had always been closed to the media except for Bob Hammel, who was always there, but now John was there, too. He sat up front with the coaches on the team plane. He rode on the bus. He stood in the food line with us at pregame meals. He attended coaches' meetings.

He tried to interview each of us away from Assembly Hall. In my case, the interview took place during the Christmas break over brunch at the Big Wheel, a restaurant on the outskirts of Bloomington.

It was a normal interview. John asked about a dozen questions, none of them threatening or prying. He asked about my New Castle years and about Dad. He asked about the Olympics. Mostly he wanted to know how I dealt with Coach Knight, how I coped with his negativism and anger.

I was a little guarded in my answers, but not overly so. On first meeting, John came off as your friendly, outspoken East Coast type, but he revealed more of himself when he got to know you. He was obviously knowledgeable about basket-ball, and that helped. Like most people, he didn't under-stand why Coach did some of the things he did, but you could tell John respected his coaching ability. The more we talked, the more I came to trust John and he came to trust me.

After that, I'd always speak to John before practice. Small talk, mostly—the things you say to friends.

But if John was really close to anyone, it seemed to be Coach Knight. They practically hung out together. When Coach went on a recruiting trip, John went along. If Coach had to do his radio show, John went along. Their relationship seemed very amiable.

"Where does John live?" someone asked me one day.

"I dunno," I said. "Isn't he staying with Coach?"

I didn't mean it as a joke. I assumed he was staying with Coach because we saw them together so much.

This was the season of the great calendar scandal.

I was approached in August by a couple of girls from the Gamma Phi Beta sorority. "Steve," one of them asked, "would you represent the basketball team in our calendar?"

"What calendar?"

"It's a male calendar. We've got all sorts of IU sports figures—baseball players, football players. We won't make any money off it—this is strictly a charitable thing. All the money goes to a specialized camp for handicapped girls."

I gave it a few seconds' thought. Charity? Handicapped girls? "Sure, why not? It's not against the rules, is it? For an athlete, I mean?"

They looked at each other. They obviously didn't know anything about the fine print in NCAA bylaws. Scholarship athletes at NCAA schools are not allowed to pose for any picture or film that is used for commercial purposes. I couldn't do a television commercial for a restaurant, for instance, or endorse a shoe store in a magazine ad. There were exceptions made for charities, I assumed, but I didn't really know.

"I'll be glad to do the calendar," I said, "but check it out for me first, please. Ask the athletic director."

They cheerfully agreed, made an appointment with me for

the shooting, and took off. The whole exchange lasted maybe three minutes.

The photo session took a little longer, but not much. They shot me one afternoon at Assembly Hall, leaning over a backboard brace. I was dressed in a sports coat and slacks with an open-collared shirt. "Head up!" the photographer said. "Look a little this way, Steve...." *Flash...flash... flash...*

End of story. Or so I thought.

We opened the season with wins over Kent State and Notre Dame. Game three had us going to Lexington to play our old rival Kentucky on a Saturday night.

Thursday at practice we were doing drills when a man in a suit and tie appeared along the baseline. He had something in his hand. He got Coach Knight's attention, and the two huddled off the court for a minute. From where I stood, I could see that the object in the man's hand was a calendar and that the calendar was open to my picture. "Mr. February."

Great, I said to myself. What's happened now?

"Alford!" Coach waved for me to come over. He introduced me to the man and said he was the university's attorney. "Because you did this"—Coach tapped my picture—"you're probably going to lose eligibility."

My jaw must have dropped. "Why? I have no interest in this calendar other than to help out some handicapped girls."

Coach made a face, but he wasn't really angry. He was just trying to figure out what was going on, and he didn't like being distracted during practice.

"Go upstairs to the AD's office," Coach said. "I'll be up in a few minutes."

I walked upstairs in my practice uniform, covered with sweat. All kinds of things ran through my mind. Could I really be punished for appearing in a charity calendar? What about the other IU athletes who had taken part? Hadn't the sorority girls said they would check it out?

Coach Knight came up a little later and we went into the conference room next to Ralph Floyd's office. The two sorority girls were there with their sorority mom, and our exchanges got pretty heated. I said that I had asked the sorority to check out the rules, but the girls said I hadn't. Coach got upset with them for the way they had handled things, and he got upset with me because I hadn't checked it out with Kit Klingelhoffer, our sports information director.

Coach didn't say we had done anything wrong, exactly. After all, no money had changed hands and the sorority had already pulled the calendars off the shelves. But Coach said we had been careless and thoughtless.

Finally, he sighed. "Let me call the NCAA."

We waited while Coach went into the secretary's office and got somebody on the phone at NCAA headquarters in Overland Park, Kansas. We could hear only his end of the conversation, but once he had told the whole story he seemed satisfied with the response at the other end. He hung up and stepped back into the conference room. "He sees no harm in it at all. He said he'd take care of it and not to worry."

Coach and I went back down to practice. We could concentrate again on Kentucky.

That evening, I called my parents and explained the whole thing, and we all breathed a sigh of relief that the great calendar caper was over.

The next day, Friday, I arrived at practice at two o'clock and was told to see Coach Knight in his upstairs office. I went up, and it was a whole different picture. Coach was extremely upset. Shouting, angry.

"You're ineligible for one game," he said. "The NCAA called back and you're going to miss a game because of your own stupidity and because you don't give a damn about anybody but yourself. I'm so sick of your screwups that I can't stand it. If we lose to Kentucky because of your selfishness, you might as well find another team to play for." And so on.

I thought Coach was totally wrong. I shot back, "Coach, I

was *not* being selfish. I couldn't care less about having my picture in some calendar. I only did it to help some girls go to a summer camp."

I had never really argued with Coach. I have to admit, it felt kind of good to snap back at him. For a few seconds, we had a full-scale argument going. In the end, of course, he threw me out of his office and told me to go sit in the locker room and wait.

I sat there alone through the whole afternoon. Coach told the team I wouldn't play at Kentucky, and he told me not to practice. But I didn't dare leave. I alternated pacing and sitting slumped in my plastic chair.

I learned afterward that I had missed a pretty intense practice. At one point, Coach threw a chair thirty feet—shades of Purdue—and it landed upright, which amazed everyone.

At the end of practice, Coach told the guys that they didn't need Mr. February to win: "We are not going down to Kentucky to lose. We are not going down just to go down. If we play with our heads and our hearts, there is absolutely no reason why we can't win this game."

The other players showered and dressed for the trip, but I wasn't sure what to do. I asked Dan Dakich, who was now a graduate assistant, "Do I go with you to Lexington or stay? Coach told me to stay, but I don't know if he meant stay at practice or *stay,* period."

Dan said I should get on the bus. "If he wants you there and you aren't, it's irreparable and you're in bigger trouble than you are now. If he doesn't want you there and you are there, then he just leaves you on the bus. You have to go unless someone tells you different."

So I got dressed and boarded the bus. It was dark, of course, and I sat in the back. When Coach Knight got on, he didn't know if I was there or not. The bus groaned away from Assembly Hall with its silent cargo.

At the airport, the players filed off the bus first, as was the custom. Coach always gave you an encouraging slap as you went by, and he gave me one before he recognized me.

"Alford!" He gave me a murderous look. "What do you think you're doing? Get back in here. Didn't you hear me tell you that you weren't making the trip?"

"No, sir."

"Well, you must be deaf. Can't you do anything right?"

"I'm just going up to support the team."

"No, you're not. I told you, you're not going."

"Coach, I never heard you tell me that."

He screamed: "Well, you're not going! Sit here and wait for us to get back! Or find your own way back!"

I retreated into the dark bus and found a seat. From the window I watched as the freshmen took the gear out of the baggage hold and lugged it across the tarmac toward the plane. A few of them gave me sly waves and sympathetic shrugs. I slumped in my seat and waited.

When everyone had boarded the plane, I got off the bus, gathered up my gear, and started walking toward Bloomington. It was very cold. I didn't have a very heavy topcoat, but I was wearing gloves, which helped. I wished I had a hat.

I saw the plane take off and disappear into the night. I should be on it, I said to myself. I didn't do anything wrong. Then I resumed walking down the side of the road through the weeds and gravel.

I had walked about three miles when I heard the downshifting of heavy gears behind me. I turned and squinted into a pair of headlights.

It was the team bus. The door hissed open and the driver called down, "Want a lift?"

I scrambled up the steps into the warmth. The door hissed closed. The bus rocked back onto the pavement and we rolled toward Bloomington. This time, I sat up front.

I watched the Kentucky game on TV the next night and hated it. Rick Calloway, a freshman from Cincinnati who was off to a hot start for us, played great, and everybody fought and hustled, but we lost, 63–58.

I had phoned home to prepare Mom and Dad for my absence, but they already knew. The news of my suspension was out, and reporters were calling them every few minutes for a quote.

"Coach Knight called," Dad said. "He said you made a mistake, but he didn't think you were a bad kid."

I had to laugh at that. One of the reasons I had chosen Indiana was that I knew we would never be on probation for cheating. And here I was, suspended for the Kentucky game.

And *Kentucky,* of all teams. Coach Knight hated their program. He called them cheaters. He said they broke the rules in recruiting and paid their players in cash and services. "There are kids on that team right now who have gotten more crap from alumni than any players in the country," Coach told Feinstein. "For Alford not to play when all their kids are playing kills me."

The national media came down hard on our side. Everyone thought it was crazy that outlaw programs got off scot-free, while an honest program like Indiana's got punished.

A few columnists pointed out the illogic in the rule itself, the one I had broken. The rule didn't actually prohibit anyone posing for promotional pictures—it said, rather, that scholarship athletes weren't allowed to pose for any picture or film made by anyone outside the athletic department. In other words, the athletic department could put my picture in a program over the words "Go to Arby's." That was fine. I found out it was done all the time. After my senior year, I ran into Tony White, the Tennessee point guard, and he was carrying a beautiful poster of himself that bore the legend "The Wiz." I said, "Where'd you get those?" He said, "Oh, they made them for me and sold them this year."

Somebody was making money with those posters, and I don't think it was handicapped girls. That's what was really sad. Those girls didn't get the money for their camp. The publicity could have sold hundreds, maybe thousands, of calendars, but only about a dozen were sold before the stock was seized and burned. Today the calendar is a rare item.

I've autographed only three, and my Dad has tried like crazy to get one, without success.

Something good did come out of it, though. When Coach Knight picked up the telephone and called the NCAA, he proved that he would not tolerate anything unethical in his program. Had he not reported the incident himself, I doubt that they would have ever found out or cared if they *had* found out. But that didn't affect his decision. "A rule was broken," he said. "I accept responsibility."

And he wasn't about to let me weasel out of it by laying all the blame on the sorority girls. "Their eligibility wasn't at stake, Steve. Yours was. You should have checked it out yourself."

I admired that in Coach. He wasn't a hypocrite.

What I didn't like was the way he used the calendar incident against me three days later, during our walk-through for a game with Kansas State. From out of the blue he started chewing me out in front of the other players.

"Alford, you really cost us that game on Saturday, and I want you to know that I really resent it. I can't forget it. I'm just out of patience with you. What you did was stupid. It wasn't a mistake, it was just plain stupid. You screwed up and cost us a game. I really have trouble forgetting that. This is a habit with you. You don't listen, whether it's defense or playing hard or this. I don't know about anyone else in here, but I resent it and it pisses me off."

What really bothered me was that he called me "selfish" in front of the team, not just once but several times. That was hard for me to swallow. I got angry again.

"Coach, I'm *not* selfish," I said when we were alone. "I told you why I did that calendar, and it hurts me that you would say that about me."

Something in his manner suggested that he really didn't think I was selfish, that he had just used me as an object lesson for the rest of the team. But he didn't apologize.

"Your not being at Kentucky really hurt us," he said.

"You owe us a great deal, and I expect you to perform the way you're capable of performing."

People who don't know Coach Knight can't believe that he gets away with stuff like that. Why doesn't somebody haul off and belt him? Why doesn't somebody get right up in his face and scream, "Shut up"?

I told myself a hundred times I was going to do that. He could only put me down so far until I finally said, "No, you're wrong." I knew in my heart he was wrong, and I told him so.

The trouble was, when it concerned basketball, he was usually right. I take that back; he was *always* right. Sometimes he jumped on me in practice—"Alford, that was your fault! Get your mind in the game or get out of the gym!" And I argued with him. "Coach, I switched with Brian," or "I went man-side, like you said." I would *know* I was right.

The next day, he would take me into the film room and show me the tape of the previous day's practice, and it would be just as he had said: my fault. I always had to apologize.

It was different with the personal attacks. When Coach questioned your manhood or your integrity, I thought that was going too far. And when he jumped on me for something that he had missed or something that hadn't really happened—that's when I gave him an ugly look or talked back.

He knew I ignored a lot of the things he told me that were not directed toward basketball. His comments on religion, for example. The expression on my face, my not looking at him sometimes when he was talking to me, the times I flat out ignored him...he *had* to know. We had a relationship in which he could tell me anything he wanted to about basketball and I would listen, but when he got personal I blocked it out. I had to maintain my sense of self-worth in the face of someone whose technique was intimidation.

The surprising thing, to me, was that so few ever stood up

to him. In the time I was at Indiana, Dakich and I were probably the only two who really challenged Coach and stood our ground. Everybody else was "Yes, sir; no, sir," no matter what the provocation.

The weird thing was, Coach respected people who stood up to him. Coach might say, "Dan, I think Uwe's playing awful well right now, don't you?" And Dan was capable of saying, "No, Coach, not really." Coach liked that.

In fact, you might say that Coach's verbal aggressiveness is designed to expose people who lack self-confidence. I've seen him take on grown men, strangers, and put them on the defensive with a simple shake of his head or a sarcastic remark. He can say something outrageous, and everyone will nod in agreement. He gets people flustered.

What is it about him that is so intimidating? It's hard to explain. There were times when I saw him up ahead in his car, waiting at a stoplight, and I turned into a side street so I wouldn't have to pull up beside him. It was like Dakich hiding under the ramp at Assembly Hall. Some days you just didn't have the energy to face the man.

The plain truth is, people seem to accept Coach's authority even when they have no reason or obligation to. They say that General George Patton had the same effect on people. I guess that's why Coach Knight is such a fan of Patton's and has Patton quotes on his walls.

Coach's way with words is legendary, but he doesn't need words to intimidate. One time we were huddled together during a time-out in a road game, and some fans seven rows up were hurling all kinds of abusive language at Coach. It was so loud that we could hardly concentrate on what he was telling us, but it took him a few seconds to pick up on it. Then, from his crouched position, he just looked up at the rowdy fans and gave them the coldest stare for ten seconds. We couldn't see the fans, because they were behind us, but the shouting stopped almost instantly, and then you could actually sense them sitting down. You could *feel* it. And Coach hadn't said a word.

Other times, he was a man of action. Our bus pulled up one time at the Wisconsin fieldhouse only to be stopped by a security guard at a big sawhorse. The security guy left his Jeep and approached the bus driver, who said through his little window, "I've got the IU basketball team. We need in."

The guard said, "Can't park here."

Coach Knight went to the window. "If you want a game tonight, you'd better move that horse."

"Well, I can't do it without a pass or some kind of approval."

"What the hell is wrong with you?" Coach said. "Don't you understand? We're playing in this game."

The guard said, "I don't care. I can't move the barrier."

"Open the doors," Coach said. He stepped off the bus, grabbed the sawhorse, and angrily threw it aside. The bus rolled through, Coach jumped on, and the security guard just gaped at us. Nothing else was said.

With the IU student body, Coach Knight tended to be paternalistic. His preseason talks filled the auditorium every fall, and he usually mixed in a stern lecture or two with his jokes and basketball talk.

"I've got a little class I teach," he said one year. "There are a lot of you who wouldn't like my class. I won't let you come in barefooted. You can't wear a hat. If you cut class, it's an automatic C. And if you cut it twice, you'd better have time to go to Drop and Add."

His thoughts on drug use were just as clear-cut: "There are some of you out here who are really screwing yourselves up on drugs. Boy, is that a shame, an unbelievable shame. We've got a lot of cruel people around who make fun of people who say no. They do so because they themselves are neither tough enough or smart enough to say no. And if you've got somebody you can't say no to, give me a call at Assembly Hall. I'll do it for you."

He was particularly severe about student behavior at Assembly Hall. At a lot of schools, the fans show their disapproval of a bad call by chanting an obscenity. Coach would not permit that, and he would take the courtside microphone, if he had to, to stop it. Another thing he would not allow was hand-waving behind the bucket when our opponents shot free throws. At some schools, the home band sits up there, beating on drums, screaming, and waving trombones in your face. Not at Indiana.

Coach's control extended to individual students, if he thought they reflected poorly on IU. We'd have guys come to nationally televised games with their bodies painted red or with shaved heads, and Coach would call security and have them thrown not. He didn't want IU represented in that fashion.

Even harmless crowd behavior risked his disapproval. By my junior year, the "Socks, shorts, one-two-three...*swish!*" chant had spread all over Assembly Hall when I shot free throws. Coach had never liked it, and he finally blew his stack in the Illinois game when I missed a free throw with two seconds left in the half. As I bounced the ball for my second attempt, Coach started waving his arms and screaming for the fans to be quiet.

I made the second, but as we left the floor at halftime, Coach stomped across the court and confronted our cheerleaders. "I'd better not hear any more of that crap in the second half when our players are shooting free throws! I'm holding you people responsible for that. That one point can cost us a ball game!"

As he turned to go, he kicked two cheerleaders' megaphones in anger, for which he apologized the next day.

I don't think I missed that free throw or any other because of the chant, but that wasn't the point. Coach just didn't like anything that disrupted or distracted from the game. He wanted attention focused on the floor at all times.

On the game.

Coach was pretty good at controlling the crowd in Assembly Hall, but he was less successful at controlling the media. Not that he didn't try. The list of media people he refuses to talk to is long and constantly changing. Jim Barbar, the sports anchor at WISH-TV in Indianapolis (and a very good friend of mine), once took a cameraman into Assembly Hall to ask Coach about a rumor that he was leaving Indiana to coach at Stanford. Coach thought he was being ambushed. He threw Jim and the cameraman out and shouted, "Don't ever come back here unless you buy a ticket." After that, Jim couldn't get a press credential at Assembly Hall, and Channel 8 had to send an alternate crew. To see us play, Jim had to go to South Bend or West Lafayette or East Lansing.

There were other untouchables. *Sports Illustrated* writers headed the list. *SI's* Barry McDermott once wrote a piece in which he joked that Coach Knight had the players over on Thanksgiving for bread and water. Coach took that as an insult to his wife, Nancy, a fine cook. He threatened to throw McDermott out a window if he ever set foot on campus again.

Another time, Coach ordered *SI's* Curry Kirkpatrick out of a postgame press conference and put him on his personal blacklist, although Kirkpatrick could still get a game pass. With time, Coach seemed to soften on Curry. At the Olympic trials, Kirkpatrick was standing on the fieldhouse floor watching scrimmages when two men in suits came up to him on either side and asked to see his credential. He patted his pockets, felt all around—it was gone. The two men flashed badges. "Sir, you'll have to come with us." They took Kirkpatrick into an office for questioning and called Coach Knight on the phone. Coach said, "Bring his butt over."

Kirkpatrick figured out the thing was a put-on when the two "FBI men" marched him across the floor and up to the coaching tower. Coach Knight tossed down Curry's credential—someone had found it on the gym floor—and said, "It's just lucky for you I'm a good guy."

Coach and I had some conflicts over his media-bashing. I enjoyed talking with the media and felt I had a good rapport with the Bloomington and Indianapolis press. They were very kind to me and my teammates, taking ample time, but not too much time, to get their jobs done. In return, I thought I owed them honest answers and reasonable access. I tried to be on time for interviews. I tried not to be defensive. And if I could, I tried to give them something to write about.

That's one thing Coach didn't like his players to do: help the media. If we *had* to say something, he wanted it to be something bland like "K State played a good game, and we feel fortunate to have won."

It didn't take much to violate that standard. Once I got in trouble for a column Bob Hammel wrote after an interview with me. We had lost a game on a Thursday, as I recall, and Bob had joked to me that it was a good thing it was a Thursday loss, because at least we had Saturday to redeem ourselves. I laughed and said, "Yeah, if we had to lose, it's better on Thursday than Saturday."

Coach read that in Bob's column and interpreted it as me saying it was okay to lose. Coach chewed me out privately. He chewed me out in front of the team. And he kept chewing me out about it for the rest of my time at Indiana.

I tried to explain: "Coach, I said it, but it was a joke."

He wouldn't buy it, and he wouldn't let it go. It's something I got real tired of.

Bob felt bad and told me he was sorry about the quote. "I wasn't trying to get you in trouble."

"I know. That's just Coach." I quickly added: "That's off the record."

Of course, Coach was media, too—he had his own shows on WIRE radio and WTTV, Channel 4. The Monday-night radio show I never listened to, because we were usually at team meals when it was on. Tanya listened, and she said it was hysterical. Someone would call in with a serious basketball question, and Coach might answer with some wild story about the team trainer in South America. Seldom did she hear him answer a question directly. Was that Coach Knight's way of showing contempt for his listeners? I really don't know.

Coach changed the format of the show while I was at

Indiana, which made it even stranger. He no longer took calls, but sat at his desk in Assembly Hall chatting with his cohost, Don Fischer. Fischer was our radio play-by-play announcer, and his job was to keep Coach interested for the whole hour, which wasn't easy. Coach would open his mail during the show, look at tapes, read catalogues—whatever he felt like doing.

His TV show was taped on Saturday and shown on Sunday afternoon. Unlike most coach shows, this one never had players on as guests. It was just Coach talking for thirty minutes with Chuck Marlowe. I thought Chuck had the hardest job around. Coach liked to tape his shows after we played on Saturdays, and sometimes that meant taping at three or four o'clock in the morning. If we lost, Chuck had to hold the show together when Coach was really hot.

The strangest thing Coach did on television, I suppose, was to bring out a jackass wearing a Purdue hat and introduce the animal as "someone who is here to represent Purdue's point of view." IU fans thought it was pretty funny. Purdue fans, I guess not.

Of course, if a player had pulled a stunt like that, Coach would have been furious. I learned that lesson my sophomore year, when I told a reporter, "We seem to be much quicker this year. We're going to play a faster tempo."

When Coach saw that in print, he really took me to task. "Why don't you just pass out our game plans, Alford?" He didn't want people knowing what we were doing or why we were doing it. He didn't want us saying, "Well, we plan to play a stick man-to-man against Michigan State." He wanted us to say, "We don't know anything about Michigan State—we're going to start preparing for them tomorrow."

Another sin was cockiness within earshot of a reporter. Our center, Dean Garrett, put his foot in his mouth my senior year when we traveled to Purdue with a game-and-a-half lead in the Big Ten. He told a reporter, "We want this game more than they want it."

"You shouldn't have said that," I told Dean.

Sure enough, Dean had a very bad game, and they beat us up there. Troy Lewis, a good friend of mine who played for Purdue, told me later that Dean's quote had been posted on the locker-room bulletin board. "It really fired us up."

For similar reasons, if we had just beaten a team badly, Coach reminded us that we would likely face that team again down the road. He never wanted us to belittle anybody or show a lack of respect. "Even if it only appears in the Bloomington paper, they'll read it, you can bet on it."

We had a pretty good intelligence-gathering operation ourselves. Our managers collected newspaper clippings from all the significant towns—Ann Arbor, South Bend, East Lansing, West Lafayette—just to keep tabs on what people were saying. If we were playing Michigan and Roy Tarpley or Gary Grant said something negative about IU, that got back to us. If the negative comment was about a particular player, a photocopy of the remark usually appeared in his locker the next day. As a player, you automatically stepped up a notch when you read something like that.

The clippings provided one kind of motivation. Coach used guest speakers to provide another. Whenever we played a big game, you could count on a succession of former Indiana stars or big-name pros turning up for pregame meals or locker-room talks. If Coach wanted to make a pitch for IU's great basketball tradition, he brought in Quinn Buckner or Kent Benson. If he wanted someone to share big-game insights with us, it might be Willie Davis of the Green Bay Packers, golf champ Fuzzy Zoeller, or baseball Hall of Famer Johnny Bench.

Sometimes he brought in people with no sports connection at all. My sophomore year, he came to practice with the world-renowned cellist Janos Starker. I don't know if Mr. Starker had ever given a locker-room talk before, but he had some interesting things to say. "The only difference in our professions," he told us, "is that when *your* game is over, the score sort of unquestionably shows whether you succeeded or not. That's a little bit different for us. But the self-respect is no different. Whether the audience cheers or not, it does not mean anything. If I know that I have done well, whether they liked it or not is not important."

Some of Mr. Starker's comments sounded eerily like Coach Knight's. "Discipline means to learn everything that helps us to the maximum performance. Discipline means concentration and concentration means discipline," Starker told us. "After a performance, if I remember that in the second movement my mind drifted for a moment, I am ashamed."

We looked forward to the guest speakers, and sometimes they provided entertainment as well as inspiration. When Johnny Bench talked to us, Coach pulled me aside afterward and dragged me over to meet him. "Johnny, you were one of the great defensive catchers of all time. Why don't you tell Alford what it's like to play defense?"

Bench looked at me and said, "Well, I played basketball in high school, and I always thought if I scored more points than my man did, I did one heck of a job on defense."

He grinned at Coach, who looked exasperated.

I laughed out loud.

Looking back, I realize I laughed pretty often my junior year. It wasn't like the sophomore season at all. The paranoia was absent. The players showed more togetherness. Basketball was fun again.

Much of the credit for that has to go to the assistant coaches, who kept their part of the bargain we had struck in Hong Kong. Now, when a player had a problem, he could go to an assistant and say, "Hey, what am I doing wrong?" The assistant would tell him. End of problem.

Same thing if one of us had a complaint about a teammate's play. If I was out of synch with one of the big men, I could take it to Joby Wright, who coached the big men. If someone had a gripe about me, he could take it to Royce Waltman, who handled the guards. The best part of it was, the opening of communications with the coaches made it easier for the players to talk with each other. There was less private grousing and backbiting.

The "keep it from Coach" conspiracy even extended to Buzz Kurpius, our academic coordinator. I had developed a trusting relationship with her over my first two years, and now we made it pay off for the team. If a player had class problems, she would tell me before telling Coach Knight, and I would confront the player myself. When the player and I had talked it out and come to an understanding, we usually went to an assistant coach. If none of our efforts solved the problem, obviously Buzz and the assistants were obliged to go to Coach Knight. But it was amazing how many problems could be solved without his ever knowing. The number of distractions fell off sharply.

Coach made his own contribution to the thawing of tensions by opening one of our preseason practices to the public. Five thousand people showed up to watch us shoot lay-ups and run drills. It was good public relations, and it was pretty good theater, too. Coach got a laugh from the crowd when he scolded Todd for putting up a midrange jump shot instead of working it inside: "I see a couple of girls in the audience I'd rather see shoot that shot than you."

Marty Simmons was missed, of course, but Evansville wasn't that far off and we did see him from time to time. (As a transfer student, he had to sit out a year of basketball before Coach Crews could use him.) Marty's place in my life was filled by Delray Brooks and Ricky Calloway. Delray had moved to my apartment complex after the world tour, and he and I spent a lot of time together in the afternoons, just talking and having fun before practice. Delray was kind of a quiet player, but he wasn't that way off the floor. He seemed to enjoy everything about Indiana University—campus life, classes, the basketball program.

Ricky was like that, too. It was unusual for a junior and a freshman to become such good friends, but Ricky's dad and my parents had gotten pretty close and Ricky's dad told him to come to me whenever he needed help. Ricky came to me a lot, and I was impressed with his high goals and willingness to work. He always seemed to have a smile on his face and a hug for everybody. Tanya called Ricky her "big buddy." She said he always looked like he wanted to dance around with somebody.

Even with Delray and Ricky around, there was no escaping Todd. From the day we moved into the same apartment complex, Todd had begun bombing my second-floor unit with bottle rockets, and I had no choice but to return his fire. We waged bottle-rocket war for three years, and I guess we're lucky that we each still have two eyes and all our fingers and toes.

I had two roommates at IU, both from New Castle and both great guys. Mike Atkins was my roomie at the dorm and for one year at the apartment. He had been a manager for Dad in high school, and he was a student manager for three years at IU. I knew I wasn't going to get along with a roommate who didn't like basketball, and Mike was great because I could bring home my frustrations without him getting mad at me. He knew when to talk to me, when to listen, and when to simply leave me alone. He made it very easy.

My other roommate, Curtis Wright, had also managed for Dad. Curtis could be called the perfect roommate: funny, orderly, considerate. When I came back from a road game at one or two in the morning, Curtis would have the portable gas heater in my room turned on. He liked to cook, too, which was a good thing—I wasn't much use in the kitchen.

Tanya transferred to the University of Evansville her junior year to pursue her degree in physical therapy, but I still saw her most every weekend. She missed only one of my home games in the two years she was "away." She'd come to Bloomington on a weeknight and stay at a girlfriend's house, and then drive back early in the morning. On weekends she'd bring her books. We'd go to church together on Sunday and then go back to my apartment, where Curtis would cook up his famous lasagna or spaghetti, of which he was very proud.

The big attraction at the apartment was Nerf ball. When I first moved in, I asked Dad to bring me my orange Nerf ball and a couple of Nerf goals from New Castle. He said, "Why two?"

I gave him my stupid-question sigh. "Full *court,* Dad."

We set up the goals at either end of the living room and put on some of the best Nerf-ball games in the country. Tanya and Todd played, of course, and Mike and Curtis and their girlfriends. Larry Gigerich, who became a great friend, lived right under my apartment, and he'd come up and play —probably because he couldn't sleep or study with all that thumping overhead. Both Curt and Larry, by the way, had a hard time beating Tanya.

The real games were with Sean, who had transferred to IU after one semester at Georgia Southern University. Sean and I had grown up playing Nerf basketball, but he was no longer my "little" brother; he was a very muscular, very aggressive young man. I took the attitude "If he drives, let him dunk; he'll throw you through the wall if you get in his way."

As kids, our Nerf games had been very competitive. The goal was over my closet, and it was not unusual for us to knock the closet doors off their tracks. That kind of banging usually drew a yell from the other room: "Quiet down!" Now, with no parents around, we let it all out. Once I went to dunk against Sean and put my foot right through the plasterboard wall. Play resumed after a brief time-out.

The only problem with full-court Nerf ball was that the ball left orange spots all over our white walls. We had to repaint the apartment when we moved out.

The early loss to Kentucky (the calendar game) didn't destroy us, as it might have a year earlier. We bounced back with a win over Kansas State and then beat Louisiana Tech

and Texas Tech in the Indiana Classic. We lost by 2 at Louisville, but answered with a 21-point win over a very good
Iowa State team led by Jeff Grayer and Jeff Hornacek, two
future NBA players. Idaho and Mississippi State went down
in the Hoosier Classic by 30 and 31 points respectively.

We had no center, of course. Magnus Pelkowski, a six-
foot-ten kid from Bogotá, Colombia, had averaged three
minutes a game for us as a freshman and had played against
Uwe every day in practice, but he had played very little basketball before coming to America. Coach decided to red-
shirt him.

That left us with a bunch of six-foot-seven guys that the
program listed as F-C, or forward-center. That role was best
filled by Daryl, who picked off 6 steals in our opening-game
win over Kent State and won a starting job. With Uwe gone,
Daryl got to use his mobility and his power-jumping skills,
and the improvement in his game was immediately apparent.
He scored 29 points against Texas Tech and was named
MVP of the Indiana Classic. He made the all-tournament
team in the Hoosier Classic. He had 11 rebounds and 31
points against Iowa State.

You wouldn't have known it from the way Coach treated
him, though. He reduced Daryl to tears more than once,
ridiculing Daryl for what he called his girlish play, although
he used a rougher word than "girlish." He called Daryl a
joke of a basketball player, a loafer, a sissy, and told him, "I
wouldn't turn you loose in a game if you were the last guy I
had." Sometimes it got so bad that the rest of us were near
tears with sympathy for Daryl, but I had been at Indiana
long enough now to know what was going on. Daryl was on
the threshold of being a really good player, and Coach was
trying to boot him through the door.

"Don't take things personal," Dakich told Daryl. "Coach
is just trying to help you." (Dakich and I should have had
that advice printed on cards, we gave it out so much.) But
that's a situation where all the talking in the world couldn't

help. Daryl had to find the strength within himself to stand up to Coach.

We celebrated New Year's with an 8–2 record, but things soured quickly. Michigan and Illinois were the preseason favorites to win the Big Ten, and we opened with Michigan at Assembly Hall. It was a wild game. We jumped out in front, 8–0, and the crowd got excited, but Michigan came right back and took the lead. Roy Tarpley was a handful for Daryl inside, and Gary Grant played me very tough. Coach was a firebrand during the time-outs, and he had plenty left for the refs, who gave him a technical for one shouted insult. Michigan took an 11-point lead in the second half, but we cut it to 3.

Daryl fouled out and Steve Eyl came in, and the crucial play came on a lay-up by Steve. His shot was rolling around on the rim when Andre Harris went up as if to tip it in, but then pulled his hand back. The ball toppled in and should have been a basket, but one of the refs said Harris had touched the ball and called basket interference. Coach had to be held back by the assistants.

In the locker room afterward, Coach seemed more weary than angry. "Boys, is this going to be last year all over again? Are we ever going to win a game that means something again?"

Coach had us in the next morning to look at the tape. He was most angry with Daryl, who hadn't managed a single rebound against Tarpley, and with me for all the usual reasons. He finally stormed out of the room, only to come right back and say, "You guys sit here for a while, and if you still want to have a team, then you come and tell us."

Winston, Stew, and I were the captains, so we had to go to the coaches' locker room to ask that the season not be canceled. Feinstein was there, doing his invisible-man routine. (He didn't take notes when things got theatrical; he observed silently and apparently wrote it down from memory when he was alone.)

We said we wanted to play, and Coach replied by glaring at me. "Yeah, but Steve doesn't guard anybody."

Stew, in his senior year, knew what to say. "That may be so, Coach, but the rest of us didn't do much guarding either."

That saved my skin for the moment, but Coach demoted me to the white team during practice the next day. Whenever he put me on the white team I got ticked off and wanted to score a lot on the reds, so Coach usually added some stipulation: "Alford, you're on the white team—and you can't shoot." That forced me to concentrate on defense and distribute the ball more.

Then we found real trouble: Daryl screamed with pain as his foot came down wrong on a rebound. He rolled around groaning, his face screwed up in agony. Within minutes he was on his way to the hospital for X-rays, and the next time we saw him he was on crutches.

"Two weeks, maybe," he said. "Minimum."

With Daryl out and Todd Jadlow in, we lost by 3 points to Michigan State, but sailed through two soft opponents, Northwestern and Wisconsin. The Wisconsin game was noteworthy in that I threw up twenty-five shots in scoring 38 points. I'd never taken twenty shots in a game before this season, but Coach had made getting me the ball for jump shots a team priority. That helped my shooting, but Coach had always made it clear that he never let a player shoot for that reason. "I hear a lot about building a shooter's confidence," he said. "Hey, I'm not worried about *his* confidence. When the guy goes up to shoot, *I* want to think it has a pretty good chance to go in."

The saddest thing that happened at this time was that Delray Brooks decided to leave Indiana. He hadn't shown much improvement on the world tour, and Coach had stopped giving him meaningful playing time. As the season wore on and as Delray struggled with his shooting, he began to share his feelings with me. He never complained—not about Coach, not about anything—but he knew he wasn't a pure point guard and probably wasn't going to get the opportunity to play much at Indiana.

We talked about where he might go: North Carolina State, Providence, a few other places. He seemed to have his heart set on Providence. Rick Pitino, the Friars' coach, liked Delray and had room for him.

Anyway, Delray talked it over with Coach after the Michigan State game and both reached the same conclusion: he'd be happier someplace where he got more playing time. It was definitely *not* a case of Coach chasing him away. Delray handled negative coaching pretty well.

When he was gone, Coach took it kind of hard, saying, "I doubt if we've ever had a nicer kid here than Delray Brooks." He could find no fault in a player's wanting to play more.

Of course, Delray left with class. "I hope everything goes well for Indiana," he said in a statement, "and I consider Coach Knight a friend."

I took his departure pretty hard myself. We had become such good friends and shared so much on the world tour, and suddenly he was gone. First Marty. Then Delray. I could see why Michael Jordan thought the odds were with him in our bet.

Fortunately, not all the news was bad. Daryl came back from his injury quicker than expected and scored 15 points and had 8 rebounds in a 69–66 win over Ohio State. Then we won consecutive home games with Purdue and Illinois— both squeakers—and we were tied for first in the Big Ten.

The Purdue game I remember for two reasons. One, I caught a knee in my thigh in the first half and was in great pain for the next week. Two, we made an incredible comeback. We were down by 5 with about three minutes left and we had lost our entire front line—Ricky Calloway to a knee injury, Daryl and Andre to fouls. But Todd made a steal and a key offensive rebound, and we cut the lead to 2.

That's when I made one of my most memorable plays. Coach was always getting on me about not taking charges, and here was Melvin McCants, all six foot nine and 215 pounds of him, streaking to the basket for a dunk with me in his way. I held my ground, got wiped out, and got to go to the line for the game-tying free throws. I made them both, and we went to overtime and an eventual 1-point win.

The Illinois game, of course, was the one where Coach kicked the megaphones and ordered an end to the "Socks, shorts, one-two-three... *swish!*" chant. That chant never entirely disappeared while I was at Indiana, but the cheerleaders now accompanied my foul shots with a loud "Shhhhh!" It didn't help—I missed another free throw in the second half. Fortunately, Daryl made both ends of a one-and-one with seventeen seconds left and we won the game by 2.

Coach was jubilant in the locker room. For once, he couldn't find anything to criticize about Daryl, who had scored 30 points. He even called Daryl a "tiger," which was a lot better than his usual name for him. And he had nothing but praise for the team. We had won a big Saturday game after a big Thursday victory—on national TV, yet—and Coach was pleased.

"You beat as talented a team as you can find anywhere," he told us. "You could play the NCAA final and not meet a better collection of players. Enjoy that. Take ten or fifteen minutes. Then start thinking about Iowa."

You guessed it. We went on the road and lost our next game, to Iowa. The Hawkeyes pressed us into countless mistakes and built up a 20-something-point lead, and it got so bad that Coach benched Daryl and me permanently with ten minutes left in the game. It wasn't for punishment, really; it was more to rest us.

That loss knocked us out of our first-place tie, but we hit the soft stretch in our schedule again and racked up wins over Minnesota, Wisconsin, and Northwestern. We were tied for first again, with Michigan.

On to Columbus, where we beat OSU by 9. In that game,

I made 14 out of 15 foul shots and told a reporter, "That's not acceptable, but it's a lot better." That quote reminded some people of something I had told *Sports Illustrated* after leading the nation in free-throw percentage my freshman year: "I could never put together a good string."

What was I saying? That anything less than 100 percent was garbage?

Well, to be honest, even *one* missed free throw bothers me. That goes back to those driveway games with my father. Shooting free throws is probably the thing I take the most pride in, because it's what I'm best at. When I led the nation as a freshman, I thought my 92 percent accuracy represented way too many misses. Why? Because as a senior in high school I shot 94.4 percent. What's more, in high school I had strings of over 50, set the state record with a string of 64, and ran out of games my senior year having made 80 in a row at home.

In college, I never made over 31 in a row. That's why I had a lot of harsh things to say about my free-throw shooting. I saw no progress.

On top of that, when I made the "acceptable" remark I was 17-for-26 from the line going back to a miss in the first Ohio State game. That's 65 percent shooting, and I shouldn't have to explain why that upset me.

We went to Champaign, where we had been blown out two straight years, and pulled off a huge victory by 1 point, pushing our record to 10–3 in the conference. We celebrated on the floor and in the locker room, and Coach was part of it. "Enjoy this one, boys," he said. "You earned it."

What made it even sweeter was that Michigan State had upset Michigan at Ann Arbor, leaving us alone in first place.

I had a remarkable fact pointed out to me: in the Bob Knight era, no Indiana player who had come in as a freshman and stayed four years had failed to win a Big Ten or an NCAA title. One year after finishing seventh in the Big Ten, it looked like I was going to get mine.

Then again, maybe not. We played at Purdue three days

after the Illinois win and got hammered. I had my worst
offensive performance of the year, scoring 8 points on 3-for-
12 from the field. That threw us back into a tie with Michigan.

Back home, we knocked off Minnesota and Iowa, and
that left us still tied for first with just two road games left—
Michigan State and Michigan. The Iowa game was the final
home game for Winston Morgan, Stew Robinson, and
Courtney Witte, and there was none of the gloom that surrounded the previous year's farewell to Uwe and Dan.
Coach took the microphone and told the fans, "Last year,
we were all kind of down because we didn't think we gave
you the kind of basketball you people are used to seeing and
enjoy seeing. I know I've enjoyed this season greatly."

It was hard not to share in the feelings of accomplishment.
We had a shot at the Big Ten title. Rick Calloway made the
freshman all-America team and was Big Ten rookie of the
year. Daryl was third-team all–Big Ten. I made the Associated Press and National Association of Basketball Coaches
all-America teams.

Our trip to cold and snowy East Lansing did nothing to
spoil things. Scott Skiles and I staged a memorable duel of
all-America guards—he scored 33 and I had 31. But we had
the stronger team and won, 97–79.

Coach's locker-room talk was short and sweet. "You've
got it down to one game for a conference championship.
We're exactly where we wanted to be when we started on
October 15. That's one hell of a turnaround."

The flight home was great fun. We joked, played cards,
and listened to our Walkman radios.

Indiana basketball was on a high.

Highlights from the game that decided the Big Ten championship:

- Roy Tarpley sailing over Daryl for a slam dunk
- Andre Harris shooting an air ball
- Tarpley swishing a hook shot

- Coach screaming at Daryl during a time-out, "Why even bother showing up, Daryl? Are you scared? What the hell are you scared of?"
- Antoine Joubert scoring 8 straight points and smirking
- Alford having the last shot of the half blocked by Gary Grant

We got bombarded. Wiped out. And on national TV. Michigan led us by 19 points at halftime and we never made a move on them after that. In the final minutes, we had to watch while Coach Frieder took his seniors out, one by one, to standing ovations from the Wolverine fans. The crowd chanted, "Throw a chair, Bobby, throw a chair!" When it was over, we had lost, 80–52, an unthinkable score.

The locker room was a morgue. Coach started to pick us apart, but his heart wasn't in it. "Okay," he said. "The hell with this game. Don't even think about it. It's one bad day, boys—it doesn't have to ruin everything that we've done. Let's get the hell out of here."

But it was hard not to think about it. Michigan hadn't just beaten us, they had dismantled us. Our confidence was badly shaken, and Coach had trouble getting our minds back to the business at hand, which was the NCAA tournament.

Our first-round opponent was a mystery team that had never appeared in the tournament before—Cleveland State. They had a very cocky coach, Kevin Mackey, who played the media beautifully. He described his players as rejects and playground players, losers in life who wanted to gain some revenge on the rich, big-time programs. We didn't know much of anything about them, except that they were an aggressive, pressing team like Iowa. It was difficult just to get game tapes of Cleveland State.

The game was at Syracuse's Carrier Dome on a Friday afternoon, so we flew in on Thursday and bused straight to the Dome for a one-hour workout. Afterward we went to a place called Grimaldi's for a good Italian dinner.

Friday dawned cold and rainy and stayed that way. Coach made his usual plea in the locker room: "Just get me to the Final Four, boys, and I'll do the rest." We felt good, we felt ready. There was no reason for what happened next.

We got beat.

The Cleveland State press was as good as Iowa's. Three times, Winston tried to throw the ball in-bounds after a Cleveland State basket, and three times he had no one to throw it to. We struggled just to keep it close in the first half, and went in trailing by 4.

Coach wasn't mad. He didn't have time to be mad. There were technical adjustments to be made. He ordered whoever was closest to the ball after an enemy basket to just grab it and throw it in-bounds before Cleveland State could set up its press. "We're all right, boys," he said. "We told you this was going to be a tough game, so this is no surprise. Plenty of time."

But time didn't seem to be working in our favor. Cleveland State scored the first 6 points of the second half, and the crowd suddenly smelled an upset. Clinton Ransey was almost unstoppable for them, making one great shot after another. We couldn't seem to cut into the lead, and with five minutes left Cleveland State led by 8. That's when they went to a spread offense, and suddenly it was a repeat of my last high school game, when I found myself chasing the ball around the court in a pathetic game of keep-away.

Time slowly clicked down. Then it was gone, and the season was over for the Indiana Hoosiers.

Coach gave us a week off for spring break, but he said, "Be back on Monday." NCAA rules allowed for practices right up through the Final Four, whether you were still in it or not. Todd Jadlow went to Florida—I got on him about that—but the rest of us hung around and stayed in shape. It was a good time to catch up on your reading, as long as you avoided the sports pages. (Headline after the Cleveland State game: HOOSIERS GET SHOCK OF LIVES.)

The workouts lasted six days. Coach left for the Final Four late in the week, but he ran the practices the first few days. They were tough workouts. Drills, mostly. When we scrimmaged, he kept up the pressure, stopping play every few seconds, yelling things like, "Get over the screen! Block out! Get in a stance!" You could tell he was evaluating us individually. It was almost as if we were trying out for the team again.

The big thing on his mind was still our mental toughness. With Daryl and Todd and me he would shake his head and say, "Three years of this team and I don't see much improvement in the mental-toughness aspect. I just don't know if we can go anywhere with this group."

He managed to underscore that point in a dramatic way. When we came in for that first day of practice, we looked at the board and saw that the score of the Miami of Ohio game, from my freshman year, had been replaced with this: CLEVELAND STATE 83, INDIANA 79.

On one of the days, Uwe dropped in for a visit. He must have been in Indianapolis with the Dallas Mavericks to play the Pacers. Anyway, he came down to see us and walked in during practice, and our eyes just about bugged out. He wore an earring, and his red hair was styled long with a tail. Coach was sitting in the stands, evaluating, and he wouldn't even acknowledge Uwe's presence. In the locker room, later, Coach said, "That is not what an Indiana player is supposed to look like." We had to fight to keep our faces straight.

John Feinstein left the day after we got back from Cleveland State. I remember Coach Knight saying goodbye to him at Assembly Hall, and they seemed no longer to be on good terms. (Coach said his exact words when John said goodbye were "Don't let the door hit you in the butt on your way out.")

John made a point of thanking all the players. Most of us were sorry to see him go. He had become a part of the Indiana scenery.

John and I said goodbye on the court at Assembly Hall.

He handed me his card, which was his way of saying, "Keep in touch."

I told him I hoped he didn't feel his time with us had been wasted. After all, it had been a pretty dull season.

He gave me a funny look.

CHAPTER SEVEN

MADE FOR INDIANA

Tanya and I first saw the movie *Hoosiers* at the Indiana Theater in Bloomington my senior year. I went back four days later.

The movie was full of stuff so real to me—the small towns, the schools, the back roads of Indiana. I had been in most of the old gyms pictured in the film, either with Dad or on my own. I recognized the Hickory gym as the old Knightstown School, just ten minutes from New Castle. Brad Long, a family friend, played Buddy in the film. His father, Gary, who played at IU from 1959 to 1961, had the role of a coach. The Hickory coach, played by Gene Hackman, not only flew off the handle like Coach Knight, he spoke lines right out of Knight's mouth. Lines like "My practices aren't designed for your enjoyment," and "Absolutely no shots until you've passed off four times!"

And the movie had the look. The camera captured the land and the sky as the seasons changed—the blowing leaves of late autumn, the blue-gray light of the woods in winter, the budding trees and green fields of early spring.

I loved it.

In a scene early in the film, the kid, Jimmy, is shooting baskets by himself on a goal outside the school. The coach comes over and talks to him, picking the ball up off the grass and passing it to Jimmy after every shot, the kid not saying a word. That scene touched me deeply. I had lived it with Dad.

What *Hoosiers* was about was something called the Indiana basketball mystique. It was about kids shooting in their driveways. It was about small-town boys playing basketball in tiny old gyms, dreaming of winning the state championship in Indianapolis.

It was about me.

I realized as early as my sophomore season that people had begun to see me not just as a good shooter on a college basketball team but as a symbol of something larger—the Indiana basketball tradition. I got, on the average, fifteen letters a day while I was in school, mostly fan mail and requests for autographs and pictures. They would pile up on my desk at the apartment, and with homework and my other commitments I needed help from Mom and Dad to answer them all.

I couldn't go out without being recognized. People approached me for autographs in restaurants. They surrounded me when I went Christmas shopping at the mall in Bloomington. If I walked into L. S. Ayres in Indianapolis, somebody would say, "Hey, aren't you..." and a crowd would start to gather.

One time I was in Washington, Indiana, where my grandparents live, and I drove over to the new Wal-Mart to pick up some propane gas for the grill at our lake home. I signed autographs there for a bunch of people, but I couldn't find what I wanted, so I drove across the street to K-Mart. I walked inside and a guy approached me, pushing his cart. He said, "We just heard you were at Wal-Mart!" I couldn't believe that such insignificant news traveled so fast.

It was an accident of fate that I came along when interest in the Hoosier mystique was so high. The connection was made in the public mind when I became Mr. Basketball and signed to play at Indiana. If I had signed with Kentucky, it wouldn't have been the same at all. To me, the player who symbolized Indiana basketball was Jerry Sichting, but he played for Purdue, and for some reason IU fans dislike Purdue even more than they dislike Kentucky.

But I have to believe that the key factor was the Olympics. I read too many articles describing me as "well-scrubbed" and "respectful" and "the sort of kid you want your daughter to marry" not to recognize that I was being held up as an example. I was the gold medal winner who didn't drink, smoke, or take drugs, who went to church faithfully, and who loved his family, hometown, and country. As a player, I stood for something, too. I was the coach's son with very ordinary athletic skills who achieved his goals through hard work, self-discipline, and a belief in teamwork.

I felt a responsibility to live up to those ideals, to sign autographs and pose for pictures graciously, to treat little kids as important people and not as pests. There is a poem on the wall in the Indiana locker room called "Little Eyes Are Upon You." Coach put it there to remind us that there would always be some little kid looking up at us, hoping for a kind word or a smile. To this day, there are times when I'm ready to scream at an adult, but it's awful tough for me to turn down a little kid who comes up to me for an autograph or a brief chat.

I know a lot of players won't do that. Patrick Ewing, at the Olympics, refused to sign autographs or get his picture taken. I like Patrick, but I don't think that's right. Coach always made the point that our fans were not inferior to us. They knew how to go to an office and turn business transactions. They knew how to practice medicine and teach children to read and make car bodies.

Let's face it, a lot of great athletes are disliked because of
the way they handle people. If we don't treat other people
with respect, why should they care that we know how to
shoot a basketball or run with a football?

That's something I've always considered carefully. There
have been times, of course, when I've failed to live up to that
ideal, when I've been tired or distracted, when I've walked
away, and it upsets me. Other times, I have had to balance
my desire to be gracious with the needs of friends and family
who are out with me in public.

Sean, in particular, suffered from the attention I got in
high school and college. It hurt him that he was always introduced to people as "Steve's younger brother." People
would come up to him, and instead of "How ya doin',"
they'd say, "What do you hear from Steve?" It reached the
point where Sean wouldn't go out with me. He hated being
someone's brother rather than himself.

Some people were surprised that Sean didn't follow me to
IU or at least play college ball in the state. He admitted later
that he chose Georgia Southern because he wanted to get out
of my shadow. "The first English class I go to," he told me,
"I'm sitting behind the starting quarterback on the football
team. He turns around to introduce himself, and when I give
my name he says, 'Hey, you're Steve Alford's younger
brother, aren't you?' That's when I realized it didn't matter
where I went, people knew you."

Ironically, being a thousand miles apart made Sean and
me closer as brothers. When he decided to give up his basketball scholarship at Georgia Southern and enroll at IU as a
paying student, that was his declaration that he would no
longer be ruled by people's expectations. He became more
comfortable with me and much more comfortable with himself.

People sometimes ask him if he was ever jealous of me.
Sean's answer surprises them: "I feel sorry for Steve. I think
he's missed a lot in life. He was always practicing, and he

seldom went out with his friends. I couldn't have done that."

To Sean, who has a real need to be with people, my obsession with basketball looks like a lonely preoccupation.

We're just different that way.

There's another line from *Hoosiers*. The scene is the locker room at Hinkle Field House, moments before the little team from Hickory High goes out to face the big school from South Bend in the state finals. The coach makes his little speech, and then he says, "Anybody want to say anything?"

One of the players swallows hard and says, "Let's win this one for all the small schools that never had the chance to get here."

I heard those words, and I thought of the little gym at Monroe City, where Dad got his start, and the gym at South Knox, where I learned to count with the scoreboard, and the gym at Martinsville, where I cried in the locker room thinking Dad's team had lost the game.

And New Castle.

No, it wasn't a little gym. But I had a strong sentimental attachment to it, all the same. More so, I'm sure, than any other kid who ever played there. It was *my* gym. I considered it my special place.

I proposed to Tanya in the New Castle gym. It was the August before my senior year at IU. I asked her to join me at the gym for a workout one evening, knowing we would have the place to ourselves. I unlocked the doors, turned on the lights, and then I made a face.

"Shoot, I left the ball in the car. Would you go up to Dad's office and get a couple of balls?"

Tanya didn't want to go alone; the stairway to Dad's office was dark. But I insisted, so she took the keys and disappeared up the stairs.

While she was gone, I got everything ready. When she returned with the basketballs, I met her on the steps and walked her out on the court with my arm around her. She looked puzzled when she saw a stepladder under the near basket. "What are you doing?"

"The net's stuck on the rim." I pointed up at the basket, where the nylon strands were all tangled up.

"Well, that's typical. It's probably just hanging from the last time you were here."

"No," I said, "it's really stuck."

Tanya thought she'd try her hand at fixing it, so she went up the ladder. She pulled and tugged and wrestled with the knots for two or three minutes, getting more and more frustrated. I held the ladder, trying not to laugh.

Finally, she gave up. "Steve, it just won't come out."

"Why don't you try shaking the back of the rim?"

Her eyes shifted toward the backboard, and that's when she saw the little felt box taped to the orange flange of the rim. She gasped.

"I can't believe you didn't see it," I said.

Then she started crying.

A minute later, we sat in the first row of seats. Tanya opened the box, put on the ring...and that's when I asked her to marry me.

Coach Knight had a wonderful line. "Basketball may have been invented in Massachusetts," he said, "but it was made for Indiana."

He called my dad the summer before my senior year. "Sam, I want Steve to play at New Castle one last time. What do you think of an intersquad game in November?"

Dad was thrilled, of course. He set everything up, and Coach Knight bused us up to New Castle on a Thursday night. The fieldhouse was packed for the scrimmage, and my hometown fans gave me a welcome I will never forget—a standing ovation.

Coach didn't want the occasion to seem maudlin, so he went for smiles by roasting me over the PA system. He turned to Ray Pavy, who starred at New Castle in the 1950s, and said, "Hey, Pavy. Why is it that every time a guard from New Castle comes to Indiana, he can't play defense?"

That wasn't the end of it. Two minutes into the game, when I stole a pass near the basket, Coach called time-out and hurried over to the spot where I had made the steal. I saw the Tisdale Maneuver coming. Sure enough, Coach squatted down and marked the spot in red with a pen. He had the PA man announce, "Steve Alford finally made a defensive play on November 20th at about seven-nineteen."

Grinning, I joined Coach under the basket. He signed the spot "Bobby Knight" and handed me the pen. I signed my name under his with a flourish.

It was only later, as the team bus pulled out of the parking lot and I looked back at the fieldhouse one last time, that it struck me: the New Castle gym had put its signature on me long before I put my signature on it.

We opened the season with two new guys, neither of them from Indiana. Dean Garrett was a junior-college player, an all-America center from San Francisco City College. He had a reputation for quick inside moves and was supposed to have a good shooting touch for a big man. Keith Smart, from Baton Rouge, Louisiana, was also a juco all-America —a small guard with slashing moves, incredible leaping ability, and a very un-Hoosier-like flamboyance.

Coach Knight didn't like to recruit junior-college players. He had nothing against junior colleges as institutions, but he didn't like the way jucos "laundered" athletes with bad grades so they could qualify for NCAA schools. He didn't like the free-lance, playground style of basketball that many junior-college coaches tolerated to let players showcase their talents. Coach also hated telling kids he had recruited as freshmen, who had put in two or three hard years at IU, that they were going to lose their jobs to outsiders who had never played or practiced a minute at Assembly Hall.

The assistant coaches understood Coach Knight's objections, but they wanted him to look at jucos on a case-by-case basis. They didn't think we could win the Big Ten without a real center—a tall person—and a quick, penetrating guard. Coach gradually came around to that view, but he put the final decision in the hands of his player selection committee: *us*.

Most people find it hard to believe, but at Indiana the players have a big say about who they'll have as teammates. When a recruit came to Bloomington on an official visit, Coach talked to him briefly, but then the players took over. We walked the kid around campus, took him to the Saturday football game, took him to the movies. We answered his questions and gave him the most accurate picture we could of what his life would be like if he came to Indiana.

When he was gone, the coaches would come to us for a report. "What's this kid like? How is he as a person?" They already knew what he could do as an athlete. They wanted to know, was he a person of good character or was he a bad actor? Someone with ego problems or someone who could get along with the players we already had?

People have always wondered why Coach Knight doesn't get all the great players who come out of Indiana, Illinois, and Ohio. They assume it's because the recruits are scared of Coach and won't sign, but often it's because the players already there give them the thumbs down. Numerous times, I told Coach that a particular recruit was a terrific player, "but I don't think he'll mesh with the rest of us."

For starters, an Indiana player has to be coachable. Coach says, "A lot of players look but don't see. A lot of players listen but don't hear."

You don't necessarily have to play with a basketball player to tell if he is coachable. If he talks nonstop about his high school accomplishments, if most of his questions are about the drinking age in Bloomington and how to get a phony ID, if he seems overly concerned about his playing time as a freshman and not at all concerned about how he might fit in on the team—those are all red flags.

An Indiana player must also communicate well and know

how to handle himself around people. Bloomington may be a small city, but Indiana basketball is big-time. A player has to be able to express himself and make a good impression, whether it's in a national TV interview or in a private conversation with a ten-year-old fan. Coach Knight doesn't want mumblers, wiseasses, or guys who wear sunglasses indoors.

An Indiana player has to be sociable, and not just with his teammates. If a recruit seemed disappointed because we didn't have an athletes-only dorm, I took that as snobbishness toward people who weren't basketball players. Coach wants players who enjoy the company of other students. He wants them to be seen on campus and to be liked and respected.

An Indiana player should be sensitive. Coach frequently invited handicapped people or learning-disabled children to our practices. Without Coach saying anything, we always made a point of going over and spending some time with our guests, making them feel welcome and appreciated. Coach wanted players who would do that instinctively, without being asked.

An Indiana player has to be responsible. We always made that point in the strongest way to recruits: "We can't cut classes, we don't get favors from professors, nobody pays our parking tickets, and nobody will bail you out if you get arrested."

And finally, an Indiana player has to be able to play for Coach Knight.

That's the toughest thing to gauge without knowing a player really well. Some players come to Indiana thinking they can handle his yelling and find out quickly that they can't. Others sail through it, collecting war stories and laughing off the tongue-lashings.

Obviously, the system isn't perfect. In my four years at Indiana, Marty Simmons and Delray Brooks transferred to other schools, Mike Giomi got kicked off the team, Andre Harris flunked out, a couple of players were suspended or lost their scholarships, and a half-dozen other guys came within an eyelash of giving up. That's why we looked very carefully at Dean and Keith when they visited Bloomington my junior year.

Dean made a very good impression. A great big guy (six-eleven), he was always smiling and laughing, but never cocky. Most recruits have a ho-hum attitude; they've seen it all. Dean wasn't that way at all. When he saw us play at Assembly Hall, he seemed in awe of the sellout crowd and the enthusiasm they showed. He asked lots of questions and seemed intrigued by Coach Knight and the whole system. I could tell he was eager to come to Indiana and be part of it. Over the season, he must have called me five or six times to ask how things were going, and he usually asked about the crowd: "Was it a sellout?"

Keith was a harder call. Most of us liked him immediately. He was warm, enthusiastic, funny, and easy to be with. The problem was, he was also dripping with gold chains and jewelry, and he had his hair cut with a little line all the way around and a tiny arrowhead shaved in the back. He told us he had gotten only one offer of a four-year scholarship out of high school—from William Penn, a tiny Iowa college. "Probably," he explained, "because I broke my arm in a motorcycle accident and only played three games my senior year."

Somehow, I couldn't see a guy who dressed like Mr. T. playing at Indiana. "If Keith comes here," I told Todd, "the chains and the haircut will be the first things to go."

Appearance aside, Keith showed us a lot of Indiana qualities. He was a good listener. He was close to his family in Baton Rouge. He was a former Boy Scout. Best of all, he expressed a strong desire to get away from the playground style of the juco conference he was in. "I'm not going to improve as a player," he said, "unless I get some discipline."

Those were the magic words. When the assistants asked me whether we should take Keith Smart, I gave the thumbs-up sign. "He's a super kid. He'll fit in."

We wasted no time in finding out. All the players stayed on campus that summer, and we played every day. Our main focus was bringing Dean and Keith into the system. The coaches had told us that they were going to play a lot. If we were going to be good, we knew we couldn't wait for the new players to catch on.

Dean probably needed the most work. He was a gangly kid, not real thick through the chest, and he threw himself into developing his power game.

With Keith—who reported minus the gold chains and with a conventional haircut—it was more a case of just learning the system. We planned to run a lot, which suited his skills, but he had to learn the basics—how to cut, how to read his defensive man on screens, things like that. In our first workouts he covered me, and he was shocked (not to mention bruised) by all the picks my teammates set for me. "Here I am, a new guy, not used to screens," he said later, "and I was just getting nailed. I think he's going inside, and he pops outside, and there's a screen. *Boom!* I'm getting frustrated, because here are all these big guys laying screens on me. And every shot goes in. I thought, Oh, man."

I thought "Oh, man" myself the first time I saw Keith use his forty-four-inch vertical jump for a two-handed reverse dunk. "He can easily outjump me," Daryl said. "If he were six-four, he'd be our center." Scott May, a former IU star who played in the Italian league, worked out with us some, and he predicted that Keith would really help my game. "If you've got a real quick guard who can penetrate, see things, and draw people to him and hit the open man...well, I tell you, Alford will either be shooting a lot of open jump shots or this guy will be shooting a lot of lay-ups."

I worked a lot with Dean and Keith, as did Daryl and Todd. We seniors had the biggest stake in making the transition successful. We were on the verge of being the only class not to win a Big Ten championship for Coach Knight. We hadn't won *anything*, when you got right down to it.

Dean and Keith were good listeners, which made our job

easier. You could tell them something and they would take it all in; they wouldn't walk away snarling. Keith, in particular, was downright apologetic when he made a bad play, saying, "My bad!" or "Sorry!" Coach finally jumped on him for apologizing all the time, saying, "Smart, there's no column in the box score for 'my bad.' Just learn from your mistakes and go on from there."

When practices started, Coach was pretty patient with Dean and Keith, because they were new. He was less patient with Daryl, who got in trouble for cutting a folklore class called "Webster: The Traditional Beliefs, Legends of People." When we flew to Gary for an exhibition intersquad game, Coach left Daryl behind. At dinner that night, he told Bob Hammel, "Daryl Thomas has been dropped from the squad because he does not think it's important enough to maintain academic standards."

Todd and I felt sick when we heard that. It had hurt enough to lose Marty at the end of the sophomore season. To lose Daryl on the threshold of our senior season was unthinkable.

We weren't the only ones who were shocked. Daryl's parents had driven down from Westchester, Illinois, for the scrimmage, and there was no Daryl. Coach talked with them after the game. Afterward, Mrs. Thomas said, "He didn't tell me if Daryl could come back, but I'm hoping. I go along with Coach Knight in whatever he does as far as academics are concerned. I'm a full believer in that myself, so I can understand why he took Daryl off the squad."

Actually, Coach hadn't said Daryl was dropped for good. Hammel, who was a good barometer of Coach's thinking, wrote, "The uniform hasn't been burned yet, nor have bridges, nor, apparently, has enough midnight oil. The last shall—or had better—be first."

A couple of days later, Daryl was back at practice as if nothing had happened. Of course, something had happened: he had promised to straighten out his priorities. End of crisis.

That's the way it went my senior year. There were the usual number of incidents—players in the doghouse, academic crises, slumps, personality clashes—but they got resolved quickly and usually to the benefit of the team.

Typical of the season was Coach's forty-sixth birthday. It had become a team tradition to celebrate October 25 in his office with ice cream and cake. The managers were always in charge of the edibles. After practice, we'd bring the cake out and the freshmen would lead the singing of "Happy Birthday" to Coach. We always ended up eating the cake ourselves, because Coach would let us.

My senior year, Coach kicked us out of practice on his birthday, so we faced the problem of rolling the cake over to Coach's office right after he had thrown us out. Some of the guys thought it might be better to give him the cake on one of his good days, even if it was a little moldy by then.

Courage won out. We rolled the cake across the floor toward the black curtain, and I'm sure everybody was thinking, Who goes in first?

To our surprise, Coach looked at the cake and brightened right up. He smiled when our two freshmen, Tony Freeman and David Minor, stepped forward to lead the singing. Tony is from inner-city Chicago, and when he cut the cake, Coach said, "You look like you're pretty familiar with that knife, Tony. It doesn't have anything to do with your background, does it?"

Tony broke up.

There was another sign that Indiana basketball was back to normal: our training meals at the Union were more like those of my freshman year, when Dakich, Chuck Franz, and the other upperclassmen told war stories and introduced us to the Hoosier way of doing things. The only difference was that Todd, Daryl, and I were the senior comedians now, and Minor, Freeman, Smart, and Garrett were our audience. (Keith and Dean, although upperclassmen, were freshmen when it came to Indiana lore. They seemed to get a big kick out of the war stories.)

We never lacked for material. We regaled the newcomers with "Coach and the Chair," "Steve Alford and the Calendar Incident," "Marty Simmons and the Twenty-Five-Pound Weight," "Mike Giomi and the Second Plane," and all the other classics. Our team meals were no longer hurried. Players didn't rush off in all different directions after gulping their food.

And if someone seemed a little down because Coach had yelled at him, Todd and Daryl and I were always there to say, "Don't take it personally. Coach is just trying to help you."

We could say that. We were seniors.

Unlike my freshman year, when people expected nothing of us, my senior year opened with us ranked number one in the *Sporting News* poll and very high in the others. Coach Knight, who had no use for the polls, used the rankings to taunt us. "How can you be rated number one when you lost to Cleveland State in your last game and you haven't won a game this year?"

His focus was again on mental toughness. He brought it up again and again and again. We won a big game up at Notre Dame at the beginning of the season, and then came home and beat Kentucky, 71–66. We played both games without Ricky Calloway, who had hurt his knee in our opener against Montana State, and winning without Ricky made us feel pretty tough.

Coach wouldn't have it. He glared at us in the locker room. "Let's don't get carried away thinking that we've made great strides. We've still got a long way to go with our mental toughness."

We flew to Nashville to play Vanderbilt, a team that had no business beating us, and, sure enough, we blew a 9-point lead in the second half and lost. We just plain fell apart in the closing minutes, and Coach was livid afterward.

It was Dean and Keith's first experience with Coach at his best. I almost risked a smile, remembering the Miami of

Ohio loss my freshman year. I couldn't smile, though, because it was Steve Alford that Coach was maddest at. "That has got to be the worst defensive play by two Indiana guards that I have ever seen! I can almost excuse Keith, because he's new, Alford, but what's your excuse? How can anybody play four years in this system and not learn one thing about playing defense? I've wasted, totally wasted, three years trying to teach you, and the minute you go into a defensive crouch I hear people laughing in the stands."

The freshmen were amazed that Coach would scorch a senior and team captain like that. We'd *told* them about it, of course, but it was something you had to see to believe.

Coach went on in the same vein on the bus to the airport, on the flight home, on the bus to Assembly Hall, in the I-Men Lounge, and for the next couple of days in practice, running our butts into the ground. Later, he confided to Bob Hammel, "Losing the game didn't really bother me that much. I just wanted to see how they'd react."

The day after the Vanderbilt game, he called Daryl and me into his office. He was very calm and down-to-earth. There was none of the abuse of the previous night. "Listen," he said, "I know what you've done for this team. A lot has been put on your shoulders in the past because the players weren't here. And now we've got a team that can play with you; we've got the talent. We need for you to be leaders, to lift them up and make them better."

I think that little meeting got us going, although it wasn't apparent our next time out. We almost got the shock of our lives in the opening round of the Indiana Classic, squeaking by North Carolina–Wilmington, 73–72. Coach started Magnus Pelkowski in place of Dean Garrett, even though Dean already had three double-figure rebounding games, and he started Dave Minor in place of Keith. We fell behind early, bounced back, and then squandered a 14-point halftime lead. At the end of the game, we were desperately blocking shots and chasing rebounds. The game wasn't safe until Steve Eyl came down with the last board.

This time, Coach saved his voice and took the blame himself. "That was my fault, not the players'," he told the media. "I was too hard on them after the Vanderbilt game. I don't think I can do that with these kids."

The media was surprised, the players were surprised, the assistant coaches were surprised. Hey, I think *Coach* was surprised. He told Rick Bozich of the *Herald-Telephone,* "For the first time in my career I said, 'Oh, well, what the hell, we won.' You have no idea what that took for me to say that. Nobody does. That's not me. That was really hard for me to do, maybe the hardest thing I've ever done in my life."

The velvet glove worked better than the iron fist. With Dean and Keith back in the starting lineup, we clobbered East Carolina the next night to win the Classic. A week later, Calloway returned from his injury and we blew away Morehead State. Then, just before Christmas, we took on defending NCAA champs Louisville. Dean outplayed their star center, Pervis Ellison, and Ricky made up for my cold shooting by scoring 19 points in a 67–58 win. We went on to easy wins over Princeton and Illinois State in the Hoosier Classic and cruised into the conference schedule with a 9–1 record.

There was no mystery about why we were better. Dean and Keith transformed our team. Dean gave us an inside scoring punch, and he was a very strong rebounder. Coach Knight's friend and mentor Pete Newell, the former University of California and Olympic coach, said, "When the shooter takes the shot, Dean expects him to miss, and consequently he's looking to get the ball off the board when he does miss. A lot of guys don't rebound that way. They watch the flight of the ball until it misses and then try to get it."

Keith was a funny case, because he felt completely lost in the early games and was actually thinking of quitting the team. He couldn't see, as we could, that his presence on the floor helped out the other starters, even when his shooting was off or his defense was shaky. He was so quick and so clever that he created terrible matchup problems for opponents who normally would have keyed on stopping my jump shots.

Those two guys had a ripple effect, making everybody's job easier. Daryl especially benefited from Dean's presence in the middle. His year as a center had really helped him, because now he could either play with his back to the bucket or go outside and shoot jump shots.

The effect on my game was just as dramatic. In my junior season, Coach had asked me to shoot more—twenty-five shots a game, if necessary—because we had to get me the ball to score. As a senior I still had the green light, but I didn't have to take twenty-five shots. I had the confidence to throw the ball to Keith, to Daryl, to Dean, to Ricky, knowing they could be creative and make things happen. I had never had the luxury of doing that with all four starters before. Now I could play instinctively, throwing at a flash of red, gambling on defense. I didn't have to think, and anytime you can play instinctively rather than mechanically, you're better off.

Another reason we were better: three seniors who could provide leadership. Coach Knight had made me team captain, but I took Daryl and Todd with me for the pregame meetings with the refs. We became three captains, and both Daryl and Todd responded beautifully to that.

It's hard to describe what experience does for a college player. In my last season I finally understood how to make my teammates better players, how to keep them in the flow of a game and take advantage of defensive mismatches. And I was no longer reluctant to lead vocally as well as by example. As a senior, I was not afraid to chew out a teammate for dogging it or get on a freshman about his grades.

Daryl could do it too, which was an amazing transformation. For three years he had been the quiet kid who crawled into his shell when Coach Knight screamed at him. Suddenly, he was a strong and positive force on the team. Dean, particularly, looked to Daryl for wisdom and guidance.

Todd? He just amazed me. His knees bothered him worse than ever and he was in constant pain, but he never bellyached or complained about his playing time. He just submitted to treatment, turned out for every practice, and gave Coach Knight everything he had. Todd pushed the rest of us. He sacrificed his body. He raised the intensity of practice to game levels.

Todd could have red-shirted. He knew he wouldn't get much playing time, not with the players we had coming in. He could have rested a year, healed his knees, and maybe come back as a starter.

Todd said no. "I just want to be part of it," he said, "even if I sit on the bench the whole time. Even if I can't play, there's young guys I can help."

I kidded him that he just couldn't face life at the apartment complex without someone to fire bottle rockets at. In truth, I admired him tremendously for his guts and leadership. Coach Knight did, too. Todd Meier was what Indiana basketball was all about.

It wouldn't have been an Indiana season, of course, without some major distraction. This time it came in the form of a publishing event. A couple of weeks before our first game, word got out on campus that a fellow named Feinstein had written a book about Indiana basketball. It was called *A Season on the Brink*. Word was that it was a bombshell. Quoted Coach word for word in some of his worst tirades.

Before practice one day, the grad assistants warned us that the book was on Coach's desk. Somebody said he had read about ten pages and put it down, extremely upset. We worried that he would carry that mood into practice, but it turned out to be a pretty good workout. Coach didn't mention the book at all.

His silence held for several days, despite growing media interest in his reaction. We heard through the grapevine that several college coaches, including Digger Phelps of Notre

Dame, were offended by things that Coach had said in the book.

Reporters were asking the players what we thought of it. Daryl said, "I haven't read it, but I've had a lot of choice passages relayed to me. It's a book I think I'll have to read."

Coach finally broke his silence in South Bend, the night before the Notre Dame game. At our team meeting, he apologized to us for giving Feinstein so much freedom. He explained that his whole objective in cooperating with Feinstein had been to give the public an idea of what it was like to play at Indiana—the academic side, the social life, the whole picture. Feinstein, he said, had violated his trust and produced something entirely different. "I'm sorry," he said. "It was a mistake."

He never mentioned Feinstein or the book to us again.

It was ironic, because I saw John Feinstein the next night at the game, sitting on press row. He was covering the game for the *Washington Post*. I looked at him, and he looked back and smiled. After the game, he caught me before we left and asked if I had gotten the book yet.

"Not yet, John. I haven't had time."

"I think you'll enjoy it," he said.

He didn't say anything about Coach Knight, but I'm sure he knew that Coach was unhappy.

Todd was the first player to get the book. He wrapped a different dust jacket around it so he could carry it on the bus and the airplane. Even then, he was careful not to read it in Coach's view.

The rest of us were curious, because the book was about us, too. It was funny, because Todd would come across a good part and say, "Read this! Read this!" We'd pass the book around, and everybody would get a good laugh out of it.

None of the players thought Feinstein was unfair to Coach, and we certainly didn't perceive the book as an attack on the team. We enjoyed it. The book was like a scrap-

book, something we could read in the years to come and
chuckle over.

Of course, I don't know how many players actually read
the whole book. The only copy we had was Todd's, and we
only read it in bits and pieces, thumbing through the book to
find our names. We'd look for "Meier," we'd look for "Dakich," we'd look for "Alford"—just to see what Feinstein
had said about us. *Sports Illustrated* published excerpts from
the book, and we all read them. They were pretty juicy.

I knew what was in the book from what people were telling me, but I didn't actually read it until much later, after I'd
left Indiana. I thought I should let some time pass. I was still
struggling with Coach Knight's mind games and probably
couldn't have read it objectively.

When I did finally read it, I enjoyed it immensely. I could
sit back and laugh out loud at incidents that had been painful at the time. I didn't find the book at all threatening.
When people came up to me and asked, "Is that book true?
Did those things really happen?" I'd laugh and say, "It's one
hundred percent fact. I know. I lived it."

I think what upset Coach about *A Season on the Brink* is
that it wasn't what he had hoped it would be—a balanced
portrait of Indiana basketball. Coach wanted people to understand how difficult it was to play there, sure, but also
how players could reap benefits from four years at a great
university. He loved *Hoosiers,* the movie. I think Coach
hoped for something with that blend of realism and poetry.

Instead, Feinstein focused on Coach's profanity and the
way he treated players. I don't blame John for that—I think
any good reporter would have done the same thing. But
that's why Coach felt betrayed.

Frankly, nobody who knew Coach could understand why
he had opened the doors to John in the first place.

If Feinstein got one thing wrong, it was the title: *A Season
on the Brink*. As I mentioned earlier, the season he spent
with us was a picnic compared to my sophomore year. *That*
was the season on the brink.

A second irony took longer to sink in. As my senior season wore on, the book got bigger and bigger, until it was the nation's number-one best-seller. Everywhere we went, people asked, "What do you think of the book? Did Feinstein do a hatchet job on Knight? Did Coach really call Daryl Thomas a you-know-what?" The questions followed us everywhere we went.

The irony: now that he was gone, John Feinstein was a greater presence in the Indiana locker room than he had been when he was actually there.

We opened the Big Ten season with a 92–80 win over Ohio State at Columbus, and 24 of our points came from shots taken behind a new line painted on the floor, nineteen feet and nine inches from the center of the basket. I hit three out of five long ones, and Keith hit five out of five—which was funny, because some people were calling the NCAA's move to the 3-point shot the "Steve Alford rule."

The new rule had several objectives. One was obvious—to encourage players like me to shoot the outside shot, which was a crowd-pleaser. The real purpose, though, was to force defenders to come out of their tightly packed zones, opening the game up for penetrating guards and inside-scoring big men. That's why the line was set at a reasonably short distance. (The NBA's 3-point line is three feet and seven inches farther out.)

Coach Knight didn't like the 3-point shot. He had voted against it. In the preseason, he wasn't even sure he was going to let us shoot it, particularly when he saw the difficulty I was having adjusting to the line. The distance was no problem for me—I had been taking twenty-foot jumpers all along, even when they counted for only 2 points. But in practice I found myself looking down to find the line instead of just shooting the shot.

One day, I missed four or five in a row. Coach slammed the ball down and went crazy. He screamed at me for a couple of minutes. "Don't ever shoot the shot again! If you can't shoot the thing, then don't shoot it! What are you, some kind of dunce?" And so on.

I knew Coach well enough by now to know what he was up to: he was testing his captain's mental toughness. He wanted to see how I'd respond.

Practice resumed, and the next time down the floor I shot another 3-pointer. And hit it.

Coach gave me a look that said, "Good thing that went in, Alford, or you'd be *outta* here."

If I'd had the guts, I would have winked at him.

Once I got the footwork down, the 3-point shot proved to be as big an edge for me as people had predicted. I put up five or six per game and hit better than 50 percent, which made things very difficult for defenders. In one crazy game against Wisconsin, I took only one shot from inside the 3-point line (and missed it), went 0-for-1 from the foul line, and had no rebounds, and I still scored 21 points. I was 7-for-8 from 3-point range.

It struck me as odd: after all the work I had put in to improve my all-around game, my primary role on the team was still that of a pure shooter.

There's one statistic of mine that I think is unusual in this era of high-flying basketball players. I scored 2,438 points at Indiana, and I would guess that about 2,000 of those points came on jump shots and free throws. I probably scored 200 points on lay-ups and put-backs and maybe another 200 on running hook shots, jump hooks, off-balance prayer shots, end-of-the-half heaves, and accidental tip-ins.

Here's the interesting number: not one dunk. *Zero.*

Well sure, you say. You're six foot one, you're white, you can't dunk.

Dad tells the story of a bunch of young coaches at a summer basketball camp who were fooling around, dunking the basketball. They saw me practicing my jump shots and started ribbing me about not being able to dunk. "C'mon, Steve, let's see your dunk!" "Show us your Michael Jordan moves!" "Is it true you can't touch the rim?"

Finally, I got provoked enough by the teasing to want to shut them up. I took two dribbles toward the hoop, jumped off my left foot, and slammed the ball through the basket with my right hand.

Jaws dropped. I then turned to the jumping experts and said, "Now let's see you hit ten jump shots in a row."

Nobody even attempted that. Their question was: "If you can dunk the ball, why don't you?"

Simple. The goal in basketball is making points for your team. I have more confidence laying the ball in than dunking it, so I always take the higher-percentage shot. Dad told me to always play to my strengths, and the dunk shot is not one of my strengths.

Coach Knight thought the same way. When one of our guys missed a dunk shot, that infuriated Coach. And if the guy missed it because he was showing off, look out! Keith Smart didn't understand that in the beginning. He thought his Michael Jordan moves would be a real crowd-pleaser at Indiana. "Coach Knight knows that was my game at Garden City," he said, "so I think if I get a steal and go in and do a 360, he's not going to say anything, as long as it goes in."

Keith soon learned otherwise, and he toned down his dunks in games.

On the other hand, Coach's theory was: "If you're going to dunk it, *dunk* it." For big guys, the two-handed power dunk was often the high-percentage shot.

Uwe! He was a horrendous dunker—those stone hands again. A lot of times he would carry the ball way over the rim and then simply release it or lay it on the board, and sometimes the ball would bounce out. That drove Coach crazy. "Cram it in the hole!" he'd scream.

One of the mysteries of basketball is why shooters are so streaky. One night you can't miss, another night it's nothing but air balls and bricks. Even in a game, you can go from cold to hot and vice versa. In our win over Louisville my senior year, I missed my first nine shots from the floor, but warmed up in the second half and scored 17. Coach grabbed me after the game and said, "I'm pleased with you that you didn't stop shooting. Not that I had any *doubt* that you would keep shooting."

I had a bad shooting slump my sophomore year, when everything was going wrong. I had another my senior year, when everything was great. In consecutive games against Northwestern, Wisconsin, and Minnesota—the three weakest teams in the Big Ten—I went 4-for-13, 4-for-19, and 7-for-20. Then against Iowa, which earlier in the season had been ranked number one in the nation, I bounced back with 8-for-15 and 4-for-7 from 3-point range. It defied explanation.

Conditions do affect shooting. Basketballs, for example, are not all alike. In high school, we never played with anything but a Spalding basketball, and I grew very familiar with its feel. Most colleges used the Spalding ball, too, but the Big Ten Conference had no official basketball. We played with whatever the home team chose—Spalding, McGregor, Rawlings. That made it tough, because it was hard to get a feel for an unfamiliar ball. Purdue always used a balloon-type Rawlings ball, and I don't think I ever had a good shooting game there.

The lighting in an arena is another influence. I shot best in the old-style fieldhouses like those at Minnesota and Wisconsin, where the majority of the light was on the court and on the baskets. Background has a lot to do with shooting, and it helps if the area behind the basket is dark. Some of the new arenas are so well lit that you can see the fans all the way up to the top row, which is distracting. From some spots on the floor you look up and are blinded by bright lights. The Iowa fieldhouse is like that—very bright, and the light is not confined to the floor. Tough place to shoot.

Domes are very hard to get used to. Larry Bird hates to play in domes, and I can understand why: the background is too far away. Anything that distorts the shooter's perspective throws his shooting off. A low ceiling makes the basket look high. A far-off crowd makes the basket look close. In the

Olympic exhibition game at the Hoosier Dome, I took a shot from the top of the key and made it. A minute later, I took a shot from the corner and air-balled it over the top of the rim. Domes are very deceiving.

I always had good shooting games at Michigan State's fieldhouse (11-for-19 in my last appearance there, 8-for-8 from the line). We played at Kansas State's old Ahearn Field House one year, and I shot well there, too. Both those gymnasiums were great places to play—very noisy, and the fans were right on top of you. Even on the road, I liked to hear that noise, I wanted to feel the presence of the crowd. I didn't want to be in the corner with fifty yards of open space behind me.

But as I say, shooting is unpredictable. Whenever I went into a slump, I'd go back to Dad for advice. We'd go to the gym in New Castle, and I'd shoot while he rebounded. He rarely found anything mechanically wrong. He'd just point at his head. "Shooters are like putters in golf," he'd say. "When they start to miss, they start to think, Did I drop my shoulder? Or...?"

He'd pat me on the back. "You're a good shooter. You don't just lose that."

The thing about my senior year is that I knew I could have a subpar shooting game and we could still win. It was no longer a case of "Shut down Alford" or "Stop Blab inside" and you'll beat Indiana. The players around me were very good players who could make the most of our continuity offense. Our attack was very spontaneous, full of touch passes and backdoor plays. That kind of basketball is the most fun to watch, and it's the most fun to play. It's just hard to get five guys doing it.

We followed the Ohio State win with a 19-point victory over Michigan State at East Lansing. Then we took on Michigan on a Monday night and got a glimpse of how our season would go.

I remember the Michigan game for two plays. We were

trailing by 3 points in the first half when I threw up a 3-point shot. Right after I released the ball, one of their freshmen, Jack Kramer, crashed into me. The shot went in, and the refs said the foul was *after* the shot, sending me to the line for a one-and-one. I made both ends, giving me a 5-point play—the first in Indiana history.

The second play was more significant. We took a 17-point lead into the locker room at halftime and still led by 15 with about eight minutes left, but Michigan made an incredible rally. Gary Grant went to the line with eight seconds left and hit a free throw to put Michigan ahead, 84–83. But he missed the second. Daryl grabbed the rebound and passed to me, and I dribbled up the left side of the floor with Gary trying to slow me down but not foul me. I veered toward the center of the court. Instead of taking the long jump shot, I suddenly cut toward the basket and just as suddenly pulled up for a leaning, ten-foot shot in traffic. I can still see that shot in my mind, the ball bouncing on the rim, bouncing, and finally toppling in. Final score: Indiana 85, Michigan 84.

What was it, mental toughness or luck? I don't have an answer for that. I only know that suddenly we were a team that could play poorly and still win. We were survivors. We escaped with a 2-point win over Northwestern—a disgraceful performance, but a win nonetheless. We beat Wisconsin in three overtimes, 86–85, when Dean caught a Joe Hillman air ball with three seconds left and laid it in. Two days later, Dean did it again. We played Minnesota at home—the same team we had beaten by 24 in our first meeting—and found ourselves in a tie with time running out. This time, *I* put up the shot, and Dean rebounded the miss and got fouled before he could shoot. He stepped to the foul line with three seconds left and coolly hit both free throws for the win. "I've never done that in my life," he said. "Now twice in one week!"

They say that good teams win when they have to. Coach

wouldn't buy that as an excuse for our bad play, but there's something to it. Those games were good for us because we hung tough and stayed together. The three-overtime game, most of all, showed the progress we had made. When things went bad, no one was pointing fingers, looking for scapegoats. Everybody pulled together. That was very different from previous seasons, when the players went five different ways in the face of adversity.

And it wasn't as if we couldn't compete against the better teams. Iowa, Purdue, and Illinois were all ranked, and we had great contests with them. The first time we played Iowa was at Iowa City, and they were ranked number one in the nation. And they deserved it. They had great players like Roy Marble and B. J. Armstrong, and a terrific sixth man in Jeff Moe. Their new coach, Tom Davis, had them pressing and fast-breaking at a frantic pace. We were trailing 93–88 with 1:25 left when I cut around a screen and swished a 3-pointer from the left side. My joy was short-lived, however, since an official ruled that my foot had touched the sideline as I squared up. No basket, and Iowa squashed us in the last minute to win, 101–88. Still, a great game.

We beat Illinois, 69–66, and Purdue, 88–77, in consecutive games at Assembly Hall. When we got our second shot at Iowa, at home, we had flip-flopped in the rankings: we were now ranked third and Iowa had dropped to seventh. This time, we outrebounded them, blew out to a 46–27 halftime lead, and won convincingly, 84–75. We followed that success with a loss to sixth-ranked Purdue at West Lafayette, and then lost a 2-point heartbreaker to Illinois at Champaign when I got trapped in the corner with time running out and had to force up a bad shot.

For comic relief, we had the midwinter battle between Coach Knight and the Bloomington Faculty Council. The council kicked it off by adopting a "statement of rights" protecting IU athletes from physical or verbal abuse. The resolution read, "Athletes shall not be subjected to physical or verbal abuse, intimidating, coercive or degrading behavior." Athletes were encouraged to report any violations to university authorities.

Did the council have any particular coach in mind? Say, a nationally known basketball coach whose strong language had recently carried a certain book to the top of the bestseller lists?

Coach Knight certainly thought so. On his next radio show, he apologized for not knowing our starting lineup for Illinois. "I wish I could give you a little bit of an idea on what our starting lineup is going to be, but I can't," he said. "The Bloomington Faculty Council was supposed to have it to me by four o'clock this afternoon, but they got caught up in a debate over whether to put petunias or daffodils in a flower bed behind the old library building."

The resolution was not a major topic of conversation among the players and coaches. Most of us thought it was ridiculous. "Coach is not going to hit you," Dakich said. "He's not going to give you a black eye. It's strange—those who get yelled at the most feel the best. He's not a big ogre like some people think. It's just that the more he expects of you, the more he yells."

I felt the same way. No one got yelled at by Coach more than I did, but I didn't need a bill of rights to shut him up. All I needed was a good game.

The truth is, Coach didn't yell at us half as much my senior year. We were a hardworking group, and we didn't screw up a lot of things with mental errors. When we got beat or didn't play well, it was usually because we didn't shoot well or somebody was extraordinarily hot on the other team. It wasn't because we weren't into the game mentally.

And Coach acknowledged that. "I probably tend to be overcritical," he admitted. "This was a team that needed a pat on the back."

Michael Jordan probably would have choked if he had heard Coach say that. Michael ran into Coach sometime in

January and told him about our Olympics-year bet that I would not last four seasons under his coaching. Michael was ready to admit defeat. "Tell Steve I owe him one hundred dollars."

"Don't pay it," Coach said. "He hasn't made it yet."

One of my last war stories dates from about this time. One afternoon, Coach started getting after me for something in practice, nagging me and yelling at me just as he had for three and a half years. I was in no mood for it and probably gave him a look. He flew into a rage and threw me out. "Take a shower and go home, Alford! I don't want to see you in here again! Don't come back till I call you on the phone!"

I wheeled around and stormed off the court, furious. When I got to the locker room, instead of sitting down and waiting for Coach to come get me, as I was supposed to, I peeled off my practice uniform and flung my sweaty stuff on the floor. I threw on my clothes, shot out the door, and practically ran to my car. I was really angry. I wanted to get away before Coach stopped me. If he asked me later why I'd left, I was prepared to tell him, "You told me to."

So I jumped in my car and drove off. My sweaty gear, meanwhile, lay in a pile in front of my locker.

That was my mistake. We were always supposed to put our laundry in a little bag, tie it up, and leave the bag in a grocery cart for the managers to take care of. No sooner had I walked into my apartment than the phone rang. It was one of the managers: "Coach Knight wants you to come in and put your practice gear where it's supposed to go."

I was still steamed. I slammed down the receiver, drove back to Assembly Hall, snuck down the steps—practice was still going on—threw my stuff in the bag, tied it up, threw it in the cart, and raced out again without Coach catching me.

I was still AWOL.

That night, of course, I had second thoughts. Walking out on Coach Knight was a nervy thing to do, a reckless thing to

do. There was no telling how he might react. He might
bench me. He might suspend me. For that matter, he might
call me. But the phone didn't ring.

The next day, I went to Assembly Hall as usual and got
ready for practice. I was on the trainer's table getting taped
when Coach peeked in the door. I was kind of tense. I knew
he had come over to our side of the building for no other
reason than to see if I was there.

Coach looked puzzled. "I can't remember, Steve—did I
have a bad dream last night where I got up, called you in my
sleep, and told you to come back in to practice?"

I said, "No, you didn't."

Coach smirked. "Okay. I just wanted to make sure." And
he turned and left.

He never mentioned the incident again.

Dakich couldn't believe that I had walked out on practice
and gotten away with it. "Nobody's ever done that! Nobody!"

That was high praise, coming from Dakich.

It was a terrific Big Ten race. Going into the second Illinois game, we were all alone in first place at 14–1. Two
blinks of an eye later, we were 14–3 and Purdue was on top
by a half game.

And now we were a little scared, because something had
to happen to Purdue. They had two games left, at Michigan
State and at Michigan, and we had one left, at home against
Ohio State. We had to win ours, and they had to lose one for
us to share the title. Otherwise, we still wouldn't have won
anything in my four years.

Purdue played Michigan State on Wednesday night and
beat them. I watched the game on TV and listened grimly as
the announcers kept saying, "This guarantees the Boiler-
makers at least a tie for the Big Ten title."

Which meant that it all came down to the final Saturday.
We had to get help from Michigan, which would play Pur-

due as the second half of an all–Big Ten doubleheader on CBS, right after we played Ohio State.

For Daryl, Todd, and me, Saturday, March 7, was a very emotional day—our last game at Assembly Hall. It just suddenly hit us that it was almost over. We still had the NCAA tournament to play, but four years had flown by and it was time to say goodbye to the fans in Bloomington. There had been times when we had wished we could leave IU right then and there, times when it was no fun, times when we lost confidence in ourselves. But now that the end was upon us, we wanted it to go on.

Assembly Hall was sold out—17,289 fans. *Noisy* fans. They were all wound up because we were playing for the conference crown, and their enthusiasm was contagious. Keith Smart was so excited in the first half that he began to hyperventilate and had to be treated with ice packs. "It was the first time my mother has *ever* gotten to see me play," Keith said afterward. "I wanted to do everything so well, it just caught up with me. I got so tired I couldn't breathe. I just got super-overheated."

It looked like a meltdown for the rest of us, too. Ohio State's star forward, Dennis Hopson, hit a long 3-pointer to put the Buckeyes ahead 38–30. We came back with a 9-point run of our own and went to the locker room trailing by just 1. In the second half, they pulled away from us again and led by 8 with ten minutes left.

Mental toughness. I'm sure Coach Knight brought it up in a time-out. I can still see him in the huddle, his face redder than his sweater, the eyebrows down and in, his jaw working overtime. "Get your heads back in the game! This is it, boys—you've got to want it more than they do!"

We did want it more than they did. It took us less than three minutes to tie the game. Everybody on the court for us scored in the last five minutes, and we won the game, 90–81, with the crowd cheering every big play.

With thirteen seconds left, Keith was in the middle of

shooting two free throws when the horn went off. I looked around, and saw Todd and Kreigh Smith running toward me. The substitutions were for Daryl and me—Coach Knight's way of letting us leave the home court for the last time to an ovation. And it was a tearful, wonderful, standing ovation. All the guys on the bench were lined up to give us high fives and hugs. Coach gave me a big, two-arm bear hug, and the crowd roared.

There wasn't much time to collect our thoughts. The seconds clicked down, and the horn sounded to end my last Big Ten game. There was a big on-court celebration, and the PA announcer reminded everyone to stay in his seat for the Senior Day ceremony. We went to the locker room for a quick comment or two from Coach Knight. Then we filed back out to a sustained ovation from the crowd.

A microphone stood on the court, waiting.

I stood with my teammates and stared at the microphone. I was reminded of Dan Dakich's words to me when I was a freshman: "The biggest thing is just to get to the mike."

He was so right. That was the biggest thing—to meet the challenge for four years and finally make it to the mike.

Coach Knight stepped forward and put his arm up to hush the crowd. "We've had some great players stand where these three kids are," he began, "some players who I think have represented Indiana, Indiana University, and Indiana basketball to the absolute highest degree. We have three kids here today who I think carry that on. I'm going to let them speak to you in reverse alphabetical order."

Laughter and applause swept the hall. I blushed.

Daryl spoke first, after a warm introduction from Coach. There was nothing shy and retiring now about the Thomas kid. He stood there with happiness in his eyes and a big smile. He thanked the fans, the assistant coaches, and, most of all, Coach Knight, for giving him the opportunity to play. "I really think if I hadn't come here, my abilities and my talents would not have been brought out the way they have been. I'm not saying I'm a great player." He glanced at the rest of us, grinning. "But I could have been a lot worse than I am now."

He finished on an emotional note: "I've saved the best for last—my parents. I love you, Mom and Dad."

Coach's introduction of Todd was a mixture of sentiment and comedy. "You've seen Todd Meier play the last two years on a couple of knees that are hard to walk on, let alone play basketball on, and I think over the four years that he has played for us, Todd has made an incredible number of big plays in games that were very, very important. Todd's father is a Lutheran minister, and I guarantee you, he leaves the university with a much broader vocabulary than he brought here."

Todd walked to the microphone with not just his parents watching but also his wife, Kris, and baby daughter, Morgan. He finished his thank-yous by saying, "I've made a lot of friends here. I would have liked to play more, but I couldn't. I thank the team for a great season, and I wish Steve and Daryl the best of luck." He got a terrific ovation.

And then it was my turn. Coach turned to me and said over the microphone, "There will probably be a time, Steve, when we're working on our defense, and we don't get back in to get the ball, and I might quickly say, 'Dammit, Alford would have had that.' I might have slipped up. I might have meant Randy Wittman and your name came out by mistake."

Having gotten in that last zinger, Coach turned serious. "But it will be because, Steve, you're on my mind as one of the truly great basketball players that we've had here."

I made it to the microphone, but those ten steps were tough to take. With each step, a memory flashed in my mind—a teammate's face, something Coach had once said, the free-throw chant, the players who had made the same walk before me. I couldn't talk at first, waiting for the applause to stop. It was just as well. I needed time to compose myself.

When I began, it was with the usual list of people I

wanted to thank: the assistant coaches, former players, the athletic department staff. And, of course, Coach Knight: "I don't even have the words to say my appreciation and thanks.... He has opened up an awful lot of doors to me."

My family was sixteen rows up, behind the Indiana bench. I searched for them in the crowd, and when I found them, I smiled.

"One thing Dan Dakich told me was 'Whatever you do, don't look up at your parents or you'll start to cry.' I just don't think I can do that, because of what they've meant to me and done for me. They know how much I love them. They know the support they've given me. I can't express that in words. I know my brother is sitting over here. He knows how much I think of him ... how much I care for him.

"Last, and definitely most important, I just want to thank the good Lord for all the things that He has done for me.

"And finally, to all of you ..." I looked up at the crowd, all decked out in red and white. "I haven't really had the chance to say thank you, but it's been an unbelievable four years, the support you've given us. We were undefeated here at home this year and I think you had an awful lot to do with it. This was a game we desperately needed and we wanted to play well in. Now, hopefully, we'll go into the NCAA on a good note.

"I didn't think I could ever make myself say this, but let's go home and root for Michigan."

The crowd cheered, and I stepped back in line with Todd and Daryl. It was one of the most wonderful moments of my life, standing with my two good friends and listening to the applause. It was one of the saddest moments as well, knowing that we would never play there again.

Within the hour, we had even more reason to celebrate. While I busily signed autographs and talked to kids outside Assembly Hall, people kept running up excitedly with updates of the Purdue score. "Michigan is killing them! Purdue's down 30!" The word spread quickly among the players. Smiles blossomed. We were co-champions of the Big Ten.

The final score in Ann Arbor was Michigan 104, Purdue 68.

It was ironic. The same thing had happened to Purdue that had happened to us the year before—getting blown out by Michigan on national TV in the final game.

"I don't feel we backdoored them," Todd said. "There might have been a little luck in there, but we had a good record, one of the best records an Indiana team has had in a long time. It just boiled down to Purdue losing and us winning."

He was right. It always boils down to losing and winning.

Fairfield University is a small college in Connecticut with a basketball team in the Metro Atlantic Athletic Conference. Their nickname is the Stags and they play in a fieldhouse that seats three thousand, which is smaller than the smallest gym in my high school conference. If the makers of *Hoosiers* decided to do a movie about college basketball, they'd pick Fairfield as the team to win the national championship.

Fairfield is the team we drew for our opening game in the sixty-four-team NCAA tournament. We were the top seed in the Midwest region. Fairfield was the sixteenth, or bottom, seed. They were 15–15, unranked, unknown, and had snuck into the tournament only by winning the Metro Atlantic postseason tournament.

And they scared us to death.

Coach Knight rebuked reporters who smirked at the matchup. "I said at last year's press conference that Cleveland State was capable of playing against anybody and that Cleveland State could very easily beat us the next day. And I don't think anybody in there paid any attention to me."

Maybe the press could forget, but we couldn't. The score was still posted in our locker room: CLEVELAND STATE 83, INDIANA 79. Again and again, Coach drove home the point that our close wins over Minnesota, Northwestern, and Wisconsin proved that we were still a team that let up against weaker opponents. If we were to avoid a repeat of those embarrassments, he said, we would have to show a real desire to win. I wrote down these words of his in my notebook: "Show the size of Indiana's heart."

We knew we could expect a very partisan crowd in the Indianapolis Hoosier Dome, but I told my teammates that the strangeness of the dome would probably negate that advantage. "It's a tough place to get used to," I said, remembering my air ball in the Olympic exhibition game.

None of us was prepared for what greeted us at Wednesday afternoon's shoot-around at the dome. Fifteen thousand people were in the stands, most of them dressed in red and screaming like crazy as we went through lay-ups and passing drills. The Fairfield coach, Mitch Buonaguro, looked at that crazy crowd and said, "That's the Indiana mystique. I just hope our kids don't get caught up in that."

If we needed a reminder that upsets were common in tournament play—and we didn't—we got it in the noon game on Thursday, when fourteenth-ranked Missouri stumbled over Xavier of Ohio. Our mood was somber at the pregame meal. Not that that was unusual.

A crowd of 29,610—an NCAA first-round record—cheered us when we took the floor that night. The tip-off came at nine thirty-seven, which was a late start for a college basketball game. We lost no time in turning the lights out for little Fairfield. We built up a 15-point lead in just seven minutes and stretched it to 25 by halftime. The final score was 92–58.

Auburn was next, on Saturday afternoon. No Charles Barkley this time, no "Round Mound of Rebound." No Chuck Person, either. Their record was an unimpressive 17–12. But some of those wins were impressive, such as their 38-point rout of LSU and a 14-point win over Florida.

Saturday's crowd at the Hoosier Dome set another record. They were 34,000 strong this time, and almost all in Hoosier red. But not as red as we were when Auburn came out and started mopping the floor with us. Coach had wanted a slow-tempoed first half, but the only thing slow was our scoring. Auburn came out in a box-and-one defense, and Gerald White was all over me, bumping, holding, practically shoving me off the floor. With six minutes gone, I hadn't scored yet and we were already 14 points behind. We hadn't come from that far behind to win all season.

Coach Knight called a time-out, and I'll never forget that huddle. He jumped all over us. "You don't have any heart. It's going to be a season just like last season." He screamed at Daryl, he screamed at me: "Show us some leadership!"

We really didn't hear him, we were so infuriated with ourselves. We didn't need *him* to tell us we were playing poorly or that we were blowing it. I looked around the huddle, and everybody was frowning, everybody was mad. "Come on, guys," somebody said, "we're embarrassing ourselves."

We took the court after the time-out with a sense of purpose that was frightening. I could be wrong, but I think the Auburn players could see it in our faces.

Whatever the reason, the game turned into a bruising match between bodies and tempers. The big guys on both teams were shoving and throwing elbows and screaming, "What's *that?*" at the refs every time somebody crashed over them for a rebound. I got into it once with White when I stepped up to the lane while Auburn was huddling for a free-throw conference. He claimed later that I was trying to eavesdrop, and his answer to that was to give me a shove. I flared up and shoved back, and that inflamed the crowd, which yelled and booed. The referees told Auburn that foul-shot situations were not a free time-out and that I had every right to be where I was.

That didn't quite square it for me. I walked over to Gerald, got right in his face, and said, "We don't need that. That's not part of the game."

I didn't say it nicely. I knew he meant to intimidate me.

Gerald and I weren't the only ones squaring off at mid-

court. Coach Knight came out and got into it verbally with
Auburn's coach, Sonny Smith, although both of them said
later they were just trying to settle things down.

The best way to settle a basketball brawl is by beating the
tar out of your opponents, and that's what we proceeded to
do. From the time-out on, we played as well as we had
played all year. Keith was sensational, driving into the lane
and kicking the ball back out to me for jump shots. Auburn
kept changing its defense: box-and-one, zone, triangle-and-
two. It didn't matter. Keith kept slicing toward the basket,
and when the defense converged he found the open man.

Scoreless in the first ten minutes, I scored my first 10
points in just two minutes. Once I was into my rhythm, I got
hot from 3-point range, going 7-for-11 for the game. When I
was covered, Keith found Daryl and Ricky on the baseline,
and both those guys were hot, too. Keith wound up with 15
assists, an IU record. More important, we roared back to
take a 53–48 lead at halftime. We wound up winning,
107–90.

It was one of the most satisfying wins of my Indiana career. Coach had asked us to play with heart, and we had.

I felt I had won my personal battle, as well. "I think White
was trying to get Steve's mind off the game," Coach said at
his press conference. "But White trying to intimidate Steve,
after Steve has played for me for four years, is like a sparrow
trying to rape an elephant."

The image wasn't pretty, but I was flattered all the same.

At game's end, Coach did a quick interview with Brent
Musberger on the floor, where we were celebrating the win.
By chance, we walked off together, and Coach slapped me
on the back.

"Well," he said, "what do you think of all this?"

I said, "I think we can go all the way." And then I ran for
the locker room, leaving him behind.

It became a ritual for Coach and me, the week of practice
leading up to the Midwest Regional in Cincinnati. Every

day, at the end of practice, he called me over, put his arm on my shoulder, and said, "Steve, you get me to New Orleans and I'll do the rest."

It was his old promise from my freshman year: if we could make it to the Final Four, he'd find a way to make us national champs.

First, we had to get by seventeenth-ranked Duke, a team that had reached the finals the year before. This game was billed as a reluctant matchup between two great coaches, one the master teacher, the other his devoted disciple. Mike Krzyzewski had played three years for Coach at West Point and had been a graduate assistant at Indiana in 1975. They were such close friends that they had never scheduled each other for a regular-season game, not wishing anything but success for each other.

When the media called attention to the similarities in their systems, both coaches got a little defensive. "I don't think Mike has stuck with anything that we did when he was a player or when he coached with me," Coach Knight said. "He has worked out his own approach to basketball and his own way of teaching the game and having the game played."

Coach K. said basically the same thing: "Everyone says we run the same system. We don't run the same system. Our man-to-man is different and our motion offense is different, because we have different types of players."

Maybe so, but in preparing for Duke it seemed like we were playing ourselves. We saw the same types of screens, the same type of discipline on shot selection, the same aggressive defense with a lot of hard man-to-man switches. That's how much they played like we played.

We flew to Cincinnati on Wednesday. As we got off the bus at the hotel, Coach grabbed me again and delivered the familiar message: "Alford, you know you've got only one job, and that's to get me to New Orleans. I'll do the rest."

On Thursday, Coach took some of us to a press conference. He was in rare form. When asked to comment on Duke, he said, "They're extremely well coached. I taught the

SOB, so they ought to be." When asked about the defensive matchups, he played dumb. "Daryl and Steve are sitting right here, and they don't know who they're going to guard tonight."

That wasn't quite true, but I didn't really expect Coach to broadcast our game plan.

It was no secret who would cover me: Billy King, a six-foot-six forward with a reputation for great man-to-man defense. King had held Byron Larkin to 7 points below his average in Duke's second-round win over Xavier, and he was used to covering a team's top scorer. What concerned me most about King was his size. I remembered the trouble I had had my sophomore season when the big guys who had usually covered Giomi had begun covering me.

As often happens, the King-Alford matchup didn't turn out to be the game story at all. The story was Ricky Calloway, playing before his hometown fans in Riverfront Coliseum. Ricky had predicted that all the women in Cincinnati would be out to see him perform, and one was, for sure— Ricky's mom, who stood up half the game holding a banner that read "Calloway Country." ("Moms never lie," he said.) Ricky missed his first three shots, but once he got going he was terrific, finishing with 21 points on 8-for-13 shooting. He also had 8 rebounds and 2 assists. Danny Ferry and Tommy Amaker had great games for Duke, but we finished with five players in double figures and never let the Blue Devils get closer than 2 points in the second half. Steve Eyl played great for us off the bench, making three great passes for baskets late in the game. Final score: 88–82.

"I really didn't enjoy this game at all," Coach said after the game. "I'm very, very happy for our players, but that was a tough ball game."

I thought that was an interesting comment. Coach loved to win, but he didn't like to see a friend lose.

Next up: Louisiana State University, winners over De Paul. "I haven't seen LSU play a minute," Coach told reporters. "I can't even begin to tell you about them."

He didn't mind telling *us,* when we gathered for a team meeting back at the hotel. "They do a good job of changing defenses and making adjustments during the game," he said. "The strength of their defense is to adjust to different offensive schemes."

There was no shortage of information on LSU: tapes, scouting reports, what-have-you. Even so, LSU was something of a mystery. A Final Four team the year before, they had managed to lose fourteen games before catching fire at tournament time. The LSU coach, Dale Brown, didn't claim to understand it. "Last year," he said, "we beat the number-one, number-two, number-three, and number-six seeds to reach the Final Four. This year, we've beaten the number-two, number-three, and number-seven. All that's missing is the number-one seed." Meaning Indiana.

This time around, LSU had additional motivation: the Final Four would be played in New Orleans at the Louisiana Superdome. If they beat us, they would practically be the home team at the Final Four.

I have funny memories of the LSU game. Three things stand out. The first is Coach Knight and the phone, which ended up costing IU ten thousand dollars. It all started when Coach waved at one of the referees during a TV time-out. He wanted an explanation for a three-second call that had just gone against Daryl. The ref didn't hear or see him, so Coach stepped out on the court to get his attention. That, in NCAA language, is "leaving the assigned coaching area." The minute the ref turned and saw Coach coming, he made a T with his hands—technical foul.

Coach got real mad real fast. He stormed over to the scorer's table to argue with tournament officials, and in arguing he pounded his fist on the table. I didn't see it—I was sitting down, resting—but I heard later that a telephone receiver popped straight up in the air, the way a spoon would if you banged the business end.

Actually, I saw it later; some photographer got a shot of the phone in midair, and the picture ran in newspapers from

coast to coast. Eventually, an NCAA committee deducted
ten thousand dollars from our tournament share for Coach's
attack on the phone.

The money didn't matter. What mattered was that An-
thony Wilson missed one of the two free throws assessed for
the technical. It was that close a game.

The second thing I remember is Ricky Calloway's misad-
venture. We hit a very dry spell in the second half—eight
trips downcourt without scoring—and suddenly we were
down 63–51. In the middle of that bad stretch, Ricky suddenly hit the floor in pain, clutching his bad knee. Tim Garl
raced out to help him, got him to his feet, and helped him
limp off the court.

Ricky recovered quickly, but to test the knee Tim decided
to take him back under the stands to jog in the corridor.
Ricky sprinted back and forth a few times, tested his mobility right and left, and said he was ready to play. The only
thing was, all the doors back to the floor were locked. The
two of them wound up banging on a locked door. Precious
seconds were lost while the hometown star made like a gate-
crasher beneath the seats.

I was relieved when Ricky reappeared and came back into
the game, but the situation was desperate. We trailed 75–66
with 4:38 to go, and that's when Ricky muscled along the
baseline and went up for a power dunk. To our horror, he
missed it. Missed it so badly, in fact, that it bounced high off
the rim and out-of-bounds. The pain in Ricky's face was
worse than when he had gone down with the knee. He was
sure he had lost the game with that miss.

The television people chose that moment for a TV time-
out. Ricky couldn't meet Coach's eyes in the huddle, but
Coach had nothing to say about the dunk. There was no
time for that, not with our whole season on the line. Coach
was hot, but he was totally in the game, totally focused on
what we had to do. "We're all right," he said. "We've got
time. You just haven't done what's been set up. What do you
say we play the way I want you to play?"

Before we took the floor again, we huddled quickly without Coach, and Daryl and I said some of the same things. "We've got plenty of time. Let's go out and play a lot harder than they do the last five minutes and see what happens."

That's the third thing that I remember clearly: what happened.

LSU tried to use the clock, but we chopped into the lead. Dean dunked a rebound, Daryl made a steal, Joe Hillman scored on a driving lay-up and got fouled for a 3-point play, and Keith made both ends of a one-and-one. That cut the lead to 1. The crowd went crazy.

With twenty-six seconds left, we had to foul Fess Irvin, a freshman who was already 6-for-7 from the floor. Luck was with us. Irvin missed his first foul shot and Daryl grabbed the rebound. We still trailed by 1, but we didn't call a time-out. Our strategy was to strike before LSU could set up a defense.

There was no set play, but the guys tried to get me the ball. Daryl set a pick, and I raced around it, but two defenders leaped out at me. That left Daryl open in the middle. He took a pass, faked a shot ten feet in front of the basket, and jumped into José Vargas, trying to draw a foul. But it didn't work, and Daryl had to force a weak shot at the basket.

The shot never had a prayer; it was an air ball all the way. And maybe the thought was just entering my consciousness: "We've lost. It's over." But that's when Ricky Calloway, the game's goat, knifed in, caught the ball just below the rim, and banked it off the glass and in.

The crowd roared itself hoarse. We led, 77–76, with only six seconds left.

I watched the final seconds from the bench. LSU called a time-out, and Coach Knight took the opportunity to replace me with Steve Eyl, a taller player, for defensive purposes. It was a good move. LSU couldn't get a shot off before the buzzer, and suddenly everybody was rushing onto the floor, fans were spilling out of the stands, everybody was mobbing

Ricky. It was complete, wonderful chaos. We went for the nets at both ends and raced around the court clutching the precious strands. Everyone was yelling, "Final Four! We're going to the Final Four!"

It was a dream come true. All our hard work had paid off. Now it was up to Coach.

Nothing changed.

We were the last team to arrive in New Orleans. The other three teams came in on Wednesday to get settled, catch the sights, talk to Dick Vitale—whatever it is Final Four teams do.

Coach didn't want that for us. He believed in making the week as normal as possible. We were scheduled to play Nevada–Las Vegas on Saturday night, so he flew us in on Friday after practice, which is exactly what he would have done if we were playing Wisconsin on a typical Big Ten weekend. Never mind that this game was for the chance to play for a national championship.

We stayed at a nice hotel with a great view of the Mississippi River. The Final Four committee assigned each team to a different hotel, so ours was the Indiana hotel. Whenever we went through the lobby we ran a gauntlet of cheering Hoosier fans wearing red jackets and sweatshirts. A popular pin was white with red lettering: HOOSIERS NO. 1!

The newspapers, both in Indiana and in New Orleans, were full of Final Four coverage—player profiles, key matchups, the coaches, predictions. The television stations ran player interviews, season highlights, expert analysis, and every kind of offbeat story you could think of, such as how many hot-dog buns were being delivered to the Super Dome and how much tickets were being scalped for. Coach let us read the papers and watch TV all we wanted. He knew we wouldn't be rattled by the hoopla, and he thought we would enjoy it, which we did.

Otherwise, everything was so normal—the bus, the meetings, the pregame meal—that there was little extra pressure on us.

Keith was our unofficial tour guide, since he was from Baton Rouge and pretended he could speak Cajun. He was the only guy on the team to have made a prior appearance at the Super Dome—as a Boy Scout ushering ticket holders to their seats at a football game.

Of the four teams left, only Providence, winners over Alabama and Georgetown in the Southeast Regional, could be called a surprise. They were ranked twenty-second in the final Associated Press poll. Syracuse, number ten, had beaten third-ranked North Carolina in the East Regional, and they came to New Orleans with the best-known big man—six-foot-ten Rony Seikaly. We knew they were good.

But the matchup that everybody was talking about was second-ranked Indiana against first-ranked Nevada–Las Vegas. UNLV had been number one for weeks and came to the Final Four with a twenty-two-game winning streak. They were a wide-open, fast-breaking team with a reputation for taking no prisoners. Someone threw some numbers at us: "These guys have an average victory margin of 20 points during the streak. You think they can't score?"

It was another great coaching confrontation, as well—Bobby Knight vs. the towel-chewing, sad-eyed Jerry Tarkanian. I had never met Tarkanian, but he gave the appearance on television of not being in control of his team the way Coach Knight was. Coach warned us not to be taken in—the UNLV style was not as disciplined as ours, but it was very effective and Tarkanian taught that style very well.

It's a credit to Coach that we felt no undue pressure. Sixty-five thousand seats were filled for the semis, and we had to hang around under the stands for almost two hours while Syracuse took care of Providence, 77–63. Even so, I felt only the usual butterflies when we took the floor to warm up. As soon as the ball went up for the center jump, it was just another very, very important basketball game. At one point in the first half, when I hit a 3-pointer and got fouled, I put my arms up and signaled "four," meaning a 4-point play. I exchanged hand slaps with some of the guys. I wouldn't have done that earlier in my career, but I had come to believe that my teammates responded well to my enthusiasm. They saw I wasn't tight, and that loosened them up as well.

It was fun. We played well from the start and led by as many as 14 in the first half, but there was no stopping UNLV's great scorers, Freddie Banks and Armon Gilliam. Banks threw up nineteen 3-point shots, which blew my mind, but he hit ten of them, and the Rebels took the lead at 59–57. We came back after a TV time-out and hit them with a 12–2 run, and the rest of the way it was just very intense, very enjoyable basketball.

The one shaky moment I remember came with about eight minutes left, when I went to the foul line for two shots. For the first time in my whole Indiana career—and I think for the first time since my senior year in high school—I missed both shots.

I was extremely upset. I knew that every player who had ever played at Indiana had probably missed two in a row, but I took a lot of pride in my foul-shooting. It was as if I had let my man go right by me for a slam dunk.

At the next dead ball, when I went over to Coach to get instructions, I apologized to him. He slapped me on the hind end and said, "Will you knock it off? How do you think we got this far?"

That made me feel good, and I immediately stopped fretting over the misses. I got eight more chances as time ran down, and I hit them all. When Steve Eyl buried a dunk that put us ahead 96–88 with thirteen seconds left, he and I did a little victory dance.

Forty minutes left for the championship.

It was bedlam back at the hotel. Our supporters clogged the lobby and the elevators, calling out congratulations and screaming, "Beat Syracuse!" Mom, Dad, and Sean had a room at the Sheraton, where the National Basketball Coaches Association was meeting, but they were at our hotel to celebrate. Grandpa and Grandma Alford were there; Grandmother Mason and her husband, Albert, were there; Uncle Morris and Aunt Patti were there. Uncle Scott and Aunt Debbie had a room down on Bourbon Street, and they were there. Tanya and her family had driven down from Indiana in a van. We managed to see each other for a few minutes in the lobby.

Dad had to be exhausted, not to mention broke. He had somehow managed to attend thirty-one of our thirty-three ball games, in addition to the games he had to coach himself. "I'm very tired," he admitted. "I don't think I'll watch you play as a pro." Mom had seen most of my games, too, but basketball wasn't her day job, teaching was.

Sunday, the team went to the dome for a short practice, but the afternoon was free for visiting with friends and family. We had a team dinner at a Cajun restaurant along the water, and they served us something that looked like scorpions in a soupy hot sauce. Keith was the only one who recognized the stuff as crawfish étouffée, and he had to show us how to eat it. He kept shaking his head, saying, "I can't believe you guys don't know how to suck 'em up." Kreigh Smith grossed him out by eating them whole—shell, tail, and all.

After dinner we had a film session without the coaches and a meeting with the coaches, and then we all went to our rooms. There was no curfew, but this was one night when nobody was going to risk a spin down Bourbon Street.

Again, nothing changed. The pregame meal on Monday featured an inspired choice of entrees: spaghetti, pancakes, hamburger patties. Todd and Daryl and I threw the food down with greater-than-normal enthusiasm, simply because we knew we would never have to eat that combination again. Keith, on the other hand, ate very little. "I was up all night with a stomachache," he said.

"What's the matter, Keith? Can't handle your crawdads?"

He gave us a weak smile. We didn't guess we'd hear much more about the pleasures of crawfish étouffée.

After dessert, Coach Knight produced the expected guest speakers. The first one was Quinn Buckner, who had scored 16 points in the 1976 championship-game victory over Michigan. "Don't go out and try to play a different game," he told us. "Go out and play like you did in January, like you did in February. Don't change a thing."

Then we heard from John Havlicek, the Boston Celtics Hall of Famer and Coach Knight's teammate on the Ohio State team that won it all in 1960. "Don't finish this game," he said, "thinking there was something else you could have done to win. When you come back into the locker room, each of you has to be able to look at himself in the mirror and say, 'I gave it everything I have.' If you can honestly say that, you've got nothing to worry about."

We were getting excited now; we could feel the roar of it all. We got a terrific send-off at the hotel from our fans. I remember looking out the bus window and spotting my seventy-year-old grandpa, all dressed in red. He was just going nuts, beating on the windows and shouting encouragement. I'd never seen my grandpa act like that.

What was the locker room like before the game? Normal. Coach Knight didn't pull a Gene Hackman and send us out with a whispered "I love you guys." But he told us he admired us and recalled how much we had been through together—my disastrous sophomore season, the world tour, the tournament games, the long hours of practice. We deserved a lot of credit for having come this far, he said.

But before he sent us out for the last time, he left us with this thought: "Nobody's gonna remember you if you finish second."

I took the floor for the last time in an Indiana uniform alongside the same four guys who had started most of our games all season: Daryl, Ricky, Dean, and Keith. The Super Dome crowd roared in anticipation as we shook hands with the five Syracuse players. It was Sherman Douglas, their great scorer and defender, who grabbed my hand. It was just a quick "Good luck," but you always feel a bond with your opponents in a championship game. The competition is real, but it's a show, too, and you respect each other as actors in the show.

The ball went up, Syracuse controlled the tip, and our last forty minutes began to tick down.

Nobody remembers the game; everybody remembers The Shot.

For the record, the score swung back and forth. Indiana by 2. Syracuse by 5. I hit a 3-pointer at the halftime horn, and we went to the locker room leading 34–33.

The second half brought no daylight for either team. Syracuse by 1. Indiana by 4. The Orangemen suddenly got hot, outscoring us 15–3, but their lead never exceeded 8. We fought back, and when Keith fed Daryl for a dunk, it was tied at 52.

And so it went, Syracuse spurting ahead, Indiana struggling to catch up. Every time we missed a shot, either Rony Seikaly, their center, or their terrific freshman forward, Derrick Coleman, seemed to come down with the ball. (Coleman finished with 19 rebounds.) Fortunately, I was hot from 3-point range (7-for-10 for the game), and Daryl and Dean were their usual strong selves inside.

But the guy who kept us in the game was Keith, who showed no ill effects from his stomachache. Syracuse jumped ahead 70–68 on a Seikaly basket, but Keith tied it up with a reverse lay-up right in the faces of their big guys. At the other end, Seikaly knocked Daryl down with an errant elbow, and Howard Triche penetrated to score for Syracuse. The score: 72–70. We missed at the other end, Triche rebounded, and I fouled him with thirty-three seconds left.

Coach Knight would be the first to admit that we were not the best team he had ever coached, but we were definitely the best in the last five minutes of a game. In fact, I can't recall a college team in recent years that played as well down the stretch.

One reason for that was our balance; four of our starting five hit last-second shots for us during the season. Another reason was Coach Knight's passing game, which was terrific under pressure. With time ticking off the clock, a motion offense is much more effective than a set play, where A has to screen for B with C cutting here, etc. If that breaks down, everyone is paralyzed on the court. The way we played, a pattern couldn't really break down. You always had a place to go or someone to pass to.

Another plus: we didn't have to call a time-out to set up a play.

Triche hit his first free throw, to make it 73–70, but he missed the second. The ball wound up in Keith's hands, and he took it straight downcourt and hit a ten-foot jumper to cut the lead to 1 with thirty seconds left. Syracuse inbounded the ball, and we quickly fouled Coleman to freeze the clock. Coach Knight immediately called time-out.

There was nothing fancy in the huddle. No A-goes-to-B plays, no impassioned speeches. Coach simply gave us the options and told us not to call a time-out if Coleman missed either end of the one-and-one. "Let's just move the ball!" he yelled over the music on the loudspeakers. "Get the good shot!" He had enough confidence in us as players to know that we would do that.

The horn sounded, and we returned to the floor, the crowd noise building under the giant roof of the dome. Coleman stood at the line, all alone, his orange jersey hanging out over his shorts. The other Syracuse players waited at the defensive end, guarding against a fast break like the one Keith had just scored on.

I lined up on the lane, a few feet from Coleman. My responsibility was to block him out after he shot. He didn't show the pressure as he bounced the ball, but I knew he couldn't feel comfortable. He was not very good at free throws, and they're much harder to shoot when you're not relaxed. There was no way he could be relaxed. As he lifted the ball to shoot, the Indiana rooters made a lot of noise.

The noise became a roar when Coleman's shot curled around the rim and out. Daryl grabbed the rebound and passed to Keith.

Twenty-five seconds left. Down by 1. How many times had I imagined that situation in my driveway? The feeling was indescribable.

There was no predetermined play. I wanted to shoot the last shot, and I was looking to shoot the last shot. But I had finally learned my biggest lesson as a player: I didn't *have* to shoot the last shot. As I ran upcourt, I recognized that Syracuse was back in its box-and-one. Sherman Douglas came up to meet me and followed me on a baseline cut. I made a stab-step back toward Daryl on the low post, and then popped back outside. I was open for an instant, but not long enough for Keith to risk a pass.

Keith dropped the ball in to Daryl, who tried to head-fake Coleman into the air, but that didn't work. Daryl had the ball with nowhere to go and the clock inside ten seconds... he kicked it back to Keith and jumped out to set a pick on Coleman...Douglas stuck to me as I made one last effort to get open...

And you have to understand that this was all going on with the crowd making the most incredible noise and the clock ticking down. Keith scraped Coleman off on Daryl and drove to the baseline. He squared up and jumped, drifting slightly left. Howard Triche raced by him, waving, but Keith was too high—that great leaping ability of his. He got the shot off over Triche's hand.

I'll never forget the instant that the ball went through the basket. I grabbed my head with both hands because I couldn't believe it. For an instant, I was frozen. And then I saw the ball bouncing, bouncing, and I rushed toward it, because nobody for Syracuse had picked it up and because nobody had called time-out. Tapes of the game show that I actually gave the ball a quick flick with my hand, but I don't remember that. I just wanted to get my body in the way of the ball, anything to slow up their in-bounds pass.

The whistles blew with 1 second left. Syracuse had lost at least three seconds by not calling time-out immediately.

We were met at the sideline by our bench players, who jumped all over us, waving towels and hugging us and screaming like crazy. I was grinning, but I went straight to Coach and said, "Let's get Eyl in the game for me. We need his height." Coach looked around for Steve, grabbed him, and told him to report in.

And that's why, with one second left in my college career, I stood as a spectator in the last huddle and sent my teammates back out on the floor with words of encouragement.

I didn't sit down, of course. Syracuse tried a desperation in-bounds pass, but Keith intercepted it and started dribbling. He was dribbling when the horn went off. Players, photographers, and fans surged onto the court. Keith wound up and tried to heave the ball into the upper deck of the Super Dome, but it landed in the Indiana cheering section, not far from where his family had seats.

We were mobbed at midcourt. Everything was crazy. People were bumping me and jostling me, screaming with joy. John Feinstein, of all people, was at my side, part of a mob of reporters. Then my mom, who gave me a tearful hug and said she loved me. A couple of minutes later, Dad and Sean fought through the crowd, as did Tanya, who was bawling with joy. She gave me another hug and a big kiss. I didn't notice that there was blood on her blouse. Todd had picked her up and spun her around, and in hugging her he had pushed one of her earrings hard enough to cut her ear.

Well, you know what those celebration scenes are like. It went on and on and on.

During a lull, I looked around for Coach Knight. I finally spotted him sitting calmly in a folding chair with his sons, Patrick and Tim, beside him. I guess he could be calm; it was his third championship, our first.

He waved me over and sat me down on his right. He put his arm around me and leaned toward my ear. "I want you to know, Steve, that I really appreciate all that you've done since you've been here. You've gotten everything you could have out of your ability."

I had tears in my eyes, and I think he had tears in his. We both knew what the moment signified: the end of our relationship as player and coach. I had to let go of him as a coach, and he had to let go of me as a player.

He gave me a little squeeze. "Steve," he said, "I've never been prouder of a player than I am of you."

I had waited four years to hear that. It was worth the wait.

In *Hoosiers*, Hickory High wins the Indiana state championship at Hinkle Field House on a last-second shot. The fans run onto the floor and carry the coach and the players around on their shoulders. The losers hang their heads. It's real loud and colorful, but gradually the scene grows dim and the music drops out. It's years later, and you see a little kid shooting all by himself in the Hickory gymnasium. Only now there's a big framed picture of the 1951 team on the wall, with the inscription "State Champions, 1951."

I was very moved by that. When I think back to my own childhood, I realize it may not have been basketball I fell in love with first, but the gymnasiums. The sound of one basketball on an old wood floor. The feeling that you have a whole building to yourself.

It took a while, after New Orleans, to find that place in my own life. There were thousands of people waiting along the runway when we landed in Bloomington the next morning. They packed Assembly Hall for a celebration rally. None of us had slept after the win, so we were all running on fumes. We were so wound up it didn't matter.

I didn't sleep well that night, or the next night either. The last month of classwork was extremely difficult. Basketball was all I could think of—the tournament, my teammates,

Coach Knight, the NBA draft. There were constant interruptions for the basketball banquet, interviews, photo sessions, and civic functions. We even flew to Washington, D.C., to meet President Reagan in the White House Rose Garden.

My first trip back home was no different. I had to show everybody the ring and the net from the Super Dome, tell the stories over and over again, and be as gracious as I could under the circumstances. There were basketballs I had to sign, all over the house, letters to answer, messages to call people on the phone. When it got to be too much, I would drive into the garage, lower the door, and hide in the house.

Gradually, the excitement subsided. The phone rang a little less often, my mind wandered shorter distances, I began to settle down.

One Sunday night, I took Dad's keys and drove over to the fieldhouse. It was late—eleven o'clock, my favorite time. I parked the car, opened the doors, and groped in the dark for the light switches. The big arena lights came on slowly— a dull glow at first, gradually building to full power. I stood for a moment on the track, my basketball under my arm, and stared down at the floor. I remembered my first game on that floor: 32 points against Richmond in the eighth-grade league. A whole bunch of other memories flooded my mind: my best high school games, the free-throw strings, the kids I played with, Dad coaching on the sidelines, Mom one row back, watching.

I walked down the steps very slowly, drinking all that in. Twenty-four rows, forty-eight steps, a thousand memories.

You could call it a workout, but I did more thinking than anything else. I went through my usual drills: the two-ball dribble, the point moves, the backboard shots, the free throws, shooting over the broom. But my mind was elsewhere. I kept envisioning Dad sitting up in the top row, watching me in silence. I saw Sean hitting that jump shot in the one game we got to play together. I saw Tanya climbing the ladder to free the net, not knowing her engagement ring was on the rim support. Most of all, I simply enjoyed the space, the light, the quiet. I took pleasure in the sound of the basketball echoing in the big gym.

I thanked the Lord for all I had been blessed with.

I practiced till after midnight. Before turning out the lights and locking up, I dribbled to the corner one last time, squared up, jumped, and fired... *swish!*

I hung the net.

Epilogue

What if we hadn't won?

In the days following the Final Four, I talked a lot with Daryl and Todd, and we all wondered the same thing: if we hadn't won a Big Ten title, if we *hadn't* won the national championship...would it all have been worth it?

That was a hard question to answer. At times, our attitude toward Coach Knight had been, "He's nuts, he's crazy. There's a part of him that just doesn't know what's going on." And then, the very next day, we'd say, "He was right. It's amazing how he always comes out smelling like a rose."

It killed us to admit that Coach was right. All the negative things he did, all the dark ugly things he threw at us...there were times we hated him for it.

Coach always told us that he understood how hard it was to play under him. "The reason it's not easy to play for me," he said, "is because I want you to be better even more than *you* want you to be better."

That's the absolute truth. If you showed Coach that you

were wholeheartedly interested in being a better player, he did everything in his power to help you.

Unfortunately, some players aren't interested in doing that, either because they aren't mature enough or because, deep down, they just don't want it enough. When you show Coach that side of yourself, it's time to leave. If you don't want to be better, Indiana is a disastrous place to be, an ugly place to be. Coach wants to make himself better every day, and he can't abide players who aren't the same way.

That's why, in the end, I found I could cope with him. I had those same thoughts. And even though he got on me and got on me, and I got madder and madder and madder, I reminded myself, He's just making me better.

I could probably have gone to any college in the country out of high school, but most coaches would have babied me and pampered me, and I wouldn't be nearly the player I am today.

But had he made me good enough?

In the weeks leading up to the 1987 NBA draft, I began to read that pro scouts regarded me as no better than a second-round pick. I was an overachiever, they said, a pure shooter whose lack of athletic ability was hidden in Coach Knight's system. One columnist wrote, "NBA teams have twenty-four seconds to hustle up the floor and get off a shot. They certainly don't have time to set up elaborate picks and screens so plodders like Alford can shoot."

I didn't mind the knocks—I thrive on people telling me I can't do something, because that gives me the chance to prove them wrong—but it did bother me that the Indiana Pacers were so vocal about my shortcomings. Every morning, I picked up the paper and read that some Pacers executive thought I was too slow, too small, couldn't guard anybody, and couldn't get my shot off against the pros.

I groaned when I read that. Other teams were going to say, "Well, the Pacers ought to know—they're just thirty minutes away."

The Pacers were on the spot. They had the eleventh pick in the first round, and there was pressure from Hoosier fans to pick me, the local hero. To justify skipping me, the Pacers apparently thought they had to downgrade me publicly. There are no hard feelings today, but I was very unhappy at the time and made some un-Alford-like comments. (I said I had a Clint Eastwood "hit list" of people I would prove wrong!)

Actually, I never expected to be picked as high as number eleven, not by Indiana or any other team. I saw myself as a low first-round selection.

On draft day, I joined Tanya and the family in the living room to watch the picks on TV. A bunch of media people turned up at the house, so Mom made stuff to eat and drink and we established a pressroom in the garage. When the first round went by and I hadn't been picked, I went out to the garage to do interviews. That's what I was doing when Tanya rushed in and told me that the Dallas Mavericks had made me their second-round choice, the twenty-sixth pick overall.

I was very excited. Dallas had a good team on the rise, it was a good geographical location, and my Uncle Scott lived there. But I also knew that I would have to make a spot for myself. The Mavericks had a lot of good guards.

I didn't know how to prepare that summer. Dad had little contact with the NBA, so he couldn't help much, and Coach Knight ignores pro basketball. I kept up with my workouts, but I wasn't sure what my role would be with the Mavericks. Anyway, there were a lot of distractions that summer.

My wedding, for one. Tanya and I were married in July at the New Castle Presbyterian Church. It was a big wedding, about five hundred people. Todd, Daryl, Ricky, and Joe Hillman were ushers, and David Minor, who has a beautiful gospel voice, sang "The Lord's Prayer" and "Through the Years."

I was pretty nervous, but I don't guess that's unusual. When Tanya came down the aisle with her dad, she started crying. That started the bridesmaids bawling, and it turned into a pretty wet wedding. The minister got teary-eyed, too.

After a honeymoon in Florida, Tanya and I moved into a house in North Dallas, Texas—Uncle Scott found it for us—and I reported to the Mavericks' training camp at Southern Methodist University. Some familiar faces greeted me there. Uwe Blab was the backup center. Sam Perkins started at one forward. Roy Tarpley, my old Michigan foe, came off the bench and was considered the league's best sixth man. Knowing those guys kept me from being in awe, but I still felt like a rookie around players like Rolando Blackman, Derek Harper, and Mark Aguirre, who had accomplished big things in the NBA.

Everybody treated me super—players, management, the coaches. John MacLeod was the head coach, and he did everything he could to help me. He said that at six-two, I would have to be more of a point guard than a shooting guard, so he gave me ball-handling drills to work on. He also made sure I went against Derek every day in practice. Derek was a powerful, quick guard, and playing against him helped my game. Brad Davis, the ten-year veteran whose role on the team I was being groomed to fill, gave me all sorts of help and became a great friend off the court as well.

The biggest adjustment I had to make involved ball handling. In the NBA, defenders pick you up at ninety feet and get away with a lot of holding and grabbing. You have to be really aggressive off the dribble. And yes, the twenty-four-second clock makes a difference. You can't walk the ball up on the lazy dribble like a college guard. The NBA game is much faster.

I had an excellent exhibition season. I scored 12 points against the Boston Celtics, which was a thrill, and I shot around 70 percent from the field for the preseason, which was unbelievable. Then Brad got hurt, and I had to play a lot in the first six games of the regular season. That was a great opportunity, but I just wasn't ready for it and I played poorly. When Brad came back, my name began to be fol-

lowed in the scoring summaries by the initials "DNP"—
"Did Not Play."

Sitting wasn't fun. The first time around the league the big
cities were entertaining, but they got monotonous on the
second and third visits. It was the same thing with the
games. Having a front-row seat to watch Larry Bird or
Magic Johnson play is great, but the second time around you
want to get in and play. After the All-Star break, it got very
old.

The worst part of sitting was knowing that my skills were
deteriorating. The Mavericks gave me only a minute here
and two minutes there, and I couldn't show anything in that
amount of time. My shooting was pitiful. If I did get a
chance to put one up, I often rushed the shot, and I was
usually cold and stiff from my hour and a half on the bench.

There were adjustments to make off the court, too. It was
a whole different atmosphere, playing basketball someplace
other than Indiana. Texas is football-oriented. For the first
time in my life, I opened up the morning paper and couldn't
find high school basketball scores. That was kind of a shock
to my system.

It was also strange not to be recognized. Tanya and I went
shopping at the Dallas Galleria that fall, and we went two or
three hours without a single person coming up and saying,
"Hey, aren't you Steve Alford?" I thought it was wonderful
at first, but a few weeks later I started missing the attention.
I guess there's no pleasing us athletes.

Fortunately, the Mavs had a great season. We finished second in our division and played great in the playoffs before
losing our semifinal series to the Lakers in seven games. I
was led to believe that I would get more playing time the
following year, so I finished the season reasonably content. I
felt I had served a valuable apprenticeship.

With a year of NBA experience, I knew what to work on
during the summer. I played in the Los Angeles summer
league on a team made up of Mavs and Cavs (Cleveland

players), and I played very well. But when I got back to
Dallas, nothing had changed: no playing time.

I got very discouraged.

In mid-December, Roy Tarpley was due to rejoin the team
after being out with an injury. It was obvious the Mavs
needed to make a roster move, and I told Tanya that I might
be the player to go. "I sort of hope it is me," I said. "I love it
here, but I'm just miserable not playing."

Coach MacLeod called me a couple of nights later and
said he'd like to see me early in the morning, before practice.
He'd never called me in like that before, so I knew what was
coming. The next morning, he and a couple of front-office
people broke the news to me: I was released. It was all very
polite. They thanked me for my effort, I thanked them for all
they had done for me, and we wished each other luck.

I walked out the door an unemployed basketball player.

It might have been a gloomy time, what with Christmas
coming up and all, but my agent told me that four or five
teams were interested in me, so I felt pretty good. The team
showing the most interest was the Golden State Warriors.
They were a struggling club that had won only twenty games
the year before, but Don Nelson had taken over as coach
and things were changing. I wanted to go someplace where I
would get a fair look, and I'd heard that Nelson was a great
"player's coach." Best of all, the Warriors had no proven
backup to point guard Winston Garland.

Golden State offered no guarantees—they said a decision
on whether to keep me would be made by Christmas—but I
thought they offered the best opportunity. I signed a Warriors contract a few days after being released by Dallas.
Coach Nelson said he'd delay practice five hours if I could
get there that very day, so I raced to the airport and caught
the first plane to San Antonio to meet the team on the road.
I felt I was getting a new start on my NBA career.

My first week was both exciting and exhausting. The
Warriors had dozens of plays, and I had to learn them almost overnight. I studied my playbook for hours in my hotel

room at the airport and tried to absorb everything I could at practices. As he had promised, Coach Nelson gave me playing time right from the start: six minutes here, eight minutes there. He was pleased to discover that I was both quicker and faster than he expected. I just needed to knock the rust off and get familiar with my role.

The Warriors were 8−12 when I joined them, and a very different team from the Mavs. Whereas Dallas had a starting five that had been together for several years, the Warriors had six guys who were twenty-five or younger. Even the veterans were pretty young, and the team's scoring leader was my old friend from the Olympics, Chris Mullin. We were a youthful, fresh team, which I liked a lot.

We became even younger and fresher shortly after I joined the team, when Ralph Sampson, our center, went out for knee surgery. Coach Nelson threw away his fat playbook and went to a three-guard lineup and a motion offense. We began to win immediately, and soon we were the talk of the NBA, everybody's choice for turnaround team of the year. Nelson played about ten guys every night, and there were times when our tallest player was six-foot-seven and the other four were all six-four and under. Manute Bol, our seven-foot-seven reserve center, came in to block shots and stir up the crowd with an occasional 3-point bomb, but our game was basically the motion offense, pressure defense, and a whole lot of hustle.

The new offense suited me. Instead of learning a whole new system, I was able to play instinctively and draw on the skills Coach Knight had taught me at Indiana. Sometimes I brought the ball up as a point guard, and other times I played more like a two-guard, running off screens. Basketball was fun again.

I got the good news on Christmas Day. My teammates and I were at a pregame walk-through when Coach Nelson came up behind me and said, "By the way, I've decided I'm going to keep you."

I grinned and said, "Thanks."

The rest of the season was a great experience. I didn't start, but I could count on fifteen to twenty-five minutes a game, which was enough for me to break a sweat and find my rhythm. My shooting percentage climbed from the dismal depths to around 50 percent, which was pretty good considering the number of 3-point shots I was asked to take. I hit 38 percent of my 3-pointers, second-best on the team, behind Rod Higgins. My free-throw touch deserted me, though, and that drove me crazy. There is absolutely no difference between a high school free throw and an NBA free throw, but there's a big difference between shooting ten free throws a night and shooting four free throws a week. I shot 94.4 percent as a high school senior, but in my second year as a pro I shot 83.1 percent.

I really liked playing for Coach Nelson. Not that I didn't like Coach MacLeod, but John is a more detached and laid-back coach, whereas Nellie is much more like Coach Knight, very excitable and competitive. We played Detroit in an overtime game, I remember, and Nellie was soaked with sweat at the end. He coaches very hard from the sidelines, just like Coach Knight.

He also yelled at me a lot, but I didn't mind that. I seem to respond better to coaches that rant and rave.

My teammates must have felt the same way. Mitch Richmond won the Rookie-of-the-Year award, Chris Mullin was third in the most-improved-player voting, and Manute led the league in blocked shots. Most important, the team won twice as many games as the year before.

We went into the play-offs as the seventh seed and were supposed to get blown out by the Utah Jazz, who had taken the Lakers to seven games the year before and had just set a franchise record for wins. Instead, we swept the Jazz in three games. We were as surprised as anybody; it was a huge confidence-builder. Phoenix, in the next round, was a different story. They matched up very well against us and beat us in five.

Even so, it was a wonderful season for the Warriors, and it

ended with the Bay Area buzzing about basketball. Two weeks after our last game, the ticket office reported over 5,000 new season tickets sold, bringing the total to more than 10,000.

And I felt like part of the success. At Dallas, I couldn't share in the good times, because I hadn't contributed. With Golden State, it was different. I had played; I had helped get us to the play-offs. Winning or losing, good or bad—I was a part of it.

That was a good feeling.

So, was it all worth it?

I have to say yes, and I'd say yes even if Indiana hadn't won the Big Ten and the NCAA championship. The benefits of my association with Coach Knight go deeper than any trophies we may have won together. I'm far ahead of most twenty-three-year-olds in terms of being able to compete against life. The things Coach stands for—mental toughness, competitiveness, perseverance—are part of my make-up now. Those are not basketball skills. Those are life skills.

We had a very unusual relationship, Coach and I. I think I got closer to him than most players do because I grew up in Indiana, went to his camp all those years, and made such an immediate impact as a freshman. The dirty looks we gave each other were real, but we never lost respect for each other. I will remember him always as a master teacher, one of the great minds of the game.

I am often asked, "Steve, what has basketball meant to you?"

That's hard to answer, because basketball has helped to mold my character, my values, even my religion. I doubt if I could live enough years to pay back what I owe the game. Perhaps that's why I enjoy my summer basketball camp so much. I love sharing my love of the game with youngsters, just as Dad and Coach Knight shared their love of the game with me.

Sometimes I daydream. In one of my daydreams the year

is 2010 and I'm lying on the couch watching a game on television with my son. (He's the star player at New Castle High School. He has a sweet jump shot, but some doubt that he's quick enough or strong enough for the big time.)

He looks at me. "Dad, what would make you happy as far as my college choice goes?"

I answer: "Do you want to be a part of the finest basketball program in the country?"

He nods.

"Do you want as fine an education as you can receive anywhere?"

He nods.

"Do you want to become a man and a better person?"

He nods.

In my daydream, the phone rings and my son answers it.

"Dad!" he yells. "It's Coach Knight at Indiana University and he wants me to become a part of his program!"

What do you think I tell my son?